# STALKER

# STALKER

## JOHN STALKER

**HARRAP**
LONDON

First published in Great Britain 1988
by HARRAP LTD
19–23 Ludgate Hill, London EC4M 7PD

Reprinted 1988 (three times)

© John Stalker Ltd

ISBN 0 245–54616–2

Printed and bound in Great Britain
by Mackays Ltd, Chatham

Typesetting by
Poole Typesetting (Wessex) Ltd., Bournemouth

*To my wife Stella, to my parents Theresa and Jack, and to my daughters Colette and Francine, for the love and strength they gave me.*

# Contents

# Introduction

The complex web of terrorism and counter-terrorism in Northern Ireland has been the subject of many books, and I have not attempted here to write yet another. What I have endeavoured to do is to set down my thoughts on what has become known as the 'Stalker Affair'. It is a story not so much of terrorism as of ambition and professional and political survival.

In May 1984 I was asked to undertake an investigation in Northern Ireland that very soon pointed towards possible offences of murder and conspiracy to pervert the course of justice, these offences committed by members of the proud Royal Ulster Constabulary. I devoted two years of my life to this task, and I failed. In May 1986, three days before I was due to complete the last and very important part of my investigation, I was removed from it and from my duties as Deputy Chief Constable of the Greater Manchester Police. Ten weeks later I resumed my job in Greater Manchester, but I was not allowed to return to Northern Ireland. A few months later I resigned from the police.

The events of those last few months of 1986 are still very recent, and as I began to write this book I found it difficult to accept that I was free of the restraints that had prevented me, at the time, from speaking out. There are matters concerning anti-terrorist measures in Northern Ireland that even now I would not wish to discuss. To do so would be irresponsible and might endanger lives. In this book I write in a detailed way about only those aspects of police activity that became public knowledge through sources other than myself.

The story is a strange one. It has left in its wake a number of casualties, and there is no point in pretending I am not one of them; but there are others. Personal reputations and police careers have suffered, probably irrecoverably. On every scale of measurement the cost of it all has been high. It was, I believe, a unique episode in the history of the modern police force. I doubt we shall ever see anything quite like it again. Indeed, procedural and financial safeguards have already been put in place by the Home Office and the Association of Chief Police Officers in order to prevent such a public spectacle ever repeating itself. But that is for the future; this book is about what happened between 1984 and 1987.

The events of those years caused me and my family great distress, and as a result of them my family's pride and faith in the fairness and efficiency of a system they trusted has been broken. Much the greater tragedy, however, is the damage caused to the reputation of the police force generally and the RUC in particular. The way in which my removal was handled has left the firm conviction in many people's minds that I was getting too close to the truth about the activities of policemen operating under cover and without proper control in Northern Ireland. There is no doubt that critics of the police and propagandists — and there are plenty of those in Northern Ireland — were in 1986 handed a powerful weapon, and that they are still in possession of it.

I have done my best to stay out of the tangled skein of Northern Ireland politics, but this story would be meaningless without some reference to the nature of policing in the Province. Since 1969 the Royal Ulster Constabulary has been locked in daily combat with the modern Irish Republican

Army and other terrorist groups. This unremitting battle has resulted in the loss of many hundreds of lives — of police, soldiers, members of the public and terrorists themselves — and in fighting it the RUC has developed over the years sophisticated and complex measures to combat the terrorist threat. Individual members of the RUC are held in high regard by British policemen. Their resourcefulness and bravery in the face of constant personal danger is clearly evident. As a senior and experienced English policeman I admired them and had for many years studied and discussed their difficulties with them. But they would be the first to say that their history and policing philosophy are in important respects different from those of the rest of the United Kingdom. They have always routinely carried arms, for example, even in times of peace. This para-militarism dates back to the inception of the Force, when, on 1 June 1922, the Royal Irish Constabulary became the Royal Ulster Constabulary. They see themselves much more as an arm of the State than do English police forces. Although they are proud servants of the British Crown, members of the RUC have historically had to perform their duties in a different way, and the differences go very deep. There has never been a time during the existence of the RUC that it has not been intermittently at war with the stubborn armed resistance of the Irish Republican Army. This means that some members of the Force have come to see themselves as soldiers. In any other country in Europe, given their problems, that is exactly what they would be.

To me all this was self-evident, and I knew it before I set foot in Northern Ireland to begin my investigation. Indeed, I have studied at first hand counter-terrorism methods around the world in recent years, and I have spent long hours talking about them with RUC men of all ranks who were working or studying in England. Theirs is a difficult and uneasy role. I knew before I began my investigation that I would inevitably encounter contradictions. What I quite failed to anticipate, however, was the studied reluctance of some senior police officers and government officials to admit that these contradictions existed — even in the face of evidence to the contrary. Neither was it the case, as was later suggested by some, that I did not understand the problems of the RUC: I understood them very well indeed. The fact was that others, including some senior officers, clearly expected that I should make allowances for them. I simply refused to do so; not because I did not sympathize or understand, but because I was not entitled under the terms of my investigation to do so. I did what I believed to be right, and I would do the same again. I saw myself, and still do, as a straightforward and experienced investigator who was not prepared to have his intelligence and experience insulted by lies and obfuscation. I was embarked on neither a cover-up nor a crusade. I merely wanted the truth, and in searching for it I undoubtedly caused grave offence to a number of people. My removal from my search for the truth was, I believe, the result of a deliberate decision made in haste and with reference to the political situation as it then existed in Ulster.

The three principal cases covered by my investigation were as follows. On 11 November 1982 three men were shot dead by members of a special Royal Ulster Constabulary anti-terrorist unit in Tullygally East Road, just outside Lurgan. The men were Eugene Toman, Sean Burns and Gervaise McKerr. They were all unarmed.

Less than two weeks later, on 24 November 1982, two youths were shot, one being killed and the other seriously wounded, by members of the same anti-terrorist unit, in a hayshed in Ballyneery Road North, also just outside Lurgan. The dead youth was Michael Justin Tighe, who was 17 years old, and his companion was Martin McCauley, who was 19. Three old pre-war rifles were recovered from the hayshed, but no ammunition was found.

Less than three weeks after that, on 12 December 1982, two more men were shot dead, yet again by a member of the same special unit, this time in Mullacreavie Park, in Armagh City. They were Seamus Grew and Roddy Carroll. Neither of them was armed.

All these shootings were investigated by other members of the Royal Ulster Constabulary, and files were sent to the Director of Public Prosecutions for Northern Ireland, Sir Barry Shaw. The first prosecution to come before the courts related to the last of the three incidents, and was that of Constable John Robinson. He appeared before Mr Justice McDermott on 3 April 1984, and was acquitted of the murder of Seamus Grew. Neither he nor any other police officer has ever been charged with the murder of Roddy Carroll, who was in the same car as Grew when they were shot. During the trial Constable Robinson gave evidence in his own defence, and it emerged publicly for the first time that the two men had been shot not, as claimed, at a random police road check, but following a long surveillance operation that had taken RUC officers into the Republic of Ireland and back again. Robinson, it was disclosed, was not an ordinary policeman as had been said, but a member of a highly trained special police squad, and the deaths of Grew and Carroll had come at the end of a planned operation involving that special squad. During the trial Constable Robinson told a story that made international headlines: he told the court that he had been instructed by senior police officers to tell lies in his official statements in order to protect the nature of that special operation. It became clear that investigating CID officers, the Director of Public Prosecutions, and finally the courts themselves, had all been quite deliberately misled in order to protect police procedures and systems. The revelations created a public outcry. Even as I write, almost five years after the deaths of those men, the story still twists and turns. In this book I try to make some sense of it all.

# 1

## *Early Days*

Despite being born with the entirely appropriate name of Stalker, in my youth I did not see myself as a policeman. My first love was writing, and had things taken a different course I would have become a journalist when, at sixteen years of age, I left the local grammar school. But the rare vacancy that occurred then on the *Oldham Chronicle* went to someone else, and after working briefly for an insurance company I joined the Manchester City Police as a teenager in 1958. I had shown no previous inclination to be a force for law and order, neither, as far as I am aware, do I have any relatives who were policemen. My impulsive decision to step into a blue uniform took me, as well as my family, by surprise.

Looking back, I can now see some logic in it. I was a young man at a loose end, compulsory military service having been recently abolished. I had no desire to leave my family but was looking for new experiences. I was naturally fit, a good athlete, and comfortable with responsibility. The thought of sitting at a desk for the best part of my life filled me with dread, and I needed to be doing something positive. I had not inherited from my father the skills of working with my hands, and my future lay in a job that could use my writing ability, my physical fitness and my natural inquisitiveness. If journalism had no place for me then the police force was not too far removed. I wish I could say I recognized some inner compulsion towards public service. The truth is I did not; or at least, not until later.

I was interviewed and accepted into the Force by Chief Superintendent Robert Mark, who was later to become Sir Robert Mark, and a Commissioner of the Metropolitan Police. Robert Mark and his two-man recruiting department were, in the fifties, responsible for bringing into the Manchester force recruits who have since been enormously influential in the policing of the United Kingdom. It is quite remarkable how so many future leaders of this country's policemen were nurtured and developed in Manchester's South Street Police Station at that time.

I was a street constable in and around the centre of Manchester for three years, and then transferred to the CID at the early age of twenty-two. I remained a detective for the next twenty years, and I often wonder whether, had I not been so quickly immersed in such a challenging work, I would have left the Force to try again to enter journalism. I learned the skills of detective work under the wing of some tough and capable men. They set high standards for themselves and for those whom they thought worthy of receiving their knowledge, and those early years as a detective constable working in the Moss Side area of inner-city Manchester taught me a great deal about tenacity, fairness and the value of teamwork. There was plenty of scope in the CID of those days for an individualist, even an eccentric, but it was no place for a loner.

I learned, in those formative years, lessons that have stayed with me ever since. By watching my older colleagues I developed a determination not to be diverted from the job in hand, and learned the art of asking the unexpected question, the one for which no answer has been rehearsed. Senior detectives, many of whom were war veterans, made sure that young men like me kept their feet firmly on the streets of the city. The message they gave to me was clear: the public paid my wages, they were entitled to be looked after to the best of my ability, and in return they would accept, if not always welcome, my presence. I was well aware that I had entered into an unwritten contract with the people of Manchester, and I was constantly reminded of this by those shrewd and wise mentors.

I was promoted to Detective Sergeant at the young age of twenty-four and immediately became involved in the first of a number of criminal investigations with a 'political' overtone. It involved allegations against policemen following a visit of the then Prime Minister, the Right Honourable Alec Douglas-Home, to a nearby town. I went from that job to the Moors murders, the deeply distressing investigations of the deaths of Manchester children at the hands of Ian Brady and Myra Hindley. Although by then I was no stranger to violent death, this was my introduction to multiple murder, and I have retained vivid memories of the four months I spent on that enquiry.

My career moved steadily and fairly rapidly upward through the CID to the rank of Detective Superintendent, once again in Manchester's Moss Side. During the intervening years I had tackled many different jobs and had worked on dozens of murder cases as well as drugs squad and robbery squad work. Also, in the mid 1970s, I was involved with the spate of bombings and shooting incidents in Manchester that formed part of the mainland campaign of both the IRA and Ulster Loyalist groups. By this time, after sixteen years of varied detective experience, I regarded myself as a thoroughly competent and experienced investigator, and I enjoyed passing on the lessons I had learned in the way they had been taught to me. In 1978, after a couple of years spent investigating serious complaints against police officers, I was promoted to the rank of Detective Chief Superintendent and moved to Warwickshire to become head of the County CID, living just outside Coventry. I was thirty-eight and had reached the highest operational rank within the CID. It was my personal pinnacle, and I was contented and busy. I had no intention of moving into the rarefied atmosphere of Chief Officer of Police. Indeed, I had publicly said so. I recognized that my training and inclinations were those of an investigator of crime. I settled my family in Warwickshire and began to put my experience to use. I did not wish to be considered for any move that would take me away from CID work.

The Chief Constable of Warwickshire saw things differently, however. He was Albert Laugharne, a former Manchester detective who had learned his skills in the same arena as I had. He was a fine policeman who later became Chief Constable of Lancashire and Deputy Commissioner at New Scotland Yard. He obviously thought I had the potential to progress further, and he encouraged me to try to obtain a place on the Senior Command Course at the Police Staff College at Bramshill in Hampshire. Interviewing for the Course is carried out over three days and is extremely competitive and challenging. This attracted me, and I told Laugharne I would make one attempt only to gain a place on the course. If I did not make it, then I would at least prove to myself that I was not destined to do so. I knew very well that success on the Senior Command Course means almost inevitable movement into the higher reaches of the police force — to Assistant Chief Constable or above.

My attempt was successful, and I attended the residential course for six months in 1979. That course made me aware of my ability to function at the highest levels of the police force. I returned to Warwickshire for a short time, and the following year was appointed Assistant Chief Constable in Greater Manchester.

The Chief Constable of the Force was then, and still is, James Anderton, a man I had first met and worked with twenty-three years earlier and who was at that time strongly tipped to be a future Commissioner of the Metropolitan Police at New Scotland Yard. I first met Cyril James Anderton in the late 1950s; he was a 24- year-old constable and was about to begin a meteoric rise that would take him, within the next eleven years, to the rank of Assistant Chief Constable. Indeed, he skipped the rank of Superintendent altogether. Since James Anderton plays an important role in this story, it is worth taking a few paragraphs now to describe how I saw him then.

He had then, as now, the fervency of a man with a sense of destiny. Whereas I felt fairly uncomfortable with the cloak of authority, James Anderton wore it with supreme confidence. Soon after leaving school he had joined the Royal Military Police, and from there he had entered the Manchester City force. He had, even then, an unshakable belief in the rightness of his calling. He was undoubtedly born to be a policeman.

I worked closely with him for some time. I remember that in 1960 he studied very hard before sitting the competitive examinations to qualify for the rank of Inspector. During those long months of preparation he showed absolute determination to pass with flying colours. Out of over two hundred entrants only seven passed; James Anderton came second in the order of merit. The man at the top was a Detective Sergeant who had studied while working shift work and long hours dealing with some very serious crimes. As he read the list of passes I saw James Anderton's face darken in disappointment and anger. To him being second was almost as bad as failure. Though he did not not know the winning candidate, he looked upon him as a serious rival, and endeavoured to find out as much as he could about him.

An air of depression wreathed him for weeks afterwards, and I think I realized then the deep and constant need he has to prove himself publicly. The strength of ambition and obsessive drive he showed to me that day long ago have not diminished with the years.

Very soon afterwards James Anderton was promoted to Inspector, and the man I had known disappeared overnight. He lost his homely Lancashire accent and dropped the name 'Cyril' from his signature. He sternly rejected first-name approaches, and his enduring love affair with Wigan Rugby League Club was never again to be mentioned. On that day he became a born again policeman. Twenty years later, when he was a Chief Constable, the mask was allowed to slip away and the young Jim Anderton emerged again. The accent returned as quickly as it had left, and Wigan's Rugby League results became important once again.

On assuming my responsibilities as Assistant Chief Constable in 1980, I found myself, for the first time since I had been a bobby on the beat, no longer a detective. (I did, however, investigate serious allegations of bribery and corruption involving a senior policeman in another police force. He was eventually convicted and sentenced to six years imprisonment.) I was now an administrator, a desk policeman, and I quickly had to understand the subtle interplay between local politicians and the Home Office, and how to talk and understand the language and stratagems of politics. I was also able to indulge in the fascinating study on a daily basis and at close quarters of the personality and leadership style of James Anderton. Then forty-eight years of age, he was at the peak of his confidence and powers as a Chief Constable. Over the next four years I learned a great deal about this controversial, complex and ambitious man. I witnessed his successes and his mistakes, and as part of a small team of six other senior officers I shared with him the leadership of the Greater Manchester Police force — the largest provincial police force in the country.

Quite unexpectedly, in late 1982, I received an invitation to undertake the course at the Royal College of Defence Studies, which is based in Belgrave Square, London. This course lasts for twelve months and is attended by selected military, diplomatic and government staff from the United Kingdom and abroad. Each year, two British police officers of the rank of Assistant Chief Constable are invited to attend. The course is very prestigious, and I accepted the invitation without hesitation. Its aims are '. . . to give selected senior military officers and officials of the United Kingdom the opportunity to study, with representatives of the Commonwealth and NATO and certain other nations, defence issues affecting the western democracies and other countries with similar interests, and the strategic, political, economic and social factors that bear on those issues.' Policemen on this course are regarded as 'civilians', not as military personnel. My fellow students were all of Brigadier or equivalent rank in the Army, Navy and Air Force and were between forty-two and fifty years of age. There were thirty-five overseas senior military or diplomatic service personnel from twenty-two countries.

I took a flat in London for the year 1983 and enjoyed the course immensely. During the year members of the course travelled to different parts of the world including China and the Far East, Africa, India, the United States of America and Canada, the Middle East and most European countries. My particular area of study was South America, and I made extended visits to look at crime and social conditions in Colombia, Chile and Brazil. The small group of which I was part was hosted at Presidential level. It was an opportunity given to very few and I enjoyed and benefited from it greatly. This year away from Manchester represented one of the high spots of my professional life. By exposing me to social, economic and military problems previously outside my experience it stretched me intellectually and broadened my vision. Its emphasis on world affairs, and the high quality of its tuition and lectures, as well as the extensive travel, helped me to put home matters in a different perspective. I spent most of that marvellous year talking with and working alongside future military and government leaders from around the globe, and I shall never forget the experience.

I successfully completed the course with a good report, and returned to Manchester just in time to celebrate the Christmas of 1983 at home with my family, of whom I had seen very little. At about that time it was announced that the then Deputy Chief Constable of Greater Manchester, Donald Elliott, was to be appointed the Chief Constable of Devon and Cornwall Police, and I applied for the vacant position. Interviews took place in February 1984, and I was subsequently appointed Deputy Chief Constable of the Force. The following month I moved into my new job, that of number two to James Anderton in a police force of almost ten thousand people. It was a proud and memorable moment for me and for my parents. I reflected on the new perspective the Royal College of Defence Studies had given me, and I was pleased to be able to apply it to my own city and region. At the age of forty-four, physically fit and personally happy, I felt as professionally comfortable in my new job as it is possible to be. I could hardly wait for it to begin.

Within a few weeks I was taken away from those familiar surroundings, and although I did not then realize it, I began the last phase of my career as a policeman. I started my work in Belfast.

# 2

## The Investigation

The 'Stalker Affair' has its beginnings in May 1984. I had barely got my feet under the table as the newly appointed Deputy Chief Constable of the Greater Manchester Police when I was asked by my Chief Constable, James Anderton, to undertake an investigation in Northern Ireland into the deaths of those six men, all referred to from the start as 'alleged terrorists'. I recall the conversation with Anderton very well. The trial had just ended at Belfast Crown Court of the Royal Ulster Constabulary policeman John Robinson on a charge of murdering Seamus Grew. The murder of Carroll was not proceeded with at this trial, because the evidence was stronger in the case of Grew. Robinson had been acquitted by Judge McDermott, sitting alone, without benefit of a jury, in what is called a 'Diplock' court. This judicial procedure is followed in certain cases because of intimidation of jurors in previous cases. Constable Robinson, giving evidence in his own defence, had described publicly for the first time how false stories were told by police in order to cover up the truth of a special police operation to capture suspected terrorists. The murder charge had been brought by the Director of Public Prosecutions for Northern Ireland, Sir Barry Shaw, and the Robinson revelations had never previously been divulged to him. He had been asked to make a judgment on this most serious of criminal matters without benefit of the full story of why Constable Robinson was where he was when he shot two men dead. The implications for the administration of justice in Northern Ireland were profoundly serious, and there were developing signs that the disagreement between Sir Barry Shaw and the Chief Constable of the RUC, Sir John Hermon, had started to spill over into the public arena. It was clear that an investigation of some sort was needed. I had been reading with moderate interest newspaper accounts of the growing political storm about what was already beginning to be described as a police 'shoot-to-kill' policy; but I had no idea how close I was to being sucked into it all. I was new in my post and very busy with the fresh responsibilities and demands of being second-in-command of the largest provincial police force in the country.

James Anderton came to my office and asked me whether I would be prepared to head a mainland investigation into the conduct of the Royal Ulster Constabulary. I knew, although he did not mention it, that a police officer from England does not actually have any power or legal authority in Northern Ireland, and that any investigation of the type I was being asked to undertake has to be voluntarily accepted. Northern Ireland is for many practical purposes a foreign country, with different police procedures and investigative rules. Had the investigation been into any other United Kingdom police force, the new Police Complaints Authority formed in April 1985 would have had an important supervisory role; but I had no authority to ask them to step in, nor did they offer, when they knew of my later problems, to extend their responsibility to Northern Ireland in order to support me.

In consequence of this, I could not be instructed to take on the investigation, nor was I in a position to instruct any other police officer to assist me. I was being asked to look into serious matters involving criminal offences committed by policemen, but without any formal authority whatsoever to do so. I say this now because I want it to be clear that I knew what my position was, and do not wish it to be thought that I used it as an excuse at some later stage for not having accomplished what I set out to do, which was to complete a thorough and professional inquiry into the conduct of some members of the Royal Ulster Constabulary.

Anderton told me (although I had already realized it) that the investigation was regarded as immensely important to the credibility and reputation of the Royal Ulster Constabulary, and of crucial political importance to the Anglo-Irish relationship. He said that the Home Office, through their Inspectorate, had asked that it should be me who investigated the matter. The decision whether I accepted, however, was mine. The Chief Constable did not try to influence me one way or the other. Mr Anderton did not appear to grasp fully the significance of it all. He is a shrewd and capable police chief but he is not an investigator. His operational CID experience is limited to a few months as a detective sergeant, a quarter of a century ago, and I could see that he was struggling to imagine what I might be thinking. I guessed at why I was being asked to do it. The investigation was without doubt the most serious enquiry ever undertaken by any senior officer into the conduct of other policemen. It involved possible offences of murder, perjury and conspiracy to pervert the course of justice. It seemed to encompass senior officers in the high reaches of the Force as well as relationships between the police, the Director of Public Prosecutions, coroners, the courts and governments in London and Dublin. Add to that formidable list the involvement with terrorist groups and the doubtful acceptability of the RUC to the substantial Catholic population of Northern Ireland and the cocktail was a volatile one indeed. But why was my name the one being put forward?

I imagined I was seen as a policeman experienced enough in serious crime investigation to take on that level of job, senior enough to carry sufficient clout operationally, and young enough, at forty-five, to carry an extra burden of duties in

24

Belfast while working part-time in Manchester, where I continued to carry out full-time my job of Deputy Chief Constable. Whatever the reasons, I did not reflect on them for too long; I accepted the task there and then. Anderton was clearly surprised by my swift response, but he made no comment about it. I had given all the thought to it I deemed necessary. It was clearly not to be an easy job, but it had to be properly and thoroughly done. Unlike many very senior officers, I was comfortable with complex criminal investigations, and I knew I had the pick of the police officers in Greater Manchester to help me. Above all, however, I looked at this request as a tribute to the Manchester Force. In short, the job had to be done and I could think of no one better equipped than me or my Force to do it. That is why I said yes. I have never regretted it — not then, and despite everything that has happened, not now.

The RUC and the British government were anxious to make an announcement to the press that I had been appointed to head the investigation, and James Anderton asked me to telephone a Home Office number to confirm with one of Her Majesty's Inspectors of Constabulary my acceptance of the task. He in turn would tell Sir John Hermon and the Secretary of State for Northern Ireland before the press release was made. British and Irish newspaper headlines using such words as 'Shoot-to-Kill' and 'Police Cover-up' were becoming larger, and television news broadcasts were leading with the story. It was in everyone's interest that something be seen to be done.

I telephoned the number given to me and spoke to Mr Philip Myers. He thanked me for my prompt response and said he would speak to me within the next day or so. He was to play a very significant part in my life over the next two years.

The Home Office exercises its influence over the police service through the Inspectorate system. The principal police adviser to the Home Secretary on police matters is the Chief Inspector of Constabulary. Working under him are several regional Inspectors of Constabulary — all of them former Chief Constables who have retired, taken their pensions and then been immediately re-engaged as civil servants. The relationship between them and the police force is often an uneasy one. Some Chief Constables, particularly those of big, busy and demanding police forces, regard them as interfering bureaucrats. They are sometimes seen as men who have found the problems of command, even of small police forces, too tough, and have taken the soft option of an Inspectorate appointment many years before normal retirement age. The majority of Chief Constables, however, regard them as a valuable source of informed second opinion when the alternative might be to confide in a more junior officer or to show their hand to Home Office politicians or career civil servants. However members of the Inspectorate are viewed, they are powerfully influential people. A regional Inspector is the link between the Home Office and that region's police force. He should be, and usually is, an objective voice speaking with the benefit of experience and with the detachment of authority. An important part of his job is to know the capabilities of the senior officers within his region, to assess their potential for advancement and to plot and influence their career path.

Undoubtedly, the most demanding of the regions is the North West. Not only does it include the great conurbations of Merseyside and Greater Manchester, with all the problems there in policing terms, it also comprises the big county police forces of Lancashire, Cheshire and Cumbria. And in 1983 the region was extended to include the entire Royal Ulster Constabulary. There are those who say that the responsibility for such an enormously diverse area, and the problems of policing within it, are too much for one man to cope with — especially when he has never personally worked within it, and when his office is situated outside it. When I was asked to take on the investigation in 1984 the Regional Inspector was the man I telephoned, Mr Philip Myers. In 1985 he was knighted. Sir Philip Myers is the former Chief Constable of the North Wales Police, and before that he was a Superintendent in Shropshire. He retired from the police at the relatively young age of fifty-one and created a flurry of controversy when, on appointment, he decided not to work from any of the regional offices that had conveniently and variously been located in Manchester, Preston and Lancaster. He opened instead a single office outside the region, at the corner of the road in which he lives, in the relatively inaccessible place of Colwyn Bay in North Wales. To a large extent this made contact with him very difficult, and much more likely to be by telephone rather than face to face. Nevertheless, he found time during my two-year investigation to see me on three occasions at his seaside office.

After I had briefly spoken to him — in order to confirm my acceptance of the Northern Ireland job — Mr Myers contacted me again by telephone and told me that I could expect a rough passage in the Province. He made it clear that this investigation, despite public pronouncements, was not welcomed by the RUC, and that its Chief Constable, Sir John Hermon, privately regarded it as unnecessary. He was already making changes, and he viewed any investigation as likely to undermine the morale of his officers. Mr Myers emphasized to me the absolute importance, to the RUC and the administration of justice in the Province, of a thorough and far-reaching investigation into the growing complaints alleging a criminal cover-up by members of the Force, and he promised me his full support should I need it. I telephoned Sir John Hermon and made an appointment to see him for 24 May 1984. He was friendly and polite in his telephone conversation with me. I then set about choosing my team to assist me. I knew that the investigation could take a considerable time, and the first and most important thing was that whoever I chose should get on together. I wanted hardworking, self-motivated, intelligent officers — determined but quiet. I chose quickly but very carefully, and spoke individually to each officer. For my number two I approached Detective Chief Superintendent John Thorburn, a gritty fifty-year-old Scot whose CID experience and stature would have been difficult to surpass anywhere in the country. He and I had joined the Force about the same time, and had worked together in the detective branch. I had a very high regard for his capabilities. I could not have made a better choice. He accepted my invitation to work with me without hesitation or reservation. That is the sort of man he is.

I decided to keep my team small in numbers. I have always taken the view that a small group of officers working purposefully around the clock achieves more than a large group with time to spare. I shall not, for safety reasons, name the rest of the team, but they were six in all. They were two detective chief inspectors (one from the Special Branch and one from the Serious Crime Squad); two inspectors (one a detective with extensive anti-corruption experience and the other a uniformed officer with a high reputation who had worked on attachment in Northern Ireland); and two detective sergeants (one from the Serious Crime Squad and the other a graduate woman officer from the Drugs Squad). Each was given the opportunity, without prejudice, to decline to come with me. None of them refused — not even one of the officers whose wife is seriously troubled with a muscular disease.

The team chosen, I opened a small office with secure telephones and cabinets, in a room adjoining my office on the eleventh floor of Police Headquarters in Manchester. I flew to Belfast on 24 May 1984 with John Thorburn. The reception there was efficient and warm. A car waited for us at the Harbour airport and we were taken to see Sir John Hermon at his sumptuous office in Police Headquarters in Knock Road, Belfast, where he is surrounded by a battery of staff officers and press relations people. We spoke cordially, and he handed me a paper outlining the terms of reference for my investigation. These were, briefly, to investigate the circumstances of the three shooting incidents in which six men were shot dead and one seriously injured, and in which certain members of the Royal Ulster Constabulary provided false or misleading evidence to members of the Criminal Investigation Department; and to investigate the conduct of members of the Royal Ulster Constabulary in connection with the investigation of all three incidents. I was also to investigate whether there was evidence to suggest that any person was guilty of perverting or attempting to pervert the course of justice, or of any other offence in connection with the shooting incidents. I was to ascertain the circumstances in which members of the Royal Ulster Constabulary entered the Republic of Ireland on 12 December 1982 while on duty, and to investigate and report on the handling of informants by police officers — which information they cannot disclose to other policemen or the courts due to the need to protect sources.

As I read these draft terms of reference I began to feel the first pangs of irritation at what I saw as an attempt to circumscribe my enquiries. I did not voice them then; firstly, I wanted to think about my response, but more importantly, I knew from past experience that open-ended investigations, even on the mainland, can easily develop into an amorphous mess, the central issues being blurred by side issues. I took the view that in Northern Ireland nothing would be straightforward, and that on balance it was probably to my advantage to know fairly precisely what were my areas of investigation. What I objected to was having the man whose Force I was investigating drawing up the parameters of those enquiries.

Sir John invited John Thorburn and me to lunch with him at a golf club, and during the meal I saw the first signs of the problems to come. The Chief Constable obviously took the view that I was in Northern Ireland to 'review' what had happened in the three separate cases involving the deaths of the six men. He expected, I think, that I would read papers, speak to some key people about what had undoubtedly gone wrong, and submit a report containing a few operational recommendations for the future. My belief was that I was there to re-examine the three cases meticulously, to look for evidence of criminal offences committed by police officers or others, and if I found it, to submit that information to the Director of Public Prosecutions for consideration of prosecution. There was clearly a difference of opinion between us, and things never really improved. Before we left the golf club he said to me, 'Remember, Mr Stalker, you are in a jungle now.'

During the meal, Hermon handed me a handwritten note, sketched on the back of a flattened-out cigarette packet. It outlined my family tree on my mother's side. She is Catholic, and her parents were born in the Irish Republic. No mention was made of my father, who is a Protestant from a Liverpool family. Sir John did not say very much about where he had obtained this information, other than to let me know he had been given it at a social function by a man whose name meant nothing to me — indeed, I cannot even remember it. This action took me by surprise, and I was never able to fully fathom why the Chief Constable gave me that piece of flattened cardboard. It had no significance to me; indeed, I had never even heard of some of the names of my mother's distant cousins. It traced her relatives back to about 1900, and included Manchester as well as Irish branches of her family. I have no idea why he should have given me such information on our first meeting, or why he should have been discussing me at obvious length with a third party before I had actually arrived in Northern Ireland. It has been suggested that it may have been a subtle way of letting me know I was vulnerable to

allegations of Catholic minority bias. I found it very puzzling;
I still do.

Sir John asked me what facilities I would need, and
suggested we should stay in secure police accommodation
under his protection and work from his police headquarters. I
declined. I had already decided that I wanted my team to be as
independent and self-contained as possible, and we had made
arrangements, despite the vulnerability issue, to stay at small
family hotels within a twenty-mile radius of Belfast. John
Thorburn had insisted on secure offices away from police
headquarters, and these were found for us at a quiet former
hotel in Knocknagoney, near the Short Brothers' factory.

I returned to Manchester and formalized my acceptance of
the terms of reference by way of a letter to Sir John Hermon. I
spoke to Mr Philip Myers, and he asked for a copy of the
correspondence for his information. I told him that I was not
too happy about the situation, that Sir John Hermon
seemingly regarded my presence in Northern Ireland as an
imposition. He appeared to have chosen not to appreciate
what my job was in Northern Ireland. He intended, it seemed,
to dictate the direction my enquiries took me in his police
force. Mr Myers showed no surprise. He is a very quietly
spoken man, a heavy smoker, and his asthmatic voice makes it
very difficult to hear what he is saying. Occasionally, on
important matters, I recorded our conversations on an official
dictating machine attached to my telephone. I found this
useful for making sure I had not misunderstood what he was
saying. He was frank about Sir John Hermon. He said that Sir
John would never welcome any outside interest in the
workings of his Force, and that I should not expect too much.
Philip Myers assured me of his full support and asked me to
keep him aware of the general direction of my investigations,
but particularly to let him know early of any obstructiveness
or developments of a politically significant nature. I cannot
say I was over-confident about this promise, and in truth I had

serious misgivings about the whole constitutional basis of my enquiry. It seemed that the entire business was founded on shifting sand. But I had accepted the job, the announcements had been made, and on the face of it I had the powerful support of the Home Office, through the Inspectorate. There were (because of the different basis of government in Northern Ireland) a number of constitutional and legal minefields, but I had recognized them and felt confident that I could avoid them. As the months went on I realized how wrong I had been.

In the second week of June 1984 I returned to Belfast. This was my first visit since the lunch with Sir John Hermon at the golf club three weeks earlier. My team were already settled into the hotel and office accommodation we had arranged. We insisted the locks be changed on the office doors, and asked for new, secure cabinets and a safe with the keys in our possession. The RUC provided two drivers and a liaison officer — a detective sergeant. I regarded this as sufficient. We refused any armed protection. The liaison officer's job was to iron out difficulties with local policemen who did not know why we were in Northern Ireland. He made appointments for us, explained structures and hierarchies to us, and generally tried to look after any internal police problems on our behalf. Within his brief, he did very well indeed, but he was not senior enough, and I was never able to obtain the services of someone with more clout within the RUC. This meant that my officers had to take on all sorts of minor skirmishes with resentful RUC officers who were particularly skilled at politely promising much but actually delivering very little. John Thorburn, and occasionally I myself, had to take petty matters to a much higher level within the RUC (at times to the Chief Constable himself) than their seriousness warranted in order to get them resolved. The result of this constant low-level friction was to slow down simple jobs and make progress difficult. Policemen, especially those who have been involved in investigations into misbehaviour by policemen in other Forces, are not unused to this. I had experienced it many times in the past. With RUC Special Branch it was an art form.

The Special Branch is a department of the RUC. It has grown enormously in the last fifteen years, and is extremely well equipped and professional. It is headed by an Assistant Chief Constable, and is responsible for obtaining, analysing and acting upon information about terrorist groups. With the military and government intelligence services, it performs a crucial intelligence-gathering role, and its recruitment and handling of informants is integral to the success it enjoys. Within the Special Branch there are a number of specialist squads, uniformed and plain clothed, whose job it is to act on the information the informants supply. The Branch is not a special department. Its members are ordinary policemen doing work of a delicate and sensitive nature. But they do not have any additional powers. Many stay for most of their police service within the department, but others rotate this work regularly with other police duties.

The 'career' special branch officers were the most difficult of people to deal with. They did not seem to understand the responsibilities of others. The internal power they wield within the RUC was a factor we had not at that time measured, but in the course of time we realized it was very pervasive indeed.

It became obvious that we could not trust anyone, and I quickly grasped the meaning of Sir John Hermon's description of living in a jungle. A week or so after we settled into the routine of our investigation I received an anonymous phone call at my hotel from a sincere-sounding man with a Northern Ireland accent who said he was an RUC sergeant, and a Catholic. He said that our suite of offices was bugged and our telephone tapped. He started to tell me names of people to beware of in the Special Branch and then suddenly hung up.

He never rang back. In fact, my team had already accepted the probability of our offices being wired, and it had become a regular joke each morning, on opening up, for us to provide a test transmission to whomever might be eavesdropping. We were exceedingly careful, and spoke about important matters either in the hotel or, more usually, in the evenings over a quiet dinner. I think we all accepted it as inevitable that what we were intending to do, whom we were arranging to see, and which directions our enquiries were taking us, could be of interest to others.

We withdrew as a group into a self-contained, self-reliant unit. The routine of early Monday morning travel to Belfast, working days of over twelve hours, and return to Manchester late Friday afternoon, became part of our lives for almost two years. The difficult day-to-day organization of work fell to John Thorburn. I divided my time between my desks at Greater Manchester Police Headquarters and in Belfast.

It did not take any of us very long to realize how unused RUC Special Branch officers were to any sort of outside scrutiny. Simple requests for explanations of basic systems or procedures were regarded with suspicion and resentment. Virtually from day one some senior members of the branch tried, unsuccessfully, to insist that we tell them why we wanted information before they agreed even to see us, let alone tell us what we wanted to know. Either John Thorburn or I had on several occasions to remind some very senior policemen that we were in the Province at the request of their Chief Constable, to investigate alleged criminal offences committed by police officers of their Force. There undoubtedly developed a strongly hostile feeling towards us at middle and senior levels in the RUC Special Branch. I am certain they saw us — in particular Thorburn and myself — as disloyal members of the same Police Service who neither knew nor cared about their special operational difficulties. They were quite wrong, of course; but their narrow perspective on

police life, protected as it is from operational responsibility
for the investigation of crime, simply did not allow them to see
that an open, honest and thorough enquiry was in the interests
of their branch and the RUC. A few key officers took a
decision, individually or collectively I know not, to obstruct
the progress of our investigations. I am convinced that most of
our difficulties flowed from the belief of influential Special
Branch officers that all I should be doing was to conduct a
review of matters past, and not commencing a new
investigation.

There are many instances of this sort of thing I could give,
but I recall one particularly vivid example: within weeks of
our arrival in Northern Ireland we discovered that four of the
men shot by the RUC in two of the incidents could be linked
by intelligence to the murders of three policemen in an IRA
land-mine explosion three weeks before. The inferences were
obvious. I had to look at the possibility of police revenge as a
motive. I started by asking for the intelligence file on the
explosion, and was told, quite unequivocally, that none
existed. I pressed further, because I did not believe that
something so important as the murder by terrorists of three
policemen could have had no Special Branch documentation.
Once again I was told, none too politely, that no file existed.
For three months my team of six police officers painstakingly
pieced together, at the expense of almost everything else, the
events and the parts played by individuals in that explosion.
By October 1984 we had painted our own picture of what had
happened on that tragic day, 27 October 1982. In March
1985 I interviewed a very senior RUC officer under caution as
a criminal suspect. He was upset, angry and defensive, and by
way of explanation and justification for certain of his actions
he asked me to consider a file of papers. He reached into his
briefcase and handed me the bulky folder whose existence he
and his colleagues had denied nine months earlier. Three
months' extra work for six of my officers could have been

avoided if this file had been provided then. The officer I was interviewing later said he had been 'doing as he had been told' — by whom I never found out — in denying me access to this file. I intended to ask the Chief Constable and his Deputy what they knew of this, but I was removed from the investigation before I could conduct interviews with them. I do not know whether this question was ever put to them.

This type of downright obstructiveness was unfortunately not rare, and it served to prolong and delay an already complex investigation even further. It also hardened our determination not to be worn down by it. As a team we were angry and disappointed at these quite indefensible tactics, but we knew we had to get on with the job in hand. A kind of war had obviously been declared between the Special Branch and my team, and my best efforts to show neutrality had been thrown back at me. If, as a fellow-policeman, I did not appear to be wholly on the side of the RUC, then some influential senior elements within it regarded me as *against* them, and by implication as disloyal to the Crown. I did not share that view. I saw my task as being to get to the truth, or as near to it as I could. Police officers are not above the law. If any in the RUC had committed criminal offences, my job was to present the evidence to the Director of Public Prosecutions. It was essential that I have a clear picture of what I was in Northern Ireland to do, and it was part of my duty to leave my team in no doubt about what that was. They were working in a difficult environment, and were entitled to know what I was thinking. Survival in a complex world is often best achieved by keeping things simple, and that is what I decided to do. I do not mean that I took a simplistic view. I thought long and hard about the problems of the Royal Ulster Constabulary and the immense difficulties of policing in Northern Ireland. I reflected on whether it would even be fair to regard some of them as being policemen at all. Were not members of that special squad in truth soldiers in a police uniform? Was it not sensible to think of them as being at war? Honest questions, but the answers came easily enough. Northern Ireland is part of the United Kingdom, its laws are our laws, and what happens there should concern us all because it happens in our name. The Royal Ulster Constabulary is a British police force and its members are policing a democracy in the name of the Crown. It was my job to reflect and to understand, perhaps even to sympathize, but it was not my job to make political judgments about the world they have to operate in. I decided that if serious breaches of the law by policemen are to be excused, then they should not be excused by other policemen. That way lies very deep trouble for a society such as ours.

After the first couple of weeks, the enormity of our task was becoming apparent. I brought my team together and told them what I deeply believed: that their job was to discover and substantiate evidence of criminal offences, whether by policemen or by anyone else, to bring that evidence to my desk, and leave the evaluation of it to me. I told them we could not allow ourselves to become bogged down in philosophical, historical and religious discussions about the nature of policing in Northern Ireland. I saw our job as providing the basis for lawyers and politicians to make those judgments; but for the moment we were to regard ourselves in the same way as if we were conducting a criminal investigation in Birmingham or Liverpool. Our interest was not in prosecutions but in presenting the best evidence to those who would make the decision whether or not to prosecute. We were to remain professional, thorough, but above all, emotionally detached from the reasons why things happened.

It has been said that this approach on my part was naive and that I showed no real understanding of the nature of policing in Northern Ireland. I knew from the start that criticism would eventually be levelled at me — unless I totally exonerated all policemen from all wrongdoing. To protect myself and to place it on record, I told Mr Philip Myers before

I commenced the enquiry that my investigative line would be straightforward and uncomplicated; that within my terms of reference I would investigate everything I could as thoroughly as I could. Philip Myers agreed fully with my decision to keep above Force politics and operational problems, and he promised continued support in my search for the truth. It was becoming clearer to me day by day that I needed all the help I could get.

Within a few days of my commencing the investigation, the trial of three more policemen on murder charges made for more international headlines. Sergeant Montgomery and Constables Brannigan and Robinson (not the same officer as in the Grew and Carroll shootings) were acquitted of the murder of Eugene Toman at a supposed road block in Tullygally East Road, Lurgan. The trial judge, Lord Justice Gibson, recognized the unusual nature of the case and commented about seriously incorrect evidence given to a court at a preliminary hearing of the charges. He then went on, in acquitting the officers of murder, to praise them for bringing the deceased men, Toman, Burns and McKerr, to 'the final court of justice'. His remarks created unprecedented uproar. They appeared to remove all doubt: there existed, it seemed, a judicially endorsed 'shoot-to-kill' policy in the Province. The judge's reference to the deaths of Burns and McKerr, whom none of the officers had been charged with unlawfully killing, was particularly unfortunate. Un-committed observers, as well as nationalists, could see no reason why the judge should be so enthusiastic about the deaths of three unarmed men at the hands of the police. Such was the widespread international condemnation of his remarks that he quickly made a prepared (and very unusual) public statement from the Bench in which he clarified his views by emphatically repudiating the idea that he approved of a shoot-to-kill policy on the part of the police. It was too late for that: the damage was done, and no denial was ever going to change the general public belief among Catholics and many others in the Province, as well as the mainland and the Republic of Ireland, that some members of the RUC were out of control and had a free rein to kill whomsoever they suspected of involvement in unlawful republicanism. Lord Justice Gibson became a marked man, and he and his wife were killed in a border car bomb explosion in April 1987.

Two of the three relevant criminal court cases were now out of the way, and I was free to start investigating in detail the deaths these cases concerned, those of Toman, Burns and McKerr, and of Grew and Carroll. The third incident, involving the death of young Michael Tighe and the shooting of his friend Martin McCauley, could not be seriously commenced until court proceedings against McCauley were concluded. It was made clear to me from within the Director of Public Prosecutions' office, however, that there was no legal impediment to my looking at the broad circumstances of the shootings, and in particular at the evidence already provided by the police officers involved by way of their official statements. The truth of what these contained was clearly crucial, having regard to the lies that had already emerged at the two earlier trials.

My team began work in earnest. We obtained, without difficulty, the routine files and information on all six deaths. The CID had in each case carried out an investigation, including forensic tests, but I was surprised and worried to see that each of these three investigations had been carried out by a different detective officer. Even though the six deaths had occurred over a five-week period in the same relatively small area of Northern Ireland, and involved in each case officers from the same specialist squad, no co-ordinated investigation had ever been attempted. It seemed that the investigating officers had never spoken to each other. Worse still, despite the obvious political and public implications, no senior officer had seen fit to draw the reports together. Even allowing for the extraordinary policing demands of Northern Ireland, this seemed inexplicable to me. Police officers do not regularly shoot people dead in the Province, and I was assured that such an event is always regarded with the utmost concern. And yet here were six deaths with a host of obviously unanswered questions attached to them. I read the papers, looked at the photographs, compared procedures based on my own previous murder investigations, and my heart sank. John Thorburn and I knew that according to our standards the files were poorly prepared and presented. We had expected a particularly high level of enquiry in view of the nature of the deaths, but this was shamefully absent. The files were little more than a collection of statements, apparently prepared for a coroner's enquiry. They bore no resemblance to my idea of a murder prosecution file. Even on the most cursory of readings I could see clearly why the prosecutions had failed. I had no doubt whatsoever that my decision to re-investigate rather than review the cases was emphatically the correct one.

I asked that each member of my team should have a good knowledge of all the matters associated with every investigation, but I allocated two officers specifically to each shooting incident. I told them I expected them to have knowledge, to the finest detail, of their particular case. When the time came to set about analysing the evidence presented to the courts, and the new evidence we had found, I wanted my officers to be unassailable in their grasp of every word, exhibit and nuance. They did not disappoint me.

We started with the investigation into the deaths of Toman, Burns and McKerr in Tullygally East Road, Lurgan. The official version of the events had been that a police officer on foot, accompanied by a colleague, had routinely attempted to stop a Ford Escort car by the traditional method of standing in the road and signalling with his torch for it to stop. The driver, it was said, stopped momentarily, then accelerated past the policeman, striking him and causing him to jump out of the way. Other policemen in a patrol car, parked by chance nearby, had witnessed the incident and had moved off to follow the car. The policemen in the car said they believed they were being fired at, and opened return fire. The Ford Escort left the road; the three men in it were all found to have died instantaneously from gunshot wounds.

The truth was quite different. We discovered that the three men had been under surveillance for many hours, and that the police plan had been to intercept them at a different place altogether. No serious attempt to attract the attention of the driver was ever made, and no policeman was struck by the car. The three officers in the police car were waiting, and they fired 108 bullets from a Sterling sub-machine gun, Ruger rifles and a handgun during a pursuit that extended over 500 yards. All the men died instantly; none was armed. I was astonished to learn that all the policemen involved had been instructed to leave the scene immediately, with their car and their weapons, and return to their base for a de-briefing by senior Special Branch officers. Detective officers were denied access for many days to them and to forensic examination of their car, clothes, hands and weapons. The same CID officers were, on the night of the killings, provided with incorrect information about where the shootings had commenced, and some forensic examination of the scene was conducted in the wrong place. Many cartridge cases were never found, and some wholly unconvincing explanations were given for their removal. One of these was that a Catholic priest who came unannounced to perform the last rites on the deceased must have swept the cases away, possibly accidentally in the hem of his cassock.

In the rest of the United Kingdom the police officers would never have been allowed to leave the scene of the shooting, unless they were injured, until the senior CID officer gave them permission. They would have been subjected to the most rigorous forensic examination and their weapons removed from them for test firing and exhibit purposes. These strict rules apply even to members of the SAS if they are deployed in earnest on the mainland. The system is designed to protect the officers involved as well as to give the best evidence to the courts. These simple rules, known as 'preservation of evidence', were blatantly ignored by Special Branch in all three of the cases I investigated.

I arranged for a reconstruction of the shootings using the original Ford Escort ridden with bullet holes. (Efforts were later made for this car to be shipped to New York to be used in a St Patrick's Day street parade as a giant collecting-box for money from Irish-American fund-raisers. This approach from Republican sympathizers was refused, and the RUC still have possession of that Ford Escort.) Our conclusion was that the first shot was probably fired by one of the officers on foot and not by the occupants of the police car. We believed also that at least one officer had been in an entirely different position from that he had claimed to be in when some fatal shots were fired. I also established that the police pursuit took place in a different manner from that described. But most damning of all, almost 21 months after the shooting we found fragments of the bullet that had undoubtedly killed the driver still embedded in the car. That crucial evidence had lain undiscovered by the RUC and the Forensic Science service. My team also traced an independent witness who had never been interviewed. Worse still, in my view, the State Pathologist who examined the bodies had not been called to the scene to see them *in situ;* photographic evidence was virtually useless — it provided no evidence of angles or distances, and was taken at night in black and white. This catalogue of ineptitude was completed when I learned that the detective officer in charge of the investigations had not attended the mortuary, or the post-mortem examinations; also, no official record of any discussions between him and the State Pathologist was ever given to me. Neither had the relatives of the dead men ever been visited or contacted by the investigating detectives.

I regarded this latter point as very important, not simply on compassionate grounds — that may be asking too much — but as a positive act of professional investigation. The relatives might in the event have refused to co-operate with the police, but that is no excuse for not making contact with them. The investigating detectives had been given an incomplete story by the Special Branch of the earlier movements of the dead men; the relatives, had they been asked, might have been able to confirm or discredit that account. In unquestioningly accepting one story when another was available, the seeds of complacency were sown. In the absence of an explanation by the police to the relatives of what had happened, rumour and terrorist propaganda was allowed to spread unchecked. No one knew what had happened, therefore everyone was free to speculate, invent and embroider. The RUC, in the eyes of the relatives of the dead men, had played out their expected role, that of a harsh, insensitive and brutal police force. The chasm widened, and the losers were the RUC.

The RUC never recovered from the poor handling of that first series of shootings. My conclusion in relation to the missing cartridge cases was that as many as twenty were deliberately removed from the scene. I could only presume that this was in order to mislead the forensic scientists and to hide the true nature and extent of the shooting. I had to regard the investigation of the matter as slipshod, and in some aspects woefully incomplete. I was left with two alternative conclusions: either that some RUC detectives were amateur and inefficient at even the most basic of murder investigation routines; or that they had been deliberately inept. I cannot say which of those is the truth, but do I know that the level of investigation would never have been tolerated on the mainland.

My team immersed themselves in the investigation. I

watched them as they pieced together the events of that night. They bore the brunt of the negative attitude of some members of the Special Branch. Their clear determination not to be diverted strengthened as each new obstacle was sighted, examined and removed. Three of my team were Scots, and I appreciated again why that country produces so many fine detectives. Apart from a natural taciturnity, they possess a stubborn streak that does not allow them to accept 'no' for an answer until they are sure that that is indeed the answer. As investigators the best of them possess a bloody-minded pride that pushes them on when others, perhaps more prag- matically, may have given up. John Thorburn was a perfect example of that breed of detective, and he was a sad loss to the police force when he decided to retire in November 1986.

We were told by the RUC that contact with Republican elements in strongly Catholic areas around Lurgan and Armagh was just not possible. The risks to us of death or capture were unacceptable to the RUC, and they could not guarantee our safety without a massive show of strength from both police and Army. For very good operational reasons this type of heavy display, put on merely to enable us to speak to a possible witness in our enquiry, was quite out of the question. I knew, however, that to do the job properly I had to spend many hours with some elements who are hostile to the RUC, and to us as representatives of the British government. The problem posed was a serious one. The RUC was un- equivocally opposed to our seeing these people, and the personal risk to us was chillingly real. If I insisted, then a big police/Army operation would reluctantly have to be arranged. We learned that the people we wished to see would not under any circumstances come near a police station. They would not come to us, and we were strongly advised not to go to them. We had reached an impasse, and I had to decide the best way round it.

I knew very well that the RUC's concerns for us were valid and sincere. But I decided that if my investigation was to mean anything it had to be seen to have tried consciously to overcome these difficulties. The method we subsequently adopted worked very well. A member of my team would make contact with a relative of one of the deceased, usually by telephone, or through a third party, and a firm appointment would be made for two of my officers to be at the local priest's house at a prearranged time. The RUC car would, at my request, drop us off a mile or so away and we would walk to the appointment. Often the young woman detective on my team made appointments direct by travelling alone to a house, usually on foot. I shall never know what the risks were, but I do know that if the IRA had wished to pick any of us off they could easily have done so. None of us was armed, at any time, while in Northern Ireland. I believe that our willingness to meet the families of the deceased on their own ground, unarmed and alone, quickly established with them our honesty of purpose and neutrality, and was probably the biggest single factor in our making the progress that we did. It has been said that in doing so I exposed myself and my team to unnecessary danger and that I risked creating a new crisis. I take a different view. I regarded our approach as having elements of necessary danger, but I saw no honest alternative. Contact with people who could help the enquiry was crucial. The members of the team knew what they were doing, but none of them expressed reservations or resentment. Even with the benefit of hindsight I would still conduct this aspect of the investigation in exactly the same way. A view could be taken that the IRA had nothing to gain by the assassination of me or of any member of my team. I was, after all, investigating obvious wrongdoing by their sworn enemies, the RUC, and until my investigation was completed I could not be accused of conducting a whitewash. I knew, however, that the fact of our walking alone and openly in certain housing estates in Lurgan and Armagh must have caused earnest discussion among terrorist elements. They knew I was there and they obviously decided I should be given a chance to complete the job.

One of the parish priests, Father Murray, was an enormous help in easing my entry into strongly Catholic enclaves in Armagh. He acted as a neutral intermediary, and lent his authority and experience to us. He was as sceptical as every other Catholic we met about what my enquiry would actually achieve, but his hopes for Northern Ireland persuaded him to keep on trying. The people we met were wary of us at first, one or two openly hostile, but all of them quickly settled into a type of polite but puzzled co-operativeness. After a while, as confidence in our objectivity grew, we were invited to some individual homes in order to take long written statements, often lasting for several hours. The television would be turned off, the kettle switched on, and this curious vignette of a British policeman sitting on their settee, taking details of the killing of their relatives and friends by other policemen, was studied at close hand. Occasionally the semi-formality of it all would be broken and someone would ask whether we were playing an elaborate game with them. None of them believed the investigation would actually achieve anything or lead to prosecutions of policemen, and several of the people I saw said prophetically that I would never finish the enquiry, particularly if it began to threaten the RUC or the British government. I recall one community leader saying to me that he just could not understand why we all seemed to be taking the whole business so seriously. He advised me to 'get in and get out' as quickly as I could: 'Tell them [the government] what they want to hear — that the RUC are a fine brave force. Whatever you say will make no difference over here — the lid has to be kept on. Only the RUC can do it — you won't be allowed to lift it off.'

I especially remember one young man in a house in Lurgan asking to see my Manchester warrant card. He gazed at it and said, 'I can't believe I have a Brit. cop in my house. I'm glad I've got witnesses because my kids will never believe it when they grow up.' Many of the older people we saw were like the people of inner-city Manchester, the area in which I was born and brought up. They gave us a respectful and polite welcome into their homes and I saw the same ornaments, wallpaper and furniture that I have seen so many times in similar houses in Manchester. But above all, they were interested in the reasons for our being in their homes. They were world-weary people, seemingly resigned to a never-changing situation but with a resilience and spirit which left its mark on my team and on me. I never had an opportunity to thank them for their hospitality, or indeed to thank the priests and others who helped us. Perhaps belatedly I can do so here — for their cool detachment and their careful choice of words, for an acceptance of our honest desire to do a professional job, but especially just for their presence and influence in those early edgy days.

Many members of the RUC, some at senior level, never accepted our need to meet and speak with Republican families. Their view, expressed forcefully and often, was that my regarding them as important witnesses, with something to contribute to my enquiry, gave Republican groups a spurious and undeserved respectability. My team was told that the IRA would regard our interest in those families as a publicity coup, and would exploit my presence on the estates for everything it was worth, either by ridiculing what they would describe as the attempts of the British government to cover up a cover-up, or by resurrecting the emotions surrounding the deaths of two years earlier. I was seen as offering myself to the IRA as a ready-made and willing stick with which they might beat the Security forces. I was very well aware then that my decision to regard relatives of the dead men, and other Republican families, as potentially legitimate witnesses was seen as naive and harmful by RUC Special Branch. Such is their understandable antipathy, hatred even, towards the IRA, they are absolutely convinced that any official contact, no matter how remote, can only add to the political stature of terrorists. I do not agree with them. The Special Branch and my team never saw eye to eye about this. I had given careful thought to it, and had recognized the propaganda value to IRA publicists, but nevertheless decided I was morally and professionally bound to do as I did. I have had plenty of time to reflect on the way I dealt with this part of my investigation, and I still believe I was right.

A strange sort of detached respect for us seemed to grow. No doubt what we represented — the police and the British Crown — was detested. We, as individuals, however, were tolerated, obviously on occasion against instinctive judgments. We were the first and possibly only policemen many of those people will ever meet in a non-confrontational, almost friendly, atmosphere.

The spokesmen for the families of the dead men were usually solicitors. They were wary towards us, very conscious, it seemed to me, of the contempt I would be held in by some policemen for entering their clients' homes. It was fascinating to see at close quarters the relationship between police and some defence solicitors in Northern Ireland. It was quite unlike anything I have ever experienced in England. In this country a defence solicitor — even the most anti-police or devious of them — is treated by policemen as a professional. He may be spoken to very coolly, in a carefully guarded way, but he will be acknowledged as doing a job. I saw very little of that type of relationship during the long days I spent at Crumlin Road Crown Court, particularly where the cases which interested me were concerned. For me and my team the Courthouse was a convenient place where we could speak to solicitors, tell them of our intentions and retain their co-operation. It was a place for new introductions, for appointment-making and courtesy contacts with a number of solicitors who specialize in representing Republican families.

The atmosphere in the big hall was electric whenever we spoke to any of these solicitors. We felt open resentment and distrust from many of the RUC officers gathered in small groups around us. I recall one conversation with a youngish RUC uniformed sergeant who left his group and approached me angrily as I walked away after a very short conversation with a solicitor representing Martin McCauley, the youth who survived the shooting at the Hayshed. The sergeant came up to me and said, 'May I speak to you, Mr Stalker? Do you know who that was you were speaking to?' I replied, 'Yes — it was Martin McCauley and his solicitor.' The sergeant said, 'The solicitor is an IRA man — any man who represents IRA men is worse than an IRA man. His brother is an IRA man also and I have to say that I believe a senior policeman of your rank should not be seen speaking to the likes of either of them. My colleagues have asked me to tell you that you have embarrassed all of us in doing that. I will be reporting this conversation and what you have done to my superiors.'

I was surprised at his studied vehemence, although I recognized his comment for the honest bigotry it clearly was, and I let the matter go. But what he had starkly illustrated to me was the bitter depths of hatred even among professionals. I began to understand just why my presence in Northern Ireland was resented so much. I had again lent respectability to alleged terrorists — a solicitor and client — merely by talking to them. This conversation with the sergeant also showed me how easy it would be in the Province to have one's name included in Special Branch files and minds as having 'possible Republican sympathies'. An open conversation in a public place with a solicitor who performs his duty to the courts was, it seems, probably sufficient evidence of such 'sympathies'.

We had settled into life in Northern Ireland and got our heads down in order to find out as much as we could in the shortest possible time. The common denominator in four of the six deaths I was investigating was a matter I had not been asked to investigate; indeed, I had not even been told about it by the Special Branch. This was the murder on 27 October 1982 of three police officers, Sergeant Sean Quinn and Constables Paul Hamilton and Alan McCloy, by a huge landmine that was exploded as their car drove over it at a place called Kinnego in Lurgan. The area around Kinnego had been regarded as on 'high alert' for some days, and out of bounds to all police officers. A telephone call was received, supposedly from a farmer reporting the theft of a battery from a tractor. The call was checked and authenticated, and the three policemen, surprisingly, were given special authority to enter the zone to investigate this minor theft. The call had been made under duress, and the theft was a lie. Their deaths prompted an internal police investigation, but no one was ever arrested. An informant, however, gave the RUC the names of the men he said were implicated in the explosion. They were never interrogated because there was no evidence other than an informant's word, but four of them, Toman, Burns, McKerr and McCauley, were shot by police within the next six weeks. Obviously the picture we had put together for ourselves from scraps of Special Branch information made the horror of Kinnego a very important event. I could not overlook the possibility that revenge killings had taken place. I spoke to some very senior police officers, including the Chief Constable, and indicated that I had extended my terms of reference to investigate the Kinnego murders and that I intended to continue along those lines.

Sir John told me that although he had been less than a mile away from the scene when his men were killed, in order to distance himself from the investigations he had not travelled immediately to the explosion. I briefly asked Sir John about the circumstances of that awful day, but he said he did not wish to discuss them with me as he felt he did not know enough about them. Quite properly, he indicated that a little knowledge in these matters is a dangerous thing and that he would prefer I obtained my information from elsewhere. Finally, he agreed that revelation of the shortcomings that he was sure I was about to discover, in relation to the investigation and background of the Kinnego landmine, could cause severe morale problems for the Force, and distress to the families of the dead policemen.

The significance of what he meant became clearer to me very soon after that conversation. We found that an IRA explosive store had been under police surveillance but that the explosives had been removed without the knowledge of the police and used in the murderous attack in Kinnego. Worse than that, we found that before the three policemen had been given clearance to enter the area, a check had supposedly been made and a message returned that the explosives were in the Hayshed all intact, and that thus the threat to police in the area was not great. This breakdown in police communications, or ineptitude — call it what you like — had never been divulged to the families of the three dead policemen, and I have no doubt that their subsequent knowledge of it caused them enormous pain. This silence may have been for reasons of compassion, or for operational or insurance reasons.

This in itself was an important piece in our picture. But even more significant was the fact that the hayshed in Ballyneery Road used for this explosives storage was the same one in which young Michael Tighe was shot dead and Martin McCauley seriously injured six weeks after the explosives had been removed. The hayshed was to play a major part in the rest of the story, but at that stage I had no idea just how important it was to be and I was not able to involve myself too deeply in that matter because, as I have said, a criminal trial in respect of Martin McCauley had still not started and the matter was still *sub judice.*

I therefore confined the team to obtaining as much information as possible about the links between the Hayshed, the Tullygally East Road shootings of Toman, Burns and McKerr, and the deaths of the three policemen at Kinnego. This was intended to put me in the position of having all the information ready for when I was free to begin actively scrutinizing the Hayshed affair.

In the meantime we worked hard at finding the truth of the shooting dead of the unarmed Roddy Carroll and Seamus Grew in Armagh City on 12 December 1982. After that shooting a public statement had been issued by the police saying that the men were shot after breaking through a random police road block and injuring a policeman. None of this was true. At the trial of Constable Robinson for the murder of Grew he gave evidence, on oath, in his own defence, in which he said that after the shooting he was taken quickly from the scene before the CID could interview him, together with his weapon, uniform and police car. He said he was told to tell lies to protect an informant source. He was instructed to tell a story that made it appear that the entire episode had been the result of a misunderstanding. My team either discovered or confirmed for me that the deaths of Grew and Carroll had, like the other shootings, come at the end of a long surveillance operation that had involved RUC officers making journeys into the Republic of Ireland. Grew and Carroll had been followed for days but had managed to avoid a joint police/Army road block after they drove back over the border into Northern Ireland. In an accidental collision between an undercover Army car and a police car a policeman had hurt his leg. We found that during the resulting confusion the suspects' Allegro car had driven past the accident undetected, followed by an RUC Special Branch Inspector who had been on their trail in the Province and in the Republic of Ireland. He saw the shambles at the side of the road, realized that Grew and Carroll had driven past unseen, and panicked. He picked up an armed RUC officer — Constable Robinson — and pursued the car containing Grew and Carroll. On the outskirts of the staunchly Catholic Mullacreavie Park housing estate in Armagh, the undercover police car pulled ahead of the suspects' car and Constable Robinson got out. He emptied his revolver into Grew and Carroll, reloaded and fired more shots. Both men died instantly. The Special Branch Inspector, who had had the opportunity to see everything and knew the truth, drove off, and his evidence was kept secret from the CID investigating the deaths and from the Director of Public Prosecutions and the courts. Records were altered to hide the use of undercover cars in that part of Northern Ireland.

These deaths, we discovered, had no connection with the others, nor with the deaths of the three policemen at Kinnego. These were men whom the Special Branch strongly believed to be associates of the much-wanted alleged terrorist murderer Dominic McGlinchey. The complex operation, the surveillance, the unauthorized journeys by police officers into the Irish Republic, and finally the shootings were all part of a plan to detain McGlinchey. He had not, however, been seen by any policemen that day despite the long periods of surveillance, and it was never established — certainly not by me — that Seamus Grew and Roddy Carroll had been in his company. An informant was at the heart of things, as so often in Northern Ireland, but we were never told so. As with Kinnego, we sat down, examined the options and worked it out for ourselves before we put requests to the Special Branch. Again, they would neither confirm nor deny that an informant was involved. They refused to give me details, despite my clear responsibility to examine the difficulties associated with the use of informants in Northern Ireland and to look at the circumstances of RUC incursions into the Irish Republic.

I protested to the Special Branch, but the officers concerned obviously regarded my undertaking as insufficient reason to discuss informants with me. It was a matter I eventually had to take up with the Chief Constable, and it illustrated yet again how stubbornly defiant the Special Branch was towards my requests. Our close examination of the evidence presented by the Special Branch to the investigating CID officers again showed a lamentable standard of professionalism in their enquiries. My team, with the assistance of Father Murray, found an independent and impressive witness to the shooting. He had never been approached by the RUC — indeed, no determined enquiries were ever made even at houses that overlooked the scene. The independent forensic findings and our own enquiries proved, in my view, that some police officers could be shown not to have been where they said they were at various times during that evening. We strongly suspected, and may even have been able to show, that the police officer injured in the crash of the two surveillance cars was later asked to roll in the dirt some distance away in order to bolster a false claim that he had been run down by Grew and Carroll's car at a road block. The same inadequate death-scene procedures unfolded for us, including unhelpful black-and-white police photographs, and poor liaison with the Forensic Scientist. The pathologist once again had not attended the scene, nor had the investigating police officer been present at the post-mortem. The shockingly low standard of basic techniques evident in the Tullygally East Road shootings had been repeated.

I examined other murder files prepared by the RUC in cases unconnected with my enquiry, and found a generally more satisfactory presentation. In the Grew and Carroll case the shooting dead of two unarmed men by a policeman had been treated as a routine coroner's file, not as a criminal matter. This had been the last of three similar incidents over a period of barely a month, and yet the significance — indeed, enormity — of what had occurred had still not been recognized at senior level in the RUC. It seemed to me that none of those six deaths was investigated as a possible murder case, with policemen as the suspects, until many months later, by which time the evidence had either been lost or forgotten.

Even as early in the investigation as this I began to worry a great deal about the impact my findings and recommendations would have on the standing and reputation of the RUC. I was not yet convinced that a shoot-to-kill policy existed, but the ineptitude of the two investigations I had looked at so far raised suspicions that some police had deliberately refused to discover evidence of murder involving their colleagues. I found this difficult to accept, as did my team; but the only alternative to this sinister interpretation was that these abysmally deficient investigations pointed to an unprofessional and careless CID. Either way, neither the Chief Constable nor the Northern Ireland Office was going to be pleased with what I would eventually have to tell them. I decided not to say anything to Sir John Hermon at this early stage, especially as I had not begun to investigate the incident at the Hayshed. Because of the potentially serious political and operational implications for the Force, however, I decided to tell Mr Philip Myers of my emerging findings. I telephoned him at the Home Office and he expressed no real surprise — indeed, he seemed almost to anticipate what I had to say. He is, of course, the civil servant responsible for inspecting the RUC in a formal sense. I gained the impression that he had been trying, without much success, to improve some aspects of the Force's procedures, and that he saw as useful any strength I could lend to his arm.

During those early months I occasionally confided my frustrations and difficulties to my own Chief Constable, James Anderton. He has a close interest in Northern Ireland affairs, and during these two years I knew he was grappling with his inner compulsion to abandon his Methodist faith and embrace Catholicism. He began taking instruction in the Catholic faith early in my investigation, and he was always ready to listen at first hand to my perceptions and impressions of the divide in Northern Ireland. He is a good friend of Sir John Hermon's and respects him greatly. I know that they see their respective jobs in very similar ways. Both are charismatic and uncompromising men who have an unfailing conviction that a strong police force is the bonding agent in a cohesive society, and they share, I believe, a dislike of politicians who 'interfere' in policing matters. James Anderton told me in one conversation that, after the job of Metropolitan Police Commissioner, that of the Chief Constable of the RUC was the one he would have liked; that it presented to a professional policeman the sternest test of strategy and tactics. He has great admiration, as do I, for the bravery and dedication of the men and women of the Royal Ulster Constabulary.

As the months of 1984 went by I realized the power of the RUC Special Branch. My team busied themselves by tracing and interviewing dozens and then hundreds of policemen. Each officer was interviewed at length and fresh written statements taken, using Greater Manchester Police forms and stationery. A clear message emerged: that Special Branch officers planned, directed and effectively controlled the official accounts given in the two incidents we had so far addressed. The Special Branch targeted the suspected terrorist, they briefed the officers, and after the shootings they removed the men, cars and guns for a private de-briefing before the CID officers were allowed any access to these crucial matters. They provided the cover stories, and they decided at what point the CID were to be allowed to commence the official investigation of what had occurred. The Special Branch interpreted the information and decided what was, or was not, evidence; they attached the labels — whether a man was 'wanted' for an offence, for instance, or whether he was an 'on-the-run terrorist'. I had never experienced, nor had any of my team, such an influence over an entire police force by one small section. We discovered an instance of a junior Special Branch officer's giving operational instructions to much more senior CID officers — and of his being meekly obeyed. Most CID officers we saw seemed resigned to the supremacy of the Special Branch. Some of them wearily said that there was no point in fighting it — that the power of Special Branch pervaded the RUC at all levels. One Chief Superintendent said to me, 'I did not ask what was going on. I knew I would not be told.'

The numbers of policemen we interviewed grew, and with it the obvious concern of the RUC. The first rumours began to reach me of what were to become familiar cries — 'Stalker is trying to make a name for himself', or 'Stalker cannot control Thorburn' or, more significantly, 'They can see who they like, butthey will get nowhere — the government won't allow it.' This last was voiced by a senior Special Branch officer to a policeman, who then told one of my team. We interviewed every policeman again, and we gave all of them the opportunity of telling us the truth. Each of them was told that we were starting with a fresh sheet, and we asked them to recognize our honesty of purpose. The response was immensely interesting. We saw over three hundred policemen, and I can recall no more than half a dozen who were hostile to us. The remainder of them either retold their original story in a straightforward way or else, with great emotional relief, recounted the true events of the shootings and the course of the operations leading up to them. For many officers it represented the end of a two-year nightmare during which they had not known to whom they could tell the truth. The RUC investigators had not, in their view, truly wanted to hear it.

The majority of these interviews were conducted by John Thorburn or the Chief Inspectors, while I interviewed all policemen of the rank of Inspector and above. In all I personally saw about thirty-five senior policemen, including four Assistant Chief Constables. Many of these interviews were conducted 'under caution', which means that the policemen interviewed were regarded by me as criminal suspects, and the interviews were formal, structured and often lasted for many hours.

The same picture emerged with both incidents. The false story had been prepared as a contingency before the shooting took place and had been put out almost immediately as a press release. One enlightening instance involved a policeman member of the special E4 Squad involved in the shooting of Grew and Carroll. While waiting to be debriefed by his Special Branch chiefs at Gough Barracks, Armagh, he watched, bewildered, a television news bulletin that broadcast an already circulated and totally false police account of what had happened. He knew it to be lies. He had fully intended, he said, to tell the truth of what had occurred at the 'road block' that never happened, and wished to be honest about the unfortunate mistake that had allowed the suspects' car to drive past them. When he went into the office to be debriefed, however, he was told that protection of informant sources was far more important than truthfulness to the press, and that he was sworn to secrecy under threat of the Official Secrets Act. He did as he was told.

Cover stories given to the press, no matter how mendacious, do not in themselves, of course, amount to a criminal offence. In rare circumstances they may be a legitimate tactic in a dirty war of disinformation designed to fool an enemy. My view is that it is dangerous and generally counter-productive. Clearly, newspapers and television reporters will clamour for details if a policeman shoots dead unarmed members of the public. They are entitled to information — but it should always be accurate. It need not — indeed, it should not — be too rich in detail, but no matter how terse it is, it must never lie. What happened in all three of these incidents should be an object lesson for all police forces in how not to deal with the press, because these false press releases set in train a course of action that was never to be reversed. The same false press story was given later to the CID officers whose job it was to investigate; the accounts became official written statements; and these in turn were passed to lawyers and then to the senior Law Officer of the Crown who made judgments on them. Finally and disastrously, the fabricated stories surfaced at the Crown Court, where the truth eventually was laid bare.

The responsibility fell to a handful of Special Branch officers whose duty it had been to plan and supervise these special operations. They were senior enough to carry a great deal of authority. After each operation, one or more of them gathered as a group with others, in what one of them described as a 'Chinese Parliament', which meant that everyone made a decision but no one was responsible for it. The prepared story would be refined to fit in with the events as they had happened, and a jointly agreed account arrived at. A press statement was then prepared and released. The officers involved were all then told what to say, irrespective of their individual misgivings. Any doubts were dispelled by telling the policemen concerned that they were helping to save innocent lives as well as those of the informants. An ever-present worry for many junior officers was prosecution under the Official Secrets Act or, at the very least, removal from the special duties with implied ostracism and disgrace. The dead men were regarded as nothing but determined and ruthless terrorists who would have killed them had they not been killed first: men who were born to die violently in one way or another.

The specially trained policemen involved in the three shootings were not what I had expected. I have met many crack SAS soldiers, and have attended their training camps in Hereford. The policemen of these RUC squads were SAS trained, and I suppose I had formed a view that they would be very similar in style. In some ways they were: they were fit, youngish (28–35) and mature men. But they differed from the soldiers in the way they spoke to us. The military SAS troops are, by and large, taciturn and anonymous. These policemen, on the other hand, several of whom were English, were prepared to talk about their work and did not see themselves as soldiers at all, although many of them had come to the police from the Army. It was clear that their confidence had taken a serious bruising. They impressed me and my team with their honesty and openness. They were glad to talk to us, and obviously felt badly let down by their own senior officers, who they believed had left them carrying the responsibility for operations that had gone seriously wrong. They had risked their lives, obeyed instructions and looked in vain for the expected support. Four of their number had been charged with murder, had been kept in custody for up to eighteen months in solitary confinement awaiting trial, and eventually acquitted. They hoped for some legal support — but it never came. A private fund contributed to by lower-ranking policemen paid for a barrister on a private basis. They seemed to me to have been abandoned and isolated by a police force that had identified a need for them, selected them, trained them, used them and then cut them adrift. Now they were being asked again, this time by a stranger from the mainland, to explain their actions. They responded positively and helpfully, but above all, honestly. I saw a great deal more to admire in that small group of constables and sergeants than I did in many of their far more senior colleagues.

By early 1985 the trial of Martin McCauley was imminent, and with it would come a chance for me to look closely at the workings of the single-judge 'Diplock' courts that sit in Northern Ireland without a jury. I had not been able, because of legal restraints, to interview formally either McCauley or the policemen involved in shooting him and his companion,

Michael Justin Tighe, at the Hayshed in November 1982. I had, however, been piecing together some interesting facts and theories. The Hayshed was a ramshackle, breeze-block and corrugated iron building owned by Kitty Kearns, the elderly widow of an old-time Republican who had died some years before. She had been away from home staying with friends at the time of the shooting. The farmhouse and barn lie close to a housing estate on the outskirts of Lurgan occupied by people of resolutely nationalist inclinations. The security forces knew that the barn had been the storage point for explosives used to kill three policemen six weeks earlier, and that the explosives had been removed undetected while the barn was supposedly under police surveillance. It had obviously remained of interest to the police, and I concluded that the watch on it had continued since the Kinnego explosion. My team tried to get some confirmation of this, but the RUC refused to confirm or deny our theories.

The search for information showed us that Tighe had no security record or criminal convictions. He was a fresh-faced young seventeen-year-old, and his death had been a bewildering tragedy for his parents. We had spoken to them at length. They told us that Michael had never shown the slightest interest in political or terrorist activity. He lived at home quietly and was a good and considerate son who had a number of friends of the same age, including Martin McCauley, who was then nineteen. McCauley's name had been mentioned by an informant in connection with the Kinnego explosion. Tighe, on the other hand, had no record whatsoever. Tighe was a lad of simple needs who was happy and contented to remain in and around his home. Mr and Mrs Tighe could not accept that their son had been shot dead for any valid reason. They will always believe that he strayed innocently into an ambush intended for anyone who entered that staked-out barn, and that he was not given the opportunity to come out before being shot. They were not bitter about it all, however. No one from the Royal Ulster Constabulary had been to see them; they were told on the first night that their son was dead, but they had learned of no official enquiry into that death. Manchester officers were the first policemen with whom they had been asked to discuss it, three years later. They were quiet and dignified people, but realists. They asked whether Michael was involved on the fringes of terrorism, perhaps without their knowledge, and they hoped to be told whether he had by his actions contributed in any way whatsoever to his death. Although not forgiving, they seemed anxious to be fair.

Until the trial was over it was not possible for me to answer those questions, but I did know that the only reference to Tighe I saw in official records was dated after his death, and associated him posthumously with IRA activity because he had been shot dead by an anti-terrorist squad. The implication was that there could be no innocent reason for any youth to be in that barn on Ballyneery Road North: its association with a Republican sympathizer owner, its recent use for explosive storage and its proximity to a Catholic housing estate seemed to confirm beyond question that Tighe must have been there in the capacity of an IRA member. The opening and closing of a new file on him a few days after his death showed the Special Branch view of his activities. I was uneasy about this intelligence record, but decided to see what emerged at the trial of Martin McCauley. This began in early February 1985.

Belfast Crown Court in Crumlin Road on a cold winter's day is a bleak and inhospitable place. Its pastel wedding cake exterior, surrounded by high fences and double check security, lends an unreal atmosphere. Inside it is much like any other busy urban court except for the flak jackets and the polished revolver handles. Witnesses, lawyers, policemen and the accused mill about together in spiky proximity to each other. The atmosphere is highly charged; stone-faced policemen stare out the accused and their sullen supporters. The use of disposable polystyrene cups seemed very appropriate: somehow the thought of either group ever drinking from the same vessel seemed unthinkable. No amount of hot water could wash off the hatred of the years. The policemen knew that they were being studied closely by people who one day might train an Armalite rifle on them, and those people in turn were on alien territory. A young man openly and skilfully sketched me, and with an arrogant gaze made it obvious what he was doing. The courts deal with the familiar run-of-the-mill cases — burglaries, car thefts and so on — as well as terrorist prosecutions. Martin McCauley, in the eyes of the policemen there, was clearly regarded as a young killer of the future. Controlled hate burned its way across the space between them.

McCauley appeared before Mr Justice Kelly charged with possessing the three old rifles that were found in the barn, without ammunition, after he and Tighe had been shot. The account first given by the police officers stated that they had been on routine patrol when one of them had seen a man with a gun move from near the cottage into the Hayshed. The police officer ran to the Hayshed and from outside heard the cocking sound of a rifle mechanism and muffled voices. A sergeant shouted 'Police! Throw out your weapons!' There was silence. He repeated the warning using the same words, but there was still no reply. Through a space in the makeshift door he saw McCauley pointing a rifle at a constable. The sergeant opened fire with an initial 14-round burst at McCauley and the constable fired a further three rounds. Within a few seconds the constable saw Tighe, also pointing a rifle, and he and another constable opened fire on him. Tighe dropped out of sight behind the bales of hay. A further volley of shots was then fired at McCauley, who had reappeared, still with the rifle, and then again at Tighe, who had also reappeared. McCauley was dragged out barely alive and

Tighe was found dead behind the straw bales. In the shed the police found three old Mauser rifles but no ammunition.

The Director of Public Prosecutions, in the light of his experience in the other two cases, was far from convinced of the truth of this account, and the police officers were given the opportunity of changing their evidence before they gave it under oath at the Crown Court. They did so. The new evidence they gave differed only in respect of their reasons for being in the vicinity, which they revealed had not been 'routine', and in that they agreed they had told lies about seeing a 'gunman' enter the Hayshed. They had seen no such thing. The evidence of the sequence of shots and of what they said they saw in the dark interior of the barn remained unchanged. If perjury were to be avoided, that rare opportunity given by the Director of Public Prosecutions to change police evidence was the time for it. The policemen, after that, were on their own. At his trial McCauley pleaded not guilty, and defence counsel Mr Andrew Harvey QC drew from police officers the admission that their lies had been told to conceal the real reasons for shooting the two youths, which had been based on information from Special Branch. The policemen told the court that the invented story had been presented to them, as the official version of what had happened, by senior officers of the Special Branch, who had also told them that the Official Secrets Act protected them in these circumstances, even though what they were saying was false. This protection does not in fact exist. The following day, at Lisnasharragh police station, another more senior Special Branch officer had told them not to tell the truth to the CID of what had happened before the shooting dead of Michael Justin Tighe. This very senior officer told them that the lives of an informant and others were at stake if the full story emerged.

McCauley, on oath, gave an entirely different story about the shooting in the Hayshed. He said he had been with Tighe to the cottage to keep a promise to check on it for its owner, Kitty Kearns, while she was away. He said he saw a window of the Hayshed open, which was unusual, and had climbed in, followed by Tighe. Inside they saw a rifle and ventured to look closer. Without any warning two shots rang out and Tighe disappeared. (He had been killed instantly.) For the first time a voice said, 'Right, come on out,' but before he could move he was hit by a burst of gunfire that severely damaged his upper leg and hand. He shouted, 'Right, right,' but he could not move because of the blood he was rapidly losing. The result was another burst of gunfire, after which policemen entered and he was dragged out. A policeman held a gun to his head outside the barn and spoke of finishing him off.

In his judgment, Lord Justice Kelly expressed new doubts about the police evidence, especially about the true position of police officers when the shots were fired, and whether they had ever seen Tighe and McCauley actually holding rifles. He roundly condemned the regrettable introduction of false stories by senior officers, and eventually decided to exclude all police evidence from his consideration and adjudication of the case. It was all tainted with lies. Nevertheless, he still disbelieved McCauley, and he found him guilty of being in possession of one of the old rifles and imposed a suspended prison sentence of two years.

What the police officers involved in the shooting did not know, what none of the players in the trial, including the judge, knew, was that the entire events at the Hayshed — the voices, the conversations, the sequence of shots and the events afterwards — had been recorded on tape by a police and Army technical unit. An electronic bug, installed by MI5, had been operating, concealed in the rafters, throughout the entire police assault on the barn. McCauley and Tighe had walked into a sophisticated operation that had been camouflaged to look like a chance encounter. The bug was of the most reliable and up-to-date kind, and was designed only to gather intelligence. No one in the Security Services or police could ever have possibly imagined that its use was to become known to the world when one day, by accident, it eavesdropped on death. This tape was to become the rope in a bitter tug-of-war between those who believe that methods of intelligence-gathering should be protected at all costs and those who regard the tape as possible evidence of murder committed by police, and therefore belonging in a wider arena.

I had discovered the existence of the tape some weeks before, in the early winter of 1984, and had been trying to obtain a copy of it. The evidence given by the policemen, on oath, at McCauley's trial made it even more crucial that I get hold of it. If the two warnings had not been shouted by the police, if McCauley had been shot for the second time after he had said he would come out, or if the tape recording indicated, by analysis, that the first shots fired were, as I suspected, from a single-shot police Ruger rifle and not a sub-machine gun, then the police had lied on oath to Lord Justice Kelly. I believed it was in the interests of the RUC to show me that their men had acted truthfully and honourably. If they had not, the offences committed would be far more serious than perjury — the evidence would have supported a charge of murder against one or more of those policemen. I was in Northern Ireland investigating what had become known as a shoot-to-kill policy. I could think of no better way of proving, or disproving, this awesomely serious allegation than to obtain a copy of that tape. This issue now transcended all others.

I took stock of what I had discovered and what I should do about it. I was faced with a choice. I could accept that war — especially an anti-terrorist campaign — will throw up an occasional civilian casualty, or I could pursue the tape vigorously because of the higher principles involved. I recognized the arguments, but eventually the single most influential factor in my deliberations was the effect on my team that any compromise of honesty on my part would have had. I had chosen these officers because they were intelligent and sharp investigators. They are also the next generation of senior officer. They would have known that I was running away from a moral and operational question that would one day catch us all up if I ignored it. As an individual, I also passionately believe that if a police force of the United Kingdom could, in cold blood, kill a seventeen-year-old youth with no terrorist or criminal convictions, and then plot to hide the evidence from a senior policeman deputed to investigate it, then the shame belonged to us all. This is the act of a Central American assassination squad — truly of a police force out of control. My team whole-heartedly supported me in my belief, and I set for us what was undoubtedly the most important single objective at which I am ever likely to aim — the obtaining of that evidence. The cover stories, the lies, the obstruction were insignificant when placed alongside possible State murder. I expected others to think the same. I was mistaken.

The knowledge of the existence of the recording device in the barn was not formally acknowledged to us. We had to find it out for ourselves. Indeed, in October 1984, when we first asked whether our suspicions about its existence were correct, they were denied. I had discovered that the barn had been under surveillance at the time Tighe and McCauley were shot, but I had believed this was surveillance by policemen with binoculars, or perhaps living under cover in the nearby housing estate or the fields surrounding it. Eventually, by prodding and poking away in Special Branch files and papers, the realization dawned that the surveillance was not just human; it was electronic. Over a period of weeks we put the jigsaw together, and by interviewing Army officers who were prepared to speak to us we learned what had happened. In the autumn of 1982 the barn had been fitted with a listening device for several weeks, even before the delivery to it of the explosives used to kill the three policemen in October of that year. The bug was unreliable — indeed, its faulty mechanisms had been the reason why the explosives were successfully removed without police knowledge. But it had been replaced by a much more sophisticated device, one that did more than merely alert the police and Army to any unusual presence in the barn. This new machine was activated by movement and voices, and from that point all noise was recorded on to tape and monitored live by police and military personnel at a listening post some distance away. The tapes were not evaluated there and then, but sent to police headquarters in Belfast, where they were transcribed and typed up by teams of women police officers and typists working from temporary buildings — unkindly referred to by the more macho Special Branch officers as the 'Bitch Squad', the 'Henhouse' or the 'Cowshed'.

The functioning of this device at the moment the shooting occurred was obviously of crucial importance. If it was running and recording properly, then the police officers' account of what happened would be either confirmed or undermined. McCauley's claims that there was an argument between the police about whether to finish him off would be tested in the best possible way. I began by speaking to the present head of the Special Branch, Assistant Chief Constable Trevor Forbes. Reluctantly he confirmed our knowledge of the tape, but enigmatically said, 'You will never be able to hear it'. I asked what he meant, and he said, 'I doubt if it exists'. He would say no more. I arranged for the police officer who had been listening to the tape as the shooting occurred to be interviewed. He was then a constable, now a sergeant. He politely told John Thorburn that he would describe to us only his general duties that day, and would not, unless instructed to do so by his own senior officers, tell us anything whatsoever of what he heard as his colleagues shot Tighe and McCauley; neither would he produce for us the tape or the transcript of it.

The situation was bizarre. Here was a constable telling a Detective Chief Superintendent that he would not co-operate with a murder enquiry unless he was instructed to do so. He was told, equally politely, that he was very close to obstructing us. He responded by saying that if that were the case he was acting only on instructions.

Our problem was that since our mainland authority did not legally extend to Northern Ireland we had no proper sanctions in situations like this. Threats from us would have been empty, so we did not make them. Neither this officer nor any of his colleagues could, in law, obstruct us because neither I nor my team had any police powers whatsoever while on Ulster soil. On more than one occasion we were reminded of this. The policeman told us that he was not obstructing our enquiries — he was merely putting them back until he had received clearance to tell us what we were asking. I took the matter higher, but received only equivocal answers. In January 1985 I went to the Chief Constable and spelled out for him the absolute importance to my enquiry of that tape, the transcript of it and the evidence of the monitoring officer who might have been a witness to murder. Sir John Hermon would not give me authority to take the matter further with the policeman. He said that he desired to co-operate with me but that the tape simply was not his to give. He agreed that the handling of it, and any action taken in respect of it, were matters for his officers, but the actual installation of it, and the ownership of any information it contained, fell within the responsibility of the Security Services. For the first time MI5 came into the picture.

On 28 January 1985 I travelled to an office in Marylebone, London, where I saw the Executive Head of Legal Services at MI5. He is an authoritative and powerful figure, and I knew he had the seniority to give me the permission I was seeking. He received me courteously and listened carefully to me. I put my request to him, and he agreed right away. He said that he could not, and would not, stand in the way of what clearly was a murder investigation. So far as MI5 was concerned, I could have access to everything I was seeking. If the RUC continued to refuse to part with the evidence, or if the role and functions of MI5 were used as a delaying tactic or as a smoke-screen, I should immediately refer the matter personally to him. I returned to Belfast, and the following day I telephoned Mr Philip Myers. He appeared to support and accept the absolute need for me to listen to the tape.

I believed the main hurdle had now been cleared. I had authority from MI5, and the expressed support of the Home Office and the Director of Public Prosecutions. I waited until the end of the McCauley trial before pursuing the matter, in case there were any new revelations, and on 20 February 1985 I wrote to Assistant Chief Constable Forbes making a formal request for access to the tape. In the same letter I also made a further request that was to add to the ill-feeling that was rapidly developing between me and the Special Branch. I had found out that the source of the information for the police operations that resulted in the shootings at both Tullygally East Road and at the Hayshed was the same man. I did not know who he was, and was never to know, but his payment record indicated that he was very active, and in return was receiving large amounts of money indeed.

The recruitment and use of informants is central to the thrust against terrorists. But I suspected that government guidelines were regularly being breached, and almost certainly in the three cases I was investigating. The absolute rule laid down by the Home Office in a document they describe as *Guidelines for the Police in the Use of Informants* is that an informant must never initiate crimes that would otherwise not take place. An informant must never be used as an *agent provocateur,* and he must not be allowed by the police freely to commit crime himself in return for giving information.

The reality in Northern Ireland is worlds away from those perfectly proper rules. In order to establish his terrorist credentials in the Province an informant may have to commit serious crime, possibly even murder. Only in this way may he become trusted and make progress within that organization. His value as an informant grows the longer he remains and the more trusted he becomes. There is a certain hypocrisy, however, inherent in considering the Home Office guidelines as workable in Northern Ireland. Nevertheless, governments, both Labour and Conservative, have ignored the dilemmas of the RUC over many years. I was not setting out to embarrass the government, but I did wish to know whether a paid police informant had been present at any of the six deaths I was looking into. I recall asking one senior RUC officer, over a bottle of whiskey, about serious breaches of the Home Office guidelines in other cases I had heard about. He had mischievously replied, 'They are only guidelines, Mr Stalker. They are not the law.' In England and Wales, so far as policemen are concerned, 'guidelines' means 'rules'; I suspected that in this case semantics hid murder, or at least knowledge of it.

Informant-handling is a murky area in the policing of a democracy. There are as many hidden problems as there are informants. My interest seemed to set off panic bells that reverberated throughout the Special Branch right up to the Chief Constable. Yet if I was to do the job properly I could not ignore the question. I started by asking ACC Forbes for full access to the file of the informant involved in the Tullygally East Road and the Hayshed.

I wanted to see where this common thread would lead me: it ran through the Kinnego murders, to the killing of Burns, Toman and McKerr and then the shootings of Tighe and McCauley, and I was anxious to know whether any other similar incidents were hidden away. I had by now learned that such information was never going to be volunteered to me. I was surprised at the very large amounts of money being paid — many thousands of pounds. I reflected on the nature of the deaths I was investigating. They had a common feature: each left a strong suspicion that a type of pre-planned police ambush had occurred, and that someone had led these men to their deaths. I did not, of course, know who it was, but I could say that in two of the three cases the informant was the same person. The third instance — that of Grew and Carroll — involved a different informant. I had serious concern about the over-dramatic, almost itchy-fingered, way in which police had responded to the actions of the dead men. I suspected that an informant had given over-inflated information about the men that heightened the flow of police adrenaline, and also raised his own value. I was also beginning to harbour doubts about the old rifles in the Hayshed. I was not happy about their convenient presence there, without ammunition, and was ready to explore the possibility that they had been planted either by the informant or by someone else. To be honest, I was starting to suspect the involvement of an *agent provocateur* — a mercenary. It seemed perfectly reasonable, given my terms of reference, to ask for access to his file. I was not, at that time, asking for his identity or to meet him.

I sent my letter to Mr Forbes by hand, and a week later received a telephone call from him turning down my requests unless the Chief Constable agreed. He had not referred my letter to him onward to the Chief Constable. On 5 March 1985 I sent a further formal request, this time addressed personally to the Chief Constable, asking for access to the tape and to any transcripts or logs, together with the identity of any person, of the police, Army or MI5, who had monitored the tape or listened in at the time of the shooting in the Hayshed.

On 13 March I received a terse letter signed by the Chief Constable which refused my request and said that the information I requested was classified 'Grade A' by his Special Branch, and therefore not for me to know. I could scarcely believe this flat refusal; but even more outrageous was the reason for it. The department I was investigating, the Special Branch, had the clear power to decide whether I should be given access to evidence that might or might not prove that some of their members had committed murder. The Chief Constable, who had almost a year earlier asked me to undertake this investigation on his behalf, had now signed a letter that prevented me from doing just that.

I called a meeting with my team and we discussed what options were open to us. Clearly any pretence at co-operation with us by the RUC had ended. We were strangers again in Northern Ireland, and the Force had closed its doors on us. It seemed to me that they had decided that my investigations were closing in on unlawful, even murderous acts, and that they no longer wished to facilitate that process. Sir John Hermon himself had signed the letter denying me the access I had been promised. Who could I now turn to? I half considered a publicly announced resignation from the investigation, and even drafted out for myself a press statement. I did not discuss this step with my team — such a decision was mine alone. I decided against it for three reasons. Firstly, I knew that when the political storm died down the investigation would still have to be continued by a policeman. I wanted to be that policeman, and a grand gesture at that stage would have burned my boats. Secondly, I knew that my team was strong in spirit and solidly behind me. If the barriers were up, we would collectively try to knock them down; the requests would still be made, and we would carefully collect the mounting refusals. More importantly, I had the backing — or so I thought — of MI5, who did not wish to be involved in any public row, and I had an open door through which I could return if my requests were refused by the Chief

Constable. I decided to stay in the Province. Perhaps, with hindsight, a well-publicized walk-out and eventual return would have achieved more. I can never know.

On 9 April 1985 I wrote a further letter to Sir John Hermon repeating in emphatic terms my absolute need for access to the tape, but this time mentioning the Director of Public Prosecutions in my request. I had confirmed to my satisfaction the commitment and determination of Sir Barry Shaw and his senior staff to get to the bottom of the affair. I also asked the Chief Constable for his authority to examine the papers on the highly-paid informant, and requested facilities in which to meet him. On the same day I wrote a separate letter to the Deputy Chief Constable, Mr Michael McAtamney, and told him formally that evidence I had obtained pointed very strongly to two of his officers, both Special Branch Detective Superintendents, Thomas George Anderson and Samuel George Flanagan, as the principal initiators, with a retired Chief Superintendent, in the cover-ups of the killings in November and December 1982. I clearly said I considered it in the best interest of the RUC, and the public in Northern Ireland, that both officers be suspended from duty immediately. Both letters, the one to Hermon and that to McAtamney, were taken from Manchester and delivered by hand. I received no response. I sought advice from Philip Myers, who said I should write again in very full terms, but this time to Sir John Hermon, repeating the request for suspension of the officers but providing him with much more of the evidence I had gathered in respect of those officers. He also hinted I should ask that, as an alternative to suspension of the two policemen, they be removed from operational duty. Mr Myers offered his full support but said that the Chief Constable was angry and offended at my persistent requests, and would need careful handling.

Frankly, I had long ago abandoned compromise in respect of my quest for the tape. The naked hostility and opposition shown to me and my officers by Special Branch left no room for it. We had been in the Province for almost twelve months, my work there was almost done, and I was wearying of the delays. I had a demanding enough job in Manchester, and I believed I held sufficient aces to get what I wanted: the expressed support of MI5, the Director of Public Prosecutions, and through him, the Attorney General and Her Majesty's Inspector of Constabulary. I saw little reason to play games. I was reluctant to spell out the nature of all the evidence I had in relation to these officers because I still had to reinterview them about some aspects. Sir John Hermon and I seemed to have locked horns again, and I wondered whom I was doing this for. My personal determination was an important factor, but I needed to be assured that Mr Myers's commitment to the search for the truth was not waning. I could not afford to lose his political support.

I wrote again to Sir John Hermon on 22 April 1985. I gave him a full outline of the evidence available to support my request for suspension. I told him the truth, that sixteen police officers of junior rank had made full statements implicating two Superintendents in the formulation of the false cover stories. I then told him that one of the Superintendents (Anderson) accepted very little of the responsibility of his rank and had blamed the conspiracy entirely on the constables and sergeants who he said had manufactured it. He stated that he, a Superintendent, had merely 'gone along' with the lies. I repeated my belief that suspension of the two Superintendents would be in the interests of the Force and, more importantly, of the public. I also requested that henceforth I be permitted to repost directly to the DPP, in the manner that obtains on the mainland. I had the letter delivered by hand; I received a reply dated the same day. It contained a flat refusal to agree to any of my requests. I was not to have the tape, neither was I to be given any further details of the informant. The police officers would not be suspended, and I was reminded of my responsibility to report to the Chief Constable and not to concern myself with the Director of Public Prosecutions. Sir John Hermon made it quite clear that he would send my report to Sir Barry Shaw, and any deficiencies in it would be commented on and rectified by Shaw. Hermon's letter to me included emphatically final words in relation to my request for the tape. He asolutely refused to allow me any information about the tape and said that to do so would create a most dangerous precedent that would demoralize policemen and others working for him. He stressed that personnel who operate in undercover and surveillance work are very carefully chosen and that he could not, and would not, expose them to the kind of external investigation I was intending to pursue. If he did so, the sense of security they enjoy, in the knowledge that their duties are fully protected, would be eroded. Sir John spelled out for me that it was his duty to protect them and that he did so, as Chief Constable, in the best interests of the public.

The Chief Constable could not have been clearer. Policemen acting under cover in anti-terrorist operations were fully protected. They were not to be exposed to external investigation. The Chief Constable was the judge of the public interest. I realized then just how great was the difference between the way Sir John Hermon saw my job in Northern Ireland and the way I saw it. I reflected on the letter and felt I was entitled to ask myself the question 'What the hell is expected of me?' The Chief Constable, after insistence from the Director of Public Prosecutions and following a public outcry, had appointed me to investigate the actions of his officers. I had not asked to be in Northern Ireland. Terms of reference for the investigation had been discussed, signed and agreed. Now he was preventing me from completing it. Firmly and unequivocally, he was saying that to allow me to carry on the type of enquiry I was conducting would be to erode the sense of security his officers were entitled to expect.

At about this time, I recall, I discussed this matter with James Anderton. Quite often, after a particularly frustrating week, I would speak to Anderton and allow my anger at Sir John Hermon, and concern for the reputation of the RUC, to show. I could not do this in any real sense in front of my team, and I never took my troubles home with me — at least not to discuss them. James Anderton was the only safety valve, apart from Sir Philip Myers, I had — and I saw Sir Philip only about three times in two years. Mr Anderton never proffered any advice but, in fairness, I never really asked for it. When he wants to be he is a good listener, and he would nod apparently sympathetically and occasionally murmur the odd word of understanding. Sometimes he would propose a balancing argument, and this was often useful to me. Any discussions we had usually centred on the near-impossible task facing the RUC in fighting a war that was not acknowledged as such, and the inadequacy of safeguards for them in filling the vacuum left as the Army retreated into barracks and contracted in size.

I remember that during a conversation about police anti-terrorist tactics James Anderton said to me, 'It is impossible to make an omelette without breaking eggs.' I hasten to say that we were not discussing any specific operation, but what I think he was voicing was a feeling that I and probably most other policemen share — that even in the most democratic and civilized of countries, anti-terrorist efforts by police or army will occasionally go wrong and excesses will be exposed. Anti-terrorist efforts often involve matching firepower with firepower, and innocent people sometimes die. I recognized that, of course. My anger in this case stemmed from the denial that things had gone wrong, that no eggs were broken even though the omelette was there to see.

# 3

# *The Tape*

I began to play the cards I thought would win me the game. On 25 April 1985 I wrote to the Director of Public Prosecutions enclosing copies of my correspondence with the Chief Constable, included in which was my request to be allowed to report directly to the DDP, or at least to have regular right of access to him and to prepare interim reports for him. The following day the DPP, Sir Barry Shaw, spoke to me on the telephone and told me that he had no authority to supervise my investigation until my request was on his desk for him to see. Since it related to the enquiry, that request had to be sent through the office of the Chief Constable, so that constitutionally and legally he was hamstrung by the same procedures that were frustrating me. The Chief Constable controlled completely the flow of paper from me to the Director of Public Prosecutions. Shaw offered some advice: he suggested that I consider myself as 'any person' (that is, not a policeman) in submitting a report to him. It was a novel and interesting idea, and I considered it carefully. What I was being invited to consider was whether I should regard myself, in essence, as a self-appointed private investigator. I would need to presume that my team and I were not police officers, or at least not acting as such. I would be engaged in a private investigation.

The idea had some attractions, but I decided against it. It seemed wrong somehow that a policeman brought in to do a job should have to act as an ordinary member of the public in order to complete it. If I was to succeed or fail I wished to do so as the Deputy Chief Constable of Greater Manchester, and not as an inquisitive civilian. I was also worried about our status as a team in using RUC accommodation, offices, telephones and transport. Without them we were even more vulnerable to delays and worse. On 29 April 1985 I again sent a hand-delivered letter to Sir John Hermon. It was short, and expressed my dismay at his decision. I asked him to release me from the requirement to report to him and to allow me to deal directly with the Director of Public Prosecutions, both for consultancy and direction, as was the practice on the mainland, where this would be commonplace during an investigation as serious as this.

There was no immediate reply, but on 9 May Philip Myers telephoned me and asked, on behalf of Sir John Hermon, that I go to Belfast on the 13th for a discussion. I took the usual flight from Manchester Airport and arrived in the morning. The meeting lasted for an hour. Sir John expressed his concern about what he saw as the undesirable involvement of Philip Myers as some sort of self-appointed intermediary. He said that there seemed to be a hidden agenda and he did not like it. I told him that Mr Myers had not in any way compromised me or my enquiry, and I saw his political interest in what was going on as perfectly legitimate. He was, after all, a government adviser. We then discussed the role of the Deputy Chief Constable, Michael McAtamney, in the investigations that took place before I was called in, and the Chief Constable said that had he been in the country at the time, he would have handled things differently from the way his deputy handled them.

I asked Sir John forcefully to reconsider his decision not to allow me to have possession of the Hayshed tape; he said he would think again about it. He was co-operative and apparently understanding of my determination to investigate the matter to the best of my abilities. He said that he was opposed to my report being submitted to anyone other than himself. This would, he believed, be unconstitutional. He asked for my assurances that I would not give any copies to Philip Myers or to the DPP. I said that I could see no harm in giving them copies provided they did not see those copies before he did. With that his mood changed dramatically, and he said that I would be quite wrong, indeed devious, to do so. I said there were a number of unanswered questions that affected him personally, and undoubtedly I would need to see him formally in due course. He asked me for examples, and I gave him one only. I referred to a letter prepared for the DPP by a Chief Superintendent that recommended a charge of murder against a police officer in one of the cases. I had discovered that Sir John Hermon had disagreed with the analysis and findings of his senior officer, and had arbitrarily overruled the recommendation. He had then written his own letter to the Director of Public Prosecutions — an almost unheard-of step — making out a more emotional and political case for not prosecuting. His plea was discarded by the DPP, who went ahead and prosecuted the policeman for murder as originally recommended. I told Sir John that as Chief Constable he had every right to disagree with and to overrule his Chief Superintendent. I did not argue with that. What I found difficult to follow was why he had not forwarded to the DPP an analytical report written by the Chief Superintendent, who is a graduate with a law degree, together with his own dissenting recommendation. I did not mention it to him at that time, but I had also learned that in another case, when the Chief Superintendent recommended no proceedings on a similar murder charge, the Chief Constable had allowed the request to go through without any comment whatsoever from him.

I told Sir John that I was puzzled at what seemed to me to be an unusual, although not improper, intervention by a Chief Constable in a prosecution, and the apparent disposal of a reasoned report recommending that a policeman be charged with murder. I decided to wait until the end of my investigation into all three incidents before I saw his Deputy and Sir John himself. He looked angry and resentful, but said he would be prepared to be interviewed by me, under criminal caution if necessary. He seemed shocked and hurt by our conversation and asked what I intended to do. I told him I was desperately anxious to make progress after what was now a quite unacceptable delay, and I asked for his co-operation. He suggested one more meeting when he had had time to consider his position. I agreed to wait forty-eight hours before I appealed again to MI5 and the Director of Public Prosecutions, but I made it clear that was as long as I wished to delay the decision.

That evening (13 May 1985) Philip Myers phoned me at my home and said he was seeing Sir John Hermon the following day in Belfast. I told Mr Myers I was weary of delays and could not allow matters to drift on any more. I spoke on 14 May to the DPP and told him that my meeting with Sir John had been inconclusive, but that I would be flying to Belfast again the following day.

I saw the Chief Constable again on 15 May in his office and we continued our conversation. He had regained his composure and was his usual powerful, confident self. He commenced briskly and uncompromisingly. He would not release me from my obligation to report directly to him, and he asked if I suspected him of serious offences. I declined to answer in detail, but said that at that moment my evidence against him was of dubious practice and possible unprofessionalism rather than criminal activity. I did not, however, rule out the latter. He then surprised me entirely by saying that he, as Chief Constable, now agreed, without any preconditions whatsoever, to release to me the tape of the activities at the Hayshed, together with all documents and also the authority to ask all the questions I needed of the police officers monitoring the tape. He added that MI5 had the most powerful interest in the tape and that they would need to be assured of the way I handled it. I was beginning to hear the same dizzying arguments I thought were behind me. I told Sir John that MI5 had already given me full authority at the highest legal level to hear the tape. All that now remained to be done was to hand it to me. Sir John then said, 'No tape may exist — you appreciate that, of course.' I said I did not appreciate it, although his Assistant Chief Constable and head of Special Branch had already hinted at it. Sir John suggested I speak to MI5 officers, but he refused to elaborate further. I was equally determined to pin the Chief Constable down to his apparently unequivocal promise to me of a few minutes earlier. I wanted that tape. I said I could not tolerate any further delays, and I would not leave his headquarters without some firm date for my access to the tape and the policemen who had heard it. Sir John paused, looked at me hard and then, without speaking, made a telephone call. About fifteen minutes later a man joined us, whose name I know, but who was introduced to me simply as a member of MI5 based in Belfast. Sir John's mood had changed again, and I was brusquely asked by him to leave his office, which I reluctantly did. I cooled my temper by walking around the grounds. About fifteen minutes later I resumed my conversation with the two of them, and the MI5 officer told me that the way was now open for me to make progress. He would speak, he said, to his senior directors in London and I could look forward to complete co-operation — subject to 'unspecified' safeguards.

Before I left I asked Sir John for his decision on my request to see the informant. He angrily refused, and would not discuss the matter further. I said that I had to accept his decision because I could not do otherwise, but that I wished to see the informant's policeman handler. He was non-committal. I told the Chief Constable and the MI5 officer that my patience was exhausted. The following day Sir John Hermon telephoned me to tell me that the way was now clear for me to deal directly with MI5 to obtain the information I was seeking about the tape. I realized then that the labyrinthine processes through which I had been groping had brought me back to exactly where I had been five months earlier in January 1985. It was obvious to me that much midnight oil had been burned.

The Belfast MI5 officer told me that the Chief Constable had suggested that MI5's role be to act as 'honest brokers' between the RUC and myself. He wished them to examine, and no doubt assess, the contents of the tape *before* it was passed to me. I told the MI5 officer I would not accept this. I was the investigator, and I would decide on the value of the evidence. I could not agree to judgments being made other than by the Director of Public Prosecutions, who was expecting me to obtain all the evidence I could to help him in that task. I said that, despite all the promises, it seemed that I would have to begin again with the Chief Constable. Within the hour Sir John Hermon telephoned me and said that he wished me to have access to all the information, and he had merely asked MI5 to look at it first to see whether they had any objections to any specific part of it being given to me. He was not keeping anything back, he said. If I were denied access to evidence, then that would be because MI5 thought it desirable, not he. I contained my rising temper and told him that MI5 had agreed to my having the tape without any argument and without conditions. He was, in my view, clouding the issue. I insisted that he speak to MI5 again and give me, by the following week, a firm answer and details of where and when I could take possession of the tape. I asked him to deal with the matter personally, and told him that if there were any further obstructions I would seriously consider whether I could continue to undertake the investigation on his behalf.

Sir John telephoned me as I had asked on the Monday of the following week. He said he had spoken to MI5 and would now ensure that I received everything I was asking for. I thanked him, and emphasized my desire to complete the enquiry as soon as I could. I honestly thought I had cleared the last hurdle. But nothing happened. No one contacted me, either from the RUC or from the offices of MI5. My calls were not returned. Eventually I received a telephone call from a junior police officer asking that I formally write to the Chief Constable explaining what I wanted. I said I had already done this several times, and had had numerous meetings and conversations with the Chief Constable and others. The intermediary expressed no real knowledge of the detail of what we were discussing — he was merely passing on a message. The Chief Constable, he said, was busy with other matters and could not speak to me. I felt the situation slipping away again. On 4 June 1985 I sent a letter by hand to the Chief Constable that detailed yet again my requirements. I also asked him for details regarding the authority to instal the device, and stated unequivocally that I regarded this part of my enquiry as an investigation into whether Michael Justin Tighe was unlawfully killed by members of the Royal Ulster Constabulary.

I learned that Sir John Hermon was attending a conference in Bristol, and arranged for Chief Superintendent Thorburn to deliver the letter to him personally on my behalf. This was done on 6 June 1985. Sir John began to ask questions that indicated his concern over my requests. He asked, for example, who else besides me would be listening to the tape, what safeguards I had made for vetting typists, and what classification and circulation my eventual file would have. None of this, in my view, was relevant. I could not begin to address most of the questions he was raising until I heard what the tape contained. He was asking for promises before I knew the extent of the evidence. I was not prepared to exclude my small team from access to anything until I personally had the full picture. Then, and only then, would I look at what I had and discuss with him the control over it. If I thought it necessary I would restrict access to it, but first I had to know what it was I was being kept from.

There was suddenly great activity. An emergency meeting was called for the morning of Friday, 14 June 1985, at the same MI5 offices in Marylebone I had visited in January. I was asked not to take John Thorburn with me. Present at the meeting were Sir John Hermon, the very senior MI5 legal officer and the MI5 Belfast representative. The meeting was opened by the senior MI5 man. He made it absolutely clear, as he had six months earlier, that his department was not standing in the way of a murder investigation. He said that MI5 was prepared to release *all* information to me. Sir John was forcibly told that MI5 should not be used as a reason for my being denied access to any evidence or information. The MI5 officer turned to me and said that he would, however, be very reluctant to discuss the authority for the use and installation of the device. He asked me to accept his word that he had personally examined the papers relating to the installation of the bug in the Hayshed at Ballyneery Road North, and that everything was politically and legally in order. He said that my report could include his assurance that the necessary legal steps had been taken. My prime need was to listen to the tape — the correctness of its installation was of secondary importance. I agreed not to pursue this. He had behaved in a briskly honourable way throughout, and I had no reason to doubt his integrity on this relatively peripheral matter.

I asked Sir John Hermon (both of us now having heard the MI5 promise to release their information) when I could have access to the tape. I said I could see no further justification for denying it to me. After a moment of silence he said dramatically, 'Never, I am afraid. The tape has been destroyed but a transcript exists.' I believe this revelation came as a surprise even to the senior MI5 officers. I asked him when the tape had been destroyed — was it during the period I had been seeking it, since October 1984? He did not answer. He then dropped another bombshell, by insisting that my team and I, before I proceeded further, sign a form designed and used by his Special Branch as a declaration of secrecy. I coldly refused. This form had been signed by all the officers who had misled the CID investigators and the courts, and had been put forward as the legal reason for so doing. I intended, in my final report, to powerfully criticize the use of this type of pseudo-Official Secrets Act declaration as being confusing and obstructive in the search for evidence in Northern Ireland, and I would certainly not sign one myself. I knew that my team, who had borne the brunt of Special Branch obstructiveness, were equally critical of it and individually would also refuse to sign. I could see another argument developing, and I realized that I was giving the Chief Constable another reason to refuse to provide the information I wanted; but I was determined that those dangerous and misleading forms should not be given any further credibility by me.

The Chief Constable's face hardened and he brought the meeting to a virtual close. He said that he could not, and would not, divulge any information about the tape. He took the view that he, as Chief Constable, could not provide it unless specifically directed to by a higher authority. He must never be seen, he said, to be voluntarily handing it over to another policeman. He was openly stating that he would not provide evidence in his possession, even of possible murder, unless he was told by the Crown that it was in the public interest to do so. He was in effect withholding information from an investigation he had himself commissioned.

I told him I could not submit an incomplete report. Professionally and personally, I was bound to obtain every shred of information, especially in a case as serious as this. Sir John was ready for this, however, and he replied by saying that my report would not be incomplete. I would have obtained all available evidence — the missing pieces were not available because he was denying them to me. I should, he said, submit my report and explain why I had not been able to hear the tape. He would then send my report — with his explanations for denying me access to this evidence — to the Director of Public Prosecutions, who would be asked to consider the public interest and make a decision.

I said that the DPP had already told me he wished me to obtain the tape, and I felt sure that the Chief Constable's decision might be seen as an obstruction of the submission of my report. I told him that he would eventually have to give me access, and that he and I both knew that. I suggested he contact the DPP, who would direct him, I felt sure, to give me the information. He said he would not do so until he had my report. We were at a complete stalemate. I saw a powerful and stubborn man who I believe was stung into a rearguard action, holding on to important evidence that he knew he would eventually have to give to me. No doubt he saw an equally stubborn, less senior officer who did not, or would not, understand his unique constitutional position as Chief Constable of the beleaguered Royal Ulster Constabulary.

The meeting was all but over. As we gathered our papers one of the MI5 men said to me that he believed I should be given the information I had been seeking for so long. I said I would speak to the Director of Public Prosecutions and would now carefully consider my position. I was bitterly disappointed by the Chief Constable's attitude, and I regarded his decision as unashamedly obstructive. It seemed that for the moment I had to accept it, because, unlike him, I did not have the authority to decide what was in the public interest. I think

I made it absolutely clear that I regarded my interpretation of that nebulous concept as much more accurate than his. I realized just how jealously a Chief Constable can guard his power and authority, no matter how inevitable the reversal of his decision might be. Just before the meeting finally ended Sir John Hermon fired a parting shot when he asked me to make any report I submitted 'for the eyes only of the Director of Public Prosecutions'. I did not need to consider my response. I told him that this was unnecessarily restrictive and declined to do it unless the DPP himself agreed to it.

This final request was, in my opinion, symptomatic of much that was unhealthy in the relationship between the Royal Ulster Constabulary and the office of the Director of Public Prosecutions. Throughout my time in Northern Ireland I received open and very professional treatment from members of the DPP's office. They welcomed my investigation but were always at pains to show their understanding of the problems of the Royal Ulster Constabulary. There existed, however, a deep-seated distrust of the Director of Public Prosecutions' office in the RUC Special Branch. There was, during my stay there, a genuinely held concern at very senior levels of the police that there were insufficient safeguards when sensitive or classified material was supplied to the Director's office. It was openly expressed to me by two or three senior officers that some members of the DPP's staff might not be entirely trustworthy, and the belief undoubtedly existed that information might, by accident or design, find its way to terrorist organizations. I tested these grave suspicions in the only way I know how, by asking for some proof. Obviously, if they were well founded and a particular lawyer, or lawyers, were suspected, I would need to be very careful indeed with whom I discussed my report. The answer I received would have been laughable had it not been so serious. The only actual example I was given was that one member of the Director's office who was a Catholic attended an occasional lunch-time service at a particular church in Belfast. In the past, families of suspected terrorists had also worshipped there, and in the eyes of some RUC officers that was sufficiently damning evidence against the man.

This atmosphere of suspicion, much of it based on raw prejudice or instinctive dislike, pervaded the relationships between police and the Crown legal service, and I regarded it as intensely worrying. My draft report made a number of recommendations for improvements, including the setting up within the Director of Public Prosecutions' office of a small secure unit for receiving and discussing sensitive information. Obviously, the DPP himself and the Chief Constable must have mutual respect and confidence in each other. A small group such as this would be chosen, vetted and trained for the purpose of dealing with police officers below the level of Chief Constable. Despite all the real or imagined problems in policing Northern Ireland, I could never accept that there should be any compromise in the doctrine of full disclosure to the Director of Public Prosecutions. For any police officer in our sort of society to be selective in judging what evidence should or should not be divulged to senior Law Officers of the Crown is never justifiable. My final report would have said so in the clearest possible terms.

I left the London meeting and walked to Euston Station feeling thoroughly defeated. I despaired of ever getting to the truth of what had happened in the Hayshed. I remembered the photographs of the dead boy with the two bullet wounds through the heart and lungs, and I recalled the lies told at the trials. I thought of his hardworking and trusting parents. I recalled also the energy and honesty of my team, who had lived away from home in a hostile world for over twelve months, and who were looking to me for continuing strength and leadership. My faith in the power and influence of MI5 to force the issue had rapidly faded. They had adopted a very proper, supportive, but essentially neutral stance, perhaps understandably so. I could not complain in any way about their response to my requests. My other allies, the Director of Public Prosecutions and Mr Philip Myers, were constitutionally handcuffed. They were powerless to instruct the Chief Constable, at this particular time, in any way at all. During the afternoon of 18 June Sir John Hermon telephoned me to say he had told the DPP of his decision not to allow me access to the tape, its transcript or the informant until he was instructed to do so in the public interest. Our conversation was short and to the point. My own position was not discussed, but he said he would be speaking to the Northern Ireland Secretary, who was then Mr Douglas Hurd, the following day.

On that day I had a long conversation with Sir Barry Shaw. I told him of my professional dismay at the Chief Constable's about-face decision. He asked me what I thought I should do, and I told him that I had seriously considered walking out of the enquiry in order to focus public attention on the situation. I said I believed, however, that this sort of action would be seen as a gesture that hid my inability to complete a job I had resolved to finish. It would be gleefully received among certain members of the Special Branch, who would see it as a clear victory for them. Reluctantly, and possibly unwisely, I had decided to submit my report without the tape evidence, but I intended to strongly condemn, in what would now be an Interim Report, the decision to exclude me from important evidence. I said that, with hindsight, I would never have accepted the terms of the enquiry as they existed, but that now, fourteen months on, it was not possible to change them. I expressed my serious concern for future enquiries of this type involving mainland policemen, and said that I believed the Chief Constable's close involvement with, and control over, an independent police investigation was unwise and wrong. I also deplored the long delays; this denial of access could have been arrived at many months before. Sir Barry listened patiently; he seemed surprised when I told him that the Chief Constable had always been unhappy about my having direct contact with the Director of Public Prosecutions staff in the same manner as in England and Wales.

On 20 June I told Mr Philip Myers about the now final and, in my view, very regrettable decision of the Chief Constable, and my reservations about the wisdom and efficacy of this type of enquiry in the future. Most surprisingly, in view of his earlier expressed and open support of me, he thanked me for calling but made absolutely no further comment.

I also kept James Anderton informed throughout of the obstructions and bitter disappointments we were experiencing. He was entitled to know — we were, after all, members of his police force, and I was worried for his reputation if there were criticisms of avoidable delays. I knew that one day someone should be brought to account for this inexcusably expensive and lengthy investigation, and I was determined it would not be the Greater Manchester Police. I was also most anxious to get back to Manchester to devote my full energies to helping him run his police force. His attitude to me throughout was out of character with the James Anderton I knew. He was essentially negative, which is not his usual style. I always felt that his support for me and his sympathy for the very real problems of the RUC were locked in conflict, cancelling each other out. As I have said, he is not an investigator, and he had never undertaken an investigation into another police force. Perhaps the truth is that he could more easily imagine himself in Sir John Hermon's role than in mine. I can only guess.

I set about preparing what I had decided to call my Interim Report, which dealt fully with the two shooting incidents at Tullygally East Road, Lurgan, and Mullacreavie Park, Armagh City, and partially with the Hayshed shooting. On 26 June I wrote what was to be my last letter to Sir John Hermon. I placed on record the serious implications of my enquiry as I now saw them. In order to protect the position of myself and the Greater Manchester Police I wished that a letter be put on his file stating that after the most careful re-investigation I believed I could present a great deal of extra evidence, including independent forensic findings, that would indicate that the five men shot dead in their cars were unlawfully killed by members of the Royal Ulster Constabulary. I believed I could safely say that the evidence available to put before the adjourned Coroner's Hearings was substantially more than that presented by the RUC at the criminal trials, and would attract much public interest when the inquests were eventually reopened. I also said that the indications were that Michael Justin Tighe might also have been unlawfully killed, but I would reserve my final recommendation on that until I had received the tape of the shooting — if it existed. I made the modest prophecy that my enquiries would undoubtedly be the subject of very close scrutiny in the months to come, and said I wished the potential for serious damage to the Royal Ulster Constabulary to be clearly understood. I sent that letter by hand from Manchester and copied it to Sir Barry Shaw, to Philip Myers and to the senior MI5 officer in London. I gave very serious consideration to forwarding a copy to Mr Douglas Hurd, but Philip Myers told me he would inform him himself.

The alleged 'cover-up' instances were now less important than they had been. I believed we were looking at possible murder, or unlawful killing, in all three cases. If that were so, then the road could lead in only one direction: to the question of whether senior police officers were involved in the formulation of any deliberate policies of shooting to kill. There was very little more I could do in Northern Ireland until the Hayshed tape controversy was resolved, and I returned to Manchester on 21 June 1985. On my way back to Manchester I spent a day at the RAF Staff College at Bracknell in Berkshire, where I presented a formal two-hour lecture to the senior students entitled 'Policing a Democratic Society.' When I arrived home my first job was to accompany Her Royal Highness the Duchess of Kent on a low-key official visit, and that was followed by a day-long seminar with senior officers and local MPs on police tactics in dealing with hooliganism at football matches. The sharp contrast between mainland and Northern Irish policing styles, separated only by a thirty-minute plane journey, is indeed a dramatic one. I retained my office in Belfast, and two of my staff remained temporarily to tie up loose ends and to maintain an occasional presence in Northern Ireland.

On 1 July I began to compile what was to be a massive file of papers. All the typing was done by my secretary on a word processor and kept in a secure room at Police Headquarters, Manchester. We had interviewed, at great length, about three hundred police officers — some of them under-cover and secret-surveillance men and women who had witnessed possible criminal acts and had not been previously interviewed. We had taken about six hundred written statements from policemen, forensic scientists, doctors, pathologists, members of the public and relatives of the dead men. Each shooting was written up, documented, prepared and arranged as a separate prosecution file but with a 'link report' showing the connections between the shootings and the Kinnego murders of the three policemen. The Hayshed shooting report was prepared up to the moment of the triggers, being pulled, and I resumed it again after Tighe was dead and McCauley grievously injured. I prepared a separate bulky report for submission to the Northern Ireland Forensic Science Service dealing with what I saw as deficiencies in their original investigations.

Each complete set of case papers ran to sixteen thick volumes, and I prepared six complete sets. I had the documents commercially bound at a Manchester printers under very close and constant police supervision. The normal type of in-house police binding is by a plastic spiral spine, but I was anxious that nothing be removed from these files until the Director of Public Prosecutions had seen his copy. Every page was classified and numbered, and I can truthfully say I have never taken such care with any police file I have prepared as I did with this one. I believed that, the Hayshed apart, every scrap of evidence had been re-examined, and that professionally I could not have done a better job. I knew it would stand up to any scrutiny. Two of my officers loaded three of the six complete sets into a van and, discreetly escorted, during the very early hours of 18 September 1985 it left for an RAF airfield in the south of England, whence the files were to be flown to Belfast. I retained three complete sets of the papers at Manchester. I had spoken to Sir John Hermon before the flight arrangements had been made, and asked him for a date convenient to him when I could deliver the report. I also asked him whether, in accordance with mainland procedures, he was content to leave the delivery of the Director of Public Prosecutions' copy to me. I knew that Sir Barry Shaw was most anxious to take delivery of the report and to look again at matters he had regarded as very urgent over eighteen months earlier, in March 1984.

I suppose that by then nothing should really have surprised me, but Sir John yet again took a tangential line. He refused me permission to give the Director of Public Prosecutions any papers connected with my investigation. I told him that, as he had demanded, my request for access to the Hayshed tape was contained within the files and that the DPP needed to consider that request very urgently. The public-interest issue was now at the heart of the enquiry, and that interest would surely not be served by delaying the decision that Sir John had insisted be made by Sir Barry Shaw. The Chief Constable's staff officer telephoned me with a convenient delivery date, which was 18 September. Sir John Hermon, he said, would be in his office that day to receive the report and to discuss it with me. John

Thorburn and I flew on a routine British Airways flight and were met at Aldergrove by a car and driver. We were taken to Police Headquarters, where we met the two Manchester officers who had escorted the bulky files from Manchester. At about 9.30 a.m. we were shown into the office of the Deputy Chief Constable, Michael McAtamney. I asked where the Chief Constable was, and was told that he had other business. I was not told what that business was. Had I been informed even a few hours before that the Chief Constable would not be in his office to receive the report, I would have delayed delivery until he was.

We opened the secure boxes and Michael McAtamney signed for the three complete sets. Little was said, but he seemed surprised at the number of bound volumes involved. We left the building, kicked our heels in and around Belfast, and returned back by the booked late afternoon flight to Manchester. On the journey home one of my Manchester team who had remained outside the Belfast Police Head-quarters, a very shrewd and sharp-eyed detective sergeant, told me he had briefly seen the Chief Constable at a window in the building while John Thorburn and I were inside. He described the window to me. I knew, although the sergeant did not, that it looked out from the Chief Constable's private apartment, which was above his office in Police Head-quarters.

I withdrew my team to Manchester and we busied ourselves with preparations for the investigation of the tape of the Hayshed shootings. I was confident that the Director of Public Prosecutions, within days of receiving his copy of the report, would agree to those further enquiries and authorize my access to the tape. The days went by, and then weeks. Routine calls from my officers were met with the standard response that the Chief Constable was 'still studying' the report. I could not afford to keep my team together any longer, and sent them back to other CID duties. One of them (now a Detective

Superintendent) I sent to the Fraud Squad, others to the Drugs Squad and Serious Crime Squad and divisional work. I learned through a friendly mole that the Chief Constable was in no hurry to send the Director of Public Prosecutions his copy of my report. Sir John had, it seems, arranged for a team of his own officers to take my report into his own Force and to dissect and analyse every word of it. I felt like Alice in Wonderland. This was quite outside any procedures I had ever come across in thirty years of mainland investigations of this nature. On the mainland the investigating officer's report would have been delivered simultaneously to the commissioning Chief Constable and the Director of Public Prosecutions. It would never be re-examined or analysed before submission to the DPP.

I was angry that the report, which had been urgently requested by the DPP eighteen months earlier and by the Chief Constable throughout the investigation, and which had been finished under pressure during the summer at the expense of our well-deserved holidays, was now gathering dust at Police Headquarters. If the Chief Constable wished to analyse what I had done, I supposed that was his obscure right, though I permitted myself the thought that if as much effort and determination had gone into the CID investigations of the original shootings, my presence in Northern Ireland might never have been required. I took exception, however, to Sir John's decision not to send the Director of Public Prosecutions his papers in order that he could analyse and decide on the matters within his sphere of responsibility. But I could not move things along, and neither, it seemed, could the DPP himself. The months went by; Christmas came and went, and the complete silence from the RUC continued. I appealed to Mr Philip Myers, but I realized just how powerless his office is to exert any real influence on a Chief Constable. He functions by persuasion — the reality of power is not his, at least not in Northern Ireland.

I had prepared a brief 10,000-word précis of my findings that dealt with a range of issues, from important matters such as recommendations for changes in the Special Branch, to the more mundane — for example, alterations in the dangerous practice of the issuance and supervision of multiple police notebooks. The summary of findings was intended for quick reading, but nevertheless it contained enough detail to indicate how and why I had arrived at my conclusions. There were, in total, 23 headings, and the document represented my thoughts not just on the things that had gone wrong but on the positive aspects and, more importantly, the way forward for investigations of the type I had undertaken. I saw it as a carefully considered and balanced evaluation by a senior mainland police officer whose only interest was to help the Royal Ulster Constabulary improve its service to all the people of Northern Ireland. It was, I believe, constructive and honest, but it has to be said it was also politically and professionally damaging to the RUC and to the Home Office Inspectorate. Most of what I was critical of, I know, would cause acute embarrassment to those whose duty it should have been to inspect and monitor the Royal Ulster Constabulary and its systems, and I did not expect it to be received with open arms. I did hope, however, that it would be regarded for what it was — a genuine attempt on my part, and that of my team, to prevent similar troubles in the future. The list of recommendations for changes was formidable, but it represented only that which my original terms of reference had encompassed. I had not strayed into areas that did not concern me, and I assumed that those responsible for asking me to undertake such a fundamental and important investigation would not expect me to pretend I had not noticed areas of policing that were inefficient, ineffective or, worse, dangerously ambiguous. I took the simple view, as I wrote that summary, that if the Chief Constable and the Home Office chose to ignore or rationalize what I had to say, that was their affair. My job was done after I had said it.

I addressed a wide range of operational matters, including the lack of accountability and dubious practices within Special Branch. I commented in general terms, and so far as I was able, on the role of informants and paid agents, and I was critical of the methods and control over the enormous payments to them. I expressed my unease at the potential for *agents provocateurs* and bounty-hunters. I spoke of the inadequacies of, and lack of definition in, CID investigations in cases in which Special Branch was involved, and of the dangerously loose use of important words such as 'wanted' when referring to suspects. Too often that word meant nothing more than 'slightly suspected', but had the effect of raising the stakes unacceptably in cases where the police were asked to make an arrest. I criticized the introduction of, and the reliance on, the unofficial Official Secrets form that prevented policemen who had signed it from telling the truth. I supported the role of the Tasking and Co-ordination Group within Special Branch, and criticized its level of staffing. I discussed at considerable length the inordinately long working hours required for some of the armed officers, and expressed my concern about the manner in which they might then be required to raise themselves at very short notice to combat pitch. It seemed to me very undesirable that tired policemen should be thrust into such situations.

I strongly disapproved of the fact that some policemen who had been involved in these fatal shootings were allowed to continue on similar armed duties before their earlier actions had been critically examined. I believed that this placed an intolerable pressure on the men themselves, and could inhibit their actions in a way that could endanger their lives. I scrutinized the selection and training methods of members of the special police squads, and reflected on the impossibility of expecting policemen to fulfil a military role in SAS style operations. In a more philosophical vein I looked at the ways in which some RUC practices had had the effect of reducing the confidence in them of the Director of Public Prosecutions, the coroners, the press, the relatives of men killed by police, and the mainland policemen investigating the conduct of the Force.

At a lower but still important level I made recommendations about the proper use of pathologists at controversial deaths, the poorly co-ordinated role of scenes-of-crime officers and forensic scientists, the abysmal quality of official photographs, and the abuse of police evidence notebooks. I made further recommendations about cross-border activities and the lack of any instructions about them. But probably the two most important issues I argued were those of Force spirit and morale, and my recommended future procedures for investigating controversial deaths at the hands of police. I spent some time in describing the traumatic effect the three incidents had had on the morale of the officers of the Special Support units. They were left to flounder on their own, and they felt ostracized, isolated and abandoned by their senior officers, to whom they had displayed, and continued to display, a high degree of loyalty. In my view, no serious attempt had ever been made to restore their confidence in the leadership of the Force, and I feared for their health and well-being. Finally, I presented three options for handling future controversial shooting enquiries, two of which involved independent mainland police supervision within the first twenty-four hours. The débâcles of the three incidents I investigated must never be allowed to happen again, and I said so strongly. I felt that my summary was forthright but considered. I can imagine, however, that it made depressing reading for the Chief Constable and his senior officers.

I was by now very busy with my duties as Deputy Chief Constable of Greater Manchester Police, and, frankly, had tried to forget Northern Ireland. Over five months had gone by since I had delivered the report to the RUC and I had begun to suspect that no one, other than my team and myself, really cared what happened to it. I could do no more. The Director of Public Prosecutions had tried and failed to speed up delivery, and I had not been contacted by Mr Philip (now Sir Philip) Myers for many weeks. In the first few days of March 1986 he telephoned me, however, and asked what my Interim Report contained. He then straightforwardly requested me to tell him what recommendations I had made about the running of the Royal Ulster Constabulary. I told him that the files had been with the Chief Constable of the RUC for five months, and asked whether he, as Her Majesty's Inspector of Constabulary, was not able to discuss the matter with Sir John Hermon? He was very honest with me. He said that Sir John would be unlikely to tell him if he did ask, and he did not wish to provoke problems. I said that my energies were now firmly committed to Manchester, and that Northern Ireland was a fast-fading memory. I knew I could do no more without his strong and unequivocal support. Could I take it that he was now offering it? Sir Philip said yes, he was; the delays were now a matter of widespread comment and political embarrassment.

I have since learned from a trusted journalist contact that Sir John's reason for delaying the delivery of my report was that he was concerned about what he saw as defamatory comments about his officers in my report, and that he wished to protect me from legal action for damages by those officers. The report was protected from such action by its very nature and circulation, however, and I cannot believe Sir John did not know that. Sir Philip asked me directly for a copy of my Interim Report. I told him that his request to me was not strictly proper: the report was now the property of the Chief Constable of the Royal Ulster Constabulary until such time as he passed it to the Director of Public Prosecutions, and I had agreed not to allow any other person to see it until Sir John had given authority. I was being asked to part with something that was not, at that moment, mine to give. Sir Philip promised that he would not divulge his approach to me and said he would lock the document in his safe at Colwyn Bay until I gave him authority to say he had read it. He emphasized how important it was that he had sight of what I had written. I promised I would think about it, but could not give him an answer there and then.

I gave the matter considerable thought and realized that I was in a difficult position. But Sir John Hermon had had five months in which to formulate his opinion. I rang Sir Philip Myers back and said that I was prepared to allow him to read my own retained and numbered copy of the Interim Report, but that I intended to formalize his request to me by way of a letter to him that could then be placed on file and would act as a form of receipt. I gained the impression that Sir Philip Myers would have preferred a less formal way, but he raised no serious objections. I also said that I had to tell my team where the copy was going, and that I would tell Sir John Hermon also, but only if he asked me. I promised Sir Philip I would not volunteer that information. On these conditions I sent him by hand, on 4 March 1986, a copy of my Interim Report. He never acknowledged it, nor did he discuss its contents with me.

By coincidence, and unknown to me, that day also saw a very important development at the office of the Director of Public Prosecutions in Belfast. A few days earlier the Chief Constable had at last, well over five months after I had given it to his Deputy, delivered a copy of my report to Sir Barry Shaw. Within a few days Shaw had read it and acted on it. On 4 March 1986 he delivered to the Chief Constable a powerful and unarguable direction to allow me access to everything and to any person, policeman or not, connected with events at the Hayshed. The response from him had been predictably swift and resolute, but still the Royal Ulster Constabulary did not tell me immediately that they knew of it. I had heard through my friendly mole that something was happening between the Royal Ulster Constabulary and the Director of Public Prosecutions; but I was not told officially until ten days later, when the Chief Constable wrote to me explaining that the Attorney General and the DPP had now judged that disclosure of all evidence to me was in the public interest, and that he was now inviting me to continue my enquiry into his police force. He asked me to let him know when I was coming to Belfast again in order that he could discuss with me certain matters relating to my terms of reference. It was a peculiarly vague letter, full of official and legal phrases. It closed by saying that he would be available only after 26 March. This absence effectively delayed my resumption of the enquiry by yet another two weeks, on top of the long delays I had already encountered. I tried continually to obtain a date to see the Chief Constable, and after a number of attempts he eventually agreed to see me on 30 April 1986. I told him that I sincerely hoped for his co-operation in allowing me access to all the information, including the tape recording and transcripts. In reply he was non-committal.

On 30 April 1986 John Thorburn and I flew to Belfast and were driven to Police Headquarters. We were met by the Chief Constable's staff officer — a Superintendent — who blandly said that Sir John Hermon was not there. I was annoyed, and said I had an appointment with the Chief Constable that *he* had made, and that this was not the first time such discourtesy had been shown. Six wasted weeks had gone by, during which I could have come on any day. I asked where the Chief Constable was and at first could not get an answer. Eventually I was told by a junior officer that he was taking a recruit passing-out parade at the Police Training Centre at Enniskillen. Such a parade must have been planned for weeks. I saw this episode as another tactic of delay, and frankly I had had enough of it. I spoke to John Thorburn in private and told him that I was not prepared to return meekly to Manchester to make yet another appointment for weeks hence that might or might not be kept. It was almost exactly two years since he and I had arrived at those Belfast headquarters for the first time, and for eighteen months of that two years I had been seeking only one thing — the tape. I did not intend to waste the rest of the day. The whole business was bizarre. I had, a few weeks earlier, submitted an interim account to the Northern Ireland office for an amount well in excess of £250,000, being the cost of my enquiry (not including my salary). Had it not been for the delays, this enormous amount from the public purse could have been reduced by half. I had no intention of adding to it unnecessarily.

I saw the head of Special Branch, Assistant Chief Constable Trevor Forbes, and told him what I wanted. He said that the Chief Constable would wish to see me before I proceeded further. I made it clear that I was here at Police Headquarters, and that if the Chief Constable wished to see me I would be here for several more hours; Enniskillen is only a short drive away. In the meantime I had a shopping list for the Special Branch. There was tremendous consternation, and a senior Assistant Chief Constable came to see me to say that what I was doing was provocative and improper, and to make efforts to stop me. I told him I would deal only with the Chief Constable and that I could not waste another expensive trip to Northern Ireland. He left me angrily and said he would get in touch with the Chief Constable. John Thorburn and I went to the Special Branch and obtained much of what we had been seeking for eighteen months. That material, however, did not include the tape. The two of us had lunch in a highly charged atmosphere in the Senior Officers' Mess restaurant, and resumed our work in the afternoon. The Special Branch obviously had not anticipated our storming their ramparts, and very few of the documents we asked for were readily available; nevertheless, we managed to obtain most of what we had been seeking. We returned to Manchester by the late afternoon flight with a variety of documents in John Thorburn's briefcase.

The following day, Thorburn began to analyse what we had and to prepare lists of work arising from this new material. In the meantime I began to give new thought to the questions I would soon have to ask of the Chief Constable, the Deputy Chief Constable and at least one Assistant Chief Constable. I also had to consider at what stage I should involve and inform the Northern Ireland Police Authority, which is a body composed of lay persons who constitute the statutory disciplinary authority for the twelve officers of Assistant Chief Constable and above in the Royal Ulster Constabulary. I felt I had grounds for belief that some offences might have been committed by one or more of those senior police officers, and I needed to put the official machinery into motion soon. During the initial probing into this area I had been requested by Philip Myers to bring him into discussions as soon as I reached that stage. In May 1986 I realized I had at last reached it. Interestingly, I received no protest by telephone from the Chief Constable about my intrusion into his Special Branch; but on 12 May a short letter was delivered by hand from him saying that 'it is unfortunate' he was absent when I visited his headquarters on 30 April. The letter made no mention that our visit was not a casual one but by appointment, and there was no hint of apology. The last paragraph was terse and pointed. It said, 'perhaps we can co-ordinate your next visit with my availability here, so that matters can be resolved before you recommence your investigations . . . I look forward to having your final report as quickly as possible.'

I did not reply. I suspected that further correspondence would waste time and be acrimonious. I telephoned Belfast and said I would be returning with my team on Monday 19 May. I asked for the use of the same suite of offices and similar facilities as before. I had decided that I would need very quickly to see the Deputy Chief Constable, Mr Michael McAtamney. I intended to interview him formally, with full notes taken of the proceedings, about his investigations into the three incidents, investigations that the Director of Public Prosecutions had decided were unsatisfactory and that had resulted in my arrival in Northern Ireland. I needed to know about his role in relation to the apparent failure to recognize the seriousness of the six deaths, coming as they did so close together, and at what stage (if at all) he had informed the Chief Constable, who was out of the country for some of the time.

Subject to his answers, I had mentally mapped out my intended interview with the Chief Constable. I required answers about the level of his involvement, if any, in restricting his Deputy's second investigation, and about his reasons for failing to send to the Director of Public Prosecutions a Detective Chief Superintendent's careful analysis and recommendation that a policeman be charged with murder. I intended to ask him how often he had done this in the past, or whether, as I suspected, that was the first and only time. I also wanted to ask three very senior officers whether they had knowledge of the false cover stories told by junior officers, and to let them know that some of those officers had indicated to me that they telephoned Police Headquarters for advice before distributing those stories. I wanted to ask whether it had been any one of them who had given that advice. I jotted down a host of questions that I hoped to turn into a structured interview before I returned to Belfast.

On Wednesday 14 May 1986, Sir Philip Myers telephoned me and I told him of my plans for the following week. He was quiet and circumspect in his reply. He told me not to go to Belfast — to cancel the flights and hotels for my team and myself. I asked him why, and he said he could not explain on the telephone. I was annoyed at the inconvenience, but assumed that his request was connected with the forthcoming Protestant marching season and the delicate state of play in the Anglo-Irish discussions. I told my team and rearranged the return to Belfast for Monday 26 May. On Friday 23 May, at 11.30 a.m., Sir Philip Myers rang me again and tersely asked me to cancel these new arrangements. I asked him, equally tersely, why? Again he said he could not trust the telephones because he was speaking from Belfast, but would explain as soon as he could. He asked me to accept his word that it was vital that I again cancel the trip.

My investigation was, on that very day, exactly two years old, and for eighteen months of that time I had been attempting to obtain a critical piece of evidence of what could amount to murder. No private individual would have been allowed to withhold such a piece of vital information. No one seemed to care about the immense damage that was being caused to the public image of the Royal Ulster Constabulary, or the immeasurable effect the saga was having on the suspected policemen and their families and the relatives of the six dead men. Less important, but still of some significance to me, was the fact that we eight police officers had been avoidably kept from our duties in Greater Manchester by what seemed to me wholly indefensible delaying tactics. I was confused by the conversation with Sir Philip Myers, and asked myself whether those tactics had now crossed the Irish Sea. I remember my thoughts as I reflected on the possible reasons for that 'phone call. I concluded that the government, because of its delicate Anglo-Irish negotiations, needed time. The Royal Ulster Constabulary, because of the heightened tension of the banned or diverted Protestant marches, also needed time. My enquiry was threatening the balance. If I did as I said I would — interview very senior officers and refer possible disciplinary offences to their Police Authority — then the one constant element that is keeping the peace in Northern Ireland, the RUC, would be under extreme threat. The original investigation was, after all, yesterday's news. My efforts now to keep it fresh were surely being seen by pragmatists in the government and the police as a pain in the neck. But I had no patience left. The enquiry was within a few weeks of completion, and had been for about fifteen months. I estimated that, at most, two months' more work would be required before my final report arrived on the desk of the Director of Public Prosecutions. I had learned enough in my two years' association with Northern Ireland to know that there would never be a good time to do what I planned to do.

The question of the tape and what was or was not on it was the most important single aspect still to be examined, and the DPP's urgent instruction for me to have access to it was now almost three months old. The Chief Constable, on the face of it, now wished for a quick conclusion, yet it seemed that unknown elements were now delaying my return to Northern Ireland.

I told James Anderton of this latest intervention by Sir Philip Myers, and expressed my doubts about whether the Inspectorate had the authority to step in between me and the operational aspect of the enquiry. More importantly, I believe I was letting Anderton know that a confrontation was imminent, because I would not brook any further inter-ference. Sir Philip Myers had promised, and failed, to tell me why he did not wish me to resume my enquiries. I told James Anderton that I would be interviewing, probably under criminal caution, several very senior police officers including the Chief Constable. I told him this, not expecting him to step in officially, but hoping he would make a discreet telephone call to the Home Office to let senior civil servants know how strongly I and my team felt about these latest, unexpected obstacles.

I instructed John Thorburn to make another — this time final — set of arrangements. We were going to Belfast on Monday 2 June 1986, whatever happened. I made an inked entry in my diary to conduct interviews in the first three days of that week. The hotels were booked, the flights confirmed and I told my team, and James Anderton, that we were going and that there would be no more postponements. The week before that was one for further preparation. I had, of course, expected to be in Northern Ireland for part of that week, and had space in my diary. Monday 26 May was a Bank Holiday and I tagged on to it, as extra leave, the next two days to enable me to prepare my thoughts at home for the interviews to come. On the Tuesday evening I had a business dinner in the Moss Nook Restaurant in Manchester, with James Anderton and two BBC TV men, Colin Cameron, the Executive Producer of *Brass Tacks,* and Peter Taylor, a reporter from the same programme. I had met Peter Taylor before in connection with his work on a *Panorama* television programme connected with the Royal Ulster Constabulary, and I knew he had been following my investigation with professional interest. The dinner was a relaxed occasion and a certain amount of bridge-building was done between the Force and the BBC; relations at that time were fractured because of what James Anderton regarded as a biased anti-police programme made by the *Brass Tacks* production team. This programme was about alleged police violence towards students when the Home Secretary had visited Manchester University, and the programme had deeply upset him and other members of the Force.

The meal was a good one, the atmosphere friendly. Northern Ireland was not mentioned. I left the restaurant about midnight and walked with James Anderton to his car. He reminded me that on the Friday of that week I was representing him at an important meeting at the Home Office in London to discuss inner-city riots and police plans for the summer. He went to the boot of his official Jaguar and handed me a blue plastic loose-leaf file of papers for the meeting. I told him that I would be back on duty on Thursday, and would read them then. He closed the boot lid and said, 'No, take them now. I have brought them for you. You may as well keep them.' I was not particularly happy about having confidential papers in my home for two days, but I took them and drove away.

The following day, 28 May, I was working in my garden when the telephone rang. My wife answered it and told me that it was Mr Roger Rees, the Clerk to the Greater Manchester Police Authority. I took the telephone through an open window. Rees was very cold and formal. He said that allegations had been made against me that might indicate a disciplinary offence on my part, and that Mr Colin Sampson, the Chief Constable of the West Yorkshire Police, would be investigating them. He asked me to be in my own office at 10.00 a.m. the following day. I asked him what on earth was going on, and what allegations had been made against me. Mr Rees refused to answer and said that Mr Sampson would tell me. I replaced the receiver. I was stunned and confused.

I leaned against the outside wall of my house and my wife came towards me. I knew then, as powerfully as it is possible to know, that what was happening to me was rooted firmly in my enquiries in Northern Ireland. It was no secret that I was within a couple of days of obtaining the vital tape, and of interviewing the highest policemen in the RUC. I knew I had nothing to fear from any fair investigation into me, but I had learned enough during the previous years to know that devious and lying policemen do exist, and that they can function without hindrance given the right conditions. In those few seconds after that 'phone call from Mr Rees, as my wife approached me across the garden, I fleetingly wondered how much I had to fear from policemen such as those.

At that time it never entered my head that I would not be allowed to finish the Northern Ireland enquiry. I did not know what Mr Sampson wanted to see me for, but whatever it was, I was confident it was a matter that could be cleared up within a few days and that I would then be allowed to complete the last few yards of what had become a painful and often circuitous marathon. I telephoned the Chief Constable, but his secretary said he was not there. It struck me that he was probably with Mr Rees. I asked that he telephone me as soon as he returned. The 'phone rang about half-past five and the Chief Constable asked me what I wanted. I told him of Mr Rees's call and asked him what was happening. He too was cold and formal, saying that he could not discuss the matter with me and that Mr Sampson would give me what information I was entitled to the following day. I told him I was concerned about my Northern Ireland enquiry, and he made a strange reply. He said, 'You must, from now on, worry only about yourself.'

I was hurt and puzzled by Mr Anderton's iciness, particularly after the pleasant and friendly evening we had spent only a few hours before; but I knew that he routinely taped his phone calls, and that he might have been merely very cautious in his choice of words. There was little more I could do. My wife and I sat on the bed to collect our thoughts. I saw the file of papers given to me by James Anderton, lying on top of my briefcase. Whatever Mr Sampson wished to see me about must have happened that day, because my own Chief Constable, in the early hours of that morning, had given me those papers to enable me to represent him at an important meeting two days hence.

I was sometimes uneasy about his evangelical style of policemanship, but I had never regarded James Anderton as a deceitful or morally dishonest man, and I suddenly felt reassured. I was certain he would not have played out an entirely unnecessary charade by giving me a file of useless papers for a meeting he never intended me to attend. Events were to prove me wrong, however. That is exactly what he had done.

# 4

## Extended Leave

I cannot truly describe my feelings as I put down the telephone after my short conversation with Mr Anderton. He had said I must now look after myself. I had no idea what he meant. But I knew there was no reason for any complaint to be made against me. I was sure there had been a mistake, and yet Anderton had been so strangely and coldly formal. It was as if he had never met me. I tried to think straight. First and most importantly, I looked my wife honestly in the eyes and told her that I had nothing to fear from any enquiry, no matter how searching, into my professional conduct. I had done nothing wrong. I then voiced the suspicion I had harboured from the moment I received the telephone call from Roger Rees: that what was happening to us was connected with my enquiry in Northern Ireland. I had learned that there were at that time some devious operators working within the RUC Special Branch, and I felt the first chill of real concern. I had made some bitter enemies, and the thought skipped across my mind that scores were being settled. I reminded myself that I had behaved scrupulously honestly and fairly in Northern Ireland, as indeed had all of my team; we had known that some elements would not hesitate to turn any suggestion of misbehaviour on our part to their own advantage.

I did not dwell too long on the reasons why this was

happening to me. I had to deal with the problems of the moment. I knew that the roof of our lives would fall in as soon as the first whiff of what was happening reached the press. The Deputy Chief Constable of the country's biggest provincial police force was in some sort of trouble, and that would be news. The Greater Manchester Police has leaked like a sieve for some years, particularly to favoured reporters, and I realized that I had to speak to the people I love before they heard a garbled story from elsewhere. I left it to my wife, Stella, to tell my two daughters, who were both out of the house at the time. I drove the twenty miles across Manchester to see my parents, who live with my brother, Michael, on the north side of the city. Both my mother and father have troublesome heart conditions and my mother especially needs to be cushioned from shocks. I told them both the little I knew, and expressed my overwhelming intuitive belief that whatever was happening to me had its roots in Northern Ireland.

I am my mother's eldest son and she can see into my soul. She is small and frail now, dwarfed by her four sons, but her wisdom, judgment and above all her values have been the bedrock of all our lives. She has the indomitable spirit and native shrewdness of inner-city working people, fired with proud ambition for her family but always demanding a standard of honesty that justifies her pride. She asked me with her compellingly direct gaze whether I had done anything to jeopardize my job or my good name. I told her with absolute honesty that I had not. 'Then you are right; it's to do with Northern Ireland,' she said. Her words were a statement, not a question. I had told her nothing of my work there, except to say it was almost finished. She was calm and at peace as I gathered myself to leave. I wished to get home to see my daughters. As I stood to go my mother took hold of me and turned me to face her as she had done when I was a child. 'Don't worry,' she said. 'I shall not worry — nor will your dad.

You will come out of this with your good name and your integrity intact. Others will be despised forever, and I think the one who will lose most will be Mr Anderton.' I had not mentioned Mr Anderton other than to refer to the 'phone call of that afternoon. At that time she knew nothing of the meal the evening before, or of the file of papers he had handed me. I had not expressed any opinion about him; but my mother had interpreted this omission to mean that he must somehow be at fault. She seemed instantly to lose the respect she had had for him.

I returned home and spoke to my daughters. The youngest of them, Francine, was due to sit her 'A' level examinations the following week. She had temporarily recovered from a long and painful orthopaedic problem associated with her knee and wrist joints, and although she had worked hard I was already anxious for her. In the event, the developments of the next weeks were a disaster for her so far as her examinations were concerned. I did not sleep that night; the words of Rees and Anderton were all I had to reason with and they had told me nothing. Only the distant iciness of their tones left any clue.

The following morning, 29 May, I listened to the early-morning radio. There was no leak yet. Two hours later than usual I drove the twelve miles to Police Headquarters and took the lift to the eleventh floor. Mr Anderton's official Jaguar was not parked in its usual place, and his police chauffeur was not at his desk. No one could tell me where the Chief Constable was. I had been in my office only a minute or so when two men came in. One I knew; he was the Chief Constable of West Yorkshire Police, Colin Sampson. The other I had never seen before; he was introduced to me as Donald Shaw, an Assistant Chief Constable in the same Force. We sat at a conference table in my office and Mr Sampson said, 'I have been asked by your Police Committee to investigate certain matters affecting yourself. This is not a formal interview and I am taking no notes.' I said, 'I will, if you don't mind.' I was beginning to regret not having asked someone to be with me. No mention had ever been made to me by either Rees or Anderton that Mr Sampson would not be on his own. Despite assurances, this was undoubtedly a formal interview. I asked what were the matters he was being requested to investigate, and he replied, 'I cannot at this moment tell you. It amounts only to rumour, innuendo and gossip about your association with people in Manchester.' I said, 'Who?' and he replied, 'I cannot tell you.' I asked, 'Cannot or will not?' and he replied, 'I am not able to tell you. I have a number of enquiries to make.'

I told him that I had done nothing wrong and asked him to make a note of this statement. I did not see either of them do so. Mr Sampson told me that no evidence had been provided to him, or any written statements, but he was sure his 'investigation — no, that's too strong a word — enquiry — should not take too long.' I asked him how long that might be. 'About a month, I should have thought.' I told him that I had a conference to attend in London the following day and, more importantly, was due back in Belfast in two days' time for a protracted stay. He said, 'I have been authorized by your Police Committee to invite you to take extra leave. You will not be going to London and you can consider yourself off the Northern Ireland investigation.' I said 'For the moment or forever?' Mr Sampson replied, 'Forever. I will now be taking over your investigations, using your team.'

He was final and quite unequivocal in relation to Northern Ireland but would give me absolutely no more information about the nature of his enquiry into me. He did, however, say that it had nothing to do with my investigations into the RUC. This was somewhat surprising. I asked him how he could be so certain. I said that I would not accept any free leave — I had plenty of unused holiday allocation and would take up that for the next month, or until he had finished his enquiry. Mr

Sampson is a slim, military-looking man with a ginger moustache and a measured Yorkshire voice. He had been polite, and had shown none of the coldness of Rees or Anderton. But at this point he changed. 'It is now my intention to ask you to leave your office and these headquarters right away,' he said. 'Either Mr Shaw or myself will be in touch with you as soon as possible.' He stood up and waited for me to leave my own office. There was no further conversation; Mr Shaw followed me to the lift and watched me enter. I felt totally humiliated.

I drove home, bewildered and numb; the meeting had lasted about a quarter of an hour, and it was about 11 a.m. when I arrived at my home.

Later that afternoon a press release was issued to every newspaper, press agency, television and radio company in the land. It was signed by Mr Rees and said:

Information has been received in relation to the conduct of a Senior Police Officer which disclosed the possibility of a disciplinary offence. To maintain public confidence the Chairman of the Police Committee, Councillor Norman Briggs, has requested the Chief Constable of West Yorkshire, C Sampson, Esq, QPM, to investigate this matter under the appropriate Statutory provisions, and the Police Complaints Authority, an independent statutory body, has agreed to supervise the investigation through its Deputy Chairman, Roland Moyle, Esq, who has approved the appointment of Mr Sampson. The Deputy Chief Constable is on temporary leave of absence whilst the matter is being investigated.

This extraordinary announcement, with its coy avoidance of actually naming me — but there is only one Deputy Chief Constable in Greater Manchester — had the obvious result. By the evening of 29 May my home swarmed with television crews and newsmen. An unrelenting, eleven-week-long media examination of me had begun. I did not know what to do. The doors of police headquarters in Greater Manchester and in West Yorkshire had now been firmly closed to the press.

Neither Anderton nor Sampson had any comment to make whatsoever. Mr Rees and the Chairman of the Police Committee would add nothing to the press release, and the Police Complaints Authority said they were awaiting the police report. No one was saying anything, and the press army understandably sniffed scandal.

The first arrivals at my door were from local newspapers and radio stations. My wife and eldest daughter dealt with them by telling the truth — that I was not able to speak to them, and that any further announcement must come from the Chief Constable or the Police Committee. We had been in our house only a few months and our telephone was ex-directory, but before long an enterprising newsman had obtained the number and began ringing us. He received the same reply. Soon many more pressmen had the telephone number, as it was passed from one to another. I sat in my own home, and with my totally bewildered family I felt the walls closing in. I knew that whatever else happened I had to make some sort of early written record about what had happened over the past twelve hours. The whole business was rapidly hurtling into the national headlines and I was not in control of anything, not even my own thoughts. I thought carefully and telephoned a man for whom I have the highest regard. Don Sharpe is a down-to-earth, pugnacious solicitor working in inner-city Coventry, whom I had met socially and liked immensely while I was in the Warwickshire CID some years before. I had not seen him for three or more years, but he is the sort of friend a man can telephone at any time. He was calm and tactful, and I made an appointment to see him in his office the following morning; he accepted my request for what it was, a plea from one friend to another for him to listen. The fact that he is a solicitor was incidental to me. I needed someone to be objective and cool, to listen and to make notes, but above all, to remember in the future what I had told him and the way I had said it.

The following morning I left the house very early to avoid the press, and drove, with my wife, the 100 miles to Coventry. My friend listened in virtual silence to the bizarre story about my sudden removal from duty and from my Northern Ireland investigation. He reduced it skilfully to eight pages of handwritten notes that I read and he signed. He placed them in a sealed envelope and then into his safe. It meant a great deal to me; I had been able to crystallize my thoughts, to record my overwhelming belief that these matters, despite Mr Sampson's premature assurance to the contrary, were connected with Northern Ireland. I had done something positive; my thoughts were safe and if, in the months to come, it was ever claimed that I had conveniently manufactured these convictions, I could show that I had not. We returned to Manchester to hear the announcement of my absence from duty on nationwide television news programmes.

The situation over the next two days was utterly chaotic. The words 'suspended from duty' and 'serious allegations' began to creep into the language of reporters. I was not suspended, and neither the words 'serious' nor 'allegation' were in Mr Rees's press release. But no one in any official position was correcting them. A reporter from ITN News came to my door with a crew on Sunday afternoon and said quite bluntly that my removal was connected with assaults on students outside Manchester University fourteen months before. I knew that he was wrong — I had not even been there — but I could not say so. I couldn't say anything. The pressures on my family and myself were becoming intolerable. On one occasion I counted eighty cameramen, reporters and technicians in my front garden. And yet the official silence was total. I was locked away in my house, with my curtains drawn, hiding from pressmen, as my wife and daughters valiantly tried to tell them we knew nothing. They simply didn't believe it, saying that if that were the case, why did I not say so?

After two days of this, I made a decision. I had three options. The first was to continue to skulk away in my own home while an increasingly disbelieving press continued to think I was guilty of serious offences. The second was to lock up my house and go away with my family. But this was impossible, since I live on a small-holding with a large number of livestock and poultry that cannot be abandoned. The third option was to do what I actually did, which was to face the cameras and the questions openly and to tell them truthfully that I had no idea why I had been removed from my desk. The *Manchester Evening News*, which played an important and leading role throughout, carried the story that the complaint against me was 'very trivial'. The Chairman of the Police Committee, Councillor Briggs, refused to give any details, but said that whatever it was 'had blown up over the last two days'. The Chief Constable, Mr Anderton, broke his silence for the only time when he issued a press statement saying he found it 'very regrettable indeed. It is my hope it will be cleared up as quickly as possible.' But still there was not the slightest indication of why such a drastic step had been taken. On Saturday morning, 31 May, two or three newspapers — the *Guardian* especially — began to speculate about my investigations into the Royal Ulster Constabulary, and a political dimension entered the story, never to leave it.

In the meantime I gave several press and television interviews at my front door, saying that I still had no idea what it was I was supposed to have done. The reporters were still sceptical, but some of them were beginning to believe me. On Monday 2 June I learned that the return of my team to Northern Ireland had again been stopped. All the appointments and important plans I had made were cancelled. Instead of being in Belfast sitting across a table from suspected senior officers, and looking for evidence of murder, I was at home, sick with worry and quite bewildered. With increasing panic I tried to imagine how serious the allegations against me must be to warrant this extraordinary state of affairs. My convictions grew that either Mr Sampson was investigating lies, or that some horrendous mistake had been made.

In due course a number of well-respected journalists with a particular interest in Northern Ireland began to arrive on the scene. Some of them had been following my investigation in the Province for the last two years, and a couple of them I had met. They included Chris Ryder from *The Sunday Times*, who flew in from Belfast, Peter Murtagh of the *Guardian*, Peter Taylor from BBC's *Panorama*, Michael McMillan from ITN and David Leigh and Jonathan Foster of the *Observer*. The pressures did not let up — from early morning to last thing at night the press were there, or else the 'phone was ringing. Friends and relatives came or called, policemen I had known for years made contact through third parties. They had been told that they should not speak to me, although many ignored those instructions. Speculation grew, and the Northern Ireland connection became stronger. Strangely, there had been no official announcement that Mr Sampson was to take on my investigation, even though almost a week had gone by since he had told me. The official doors were still firmly barred to the press, but I had decided that mine was now open. I could not prevent them coming; they had a job to do, and they were flesh and blood and real. What was happening elsewhere involving Mr Sampson was not real.

Each morning of the next week I drove my daughter Francine to school to take her 'A' level examinations, followed the three miles there and back by a posse of press cars. The narrow bend in the road on which I live was dangerously choked with press and sightseers. My wife telephoned Mr Anderton's office, pleading that he say something to the press. He did not return her calls and remained silent. She asked his office for some police assistance before an accident happened outside our home, but none was sent, although the local policeman, on his own account, called by when he could. No information of any kind was given out, and I found myself united in ignorance with the world's press. The *Manchester Evening News*, for instance, is a newspaper that is consistently and thoroughly well informed about police matters; but even they could not discover what was going on. Every day for almost a week, television news bulletins, local and national, carried close-ups of my face as I said that I had no more idea then of what was being investigated than I had had on the first day.

At 5.15 p.m. on 2 June my wife again telephoned the Chief Constable intending to beg him to say something — anything — to the press. The position was untenable. We had had four days of unceasing press demands, during which time we had hardly slept. My family, my parents, and our friends listened in stunned disbelief when I told them I still had not heard a thing beyond the uninformative press release of a week earlier. By the afternoon of 3 June the first political stirrings began. Seamus Mallon, Member of Parliament for Newry and Armagh, asked in the House of Commons what was going on in Manchester. He said, 'At the very least, it is highly coincidental that this should have happened to a man chosen to spear-head this investigation in Northern Ireland.' From that moment the press took up the growing political speculation. I had been nobbled, muzzled, gagged, stitched-up, set up or shot down. Headline writers ran riot. Allegations were made that my critical report into the management and practices of the RUC had been shelved and that my removal from the scene had been engineered in order to discredit what I had already said, in advance of its landing on the public lap. These claims were met with absolute silence from this side of the Irish Sea. There were no official denials whatsoever, although there were some indignant but impotent protests from Belfast.

Some newspapers were more careful, saying that even if my

mysterious enforced absence were not directly connected with Ulster, it had now been pounced on by the authorities, who were seeking any pretext they could find to refuse to act on my report and recommendations. Several newspaper leader articles spelled out the iniquity of my not being told the nature of the complaint about me. My name was swept along on a flood-tide of newspaper accusations of dirty tricks by government and the RUC. I continued to speak to the press, several times daily, telling them I had heard nothing. I spoke the truth — neither Mr Sampson nor any representative of the Police Committee had been in touch with me.

A cruel twist came on the eighth day after I had been asked to take extra leave. The *Daily Mail* carried a story that I was 'suspended' because of my 'associations with a criminal' (unnamed), and the reporter suggested that I had accepted 'lavish hospitality' from 'a criminal contact'. The story was a lie, and I was devastated. Up to this moment I had coped with the press myself and had, perhaps naively, regarded an honest approach on my part as the best weapon against mis-information. I might not have been able to tell the press anything, but at least I made myself regularly available. The evening before the *Mail* carried this story, I was visited at home by two of their reporters who half apologetically declared the paper's intention to publish it. I told them unequivocally that there was no truth whatsoever in their information, and that it would be discredited. I told them that I had never accepted any hospitality from a criminal. The reporters replied that the story was going in the following day, whatever I said. They were at my home 'out of courtesy' and to obtain a reaction from me, not to check its authenticity. I told the reporter, Margaret Henfield, that I would wait to see what the report said and then take the matter further. I made full notes of the conversation.

The following day confirmed my worst fears. The *Mail* carried the story, but without the majority of the vehement

121

denials made by my wife and myself. No names were mentioned in the article other than mine. The same day the *Manchester Evening News*, in the searching and balanced way that characterized its coverage of the story throughout, began to throw some true light on the matter. For the first time I saw a glimmer of what Mr Sampson's oblique reference to 'people in Manchester' may have meant. A long-time friend of mine, Kevin Taylor, gave an interview in which he said that he believed he was under police investigation, but bitterly rejected any suggestion that he was 'the known criminal' referred to in the *Daily Mail*. Kevin Taylor is a 55-year-old Manchester businessman whom I had met on the Parent/Teachers Committee of our children's junior school about thirteen years earlier, and whom I regarded as a friend. He is a man with no criminal convictions whatsoever, nor has he ever in his life been accused of any wrongdoing. Apart from his friendship with me, I don't think he had ever spoken to a policeman in any meaningful way during the time I had known him. The *Manchester Evening News* article made reference to a holiday taken by Kevin Taylor and myself some years earlier, and in response he made it clear that I had fully paid my share of the costs, which I had. Was this the 'lavish hospitality' the *Mail* was referring to? Later events showed that it was. The entire fuss and the immense national interest in what was going on in the Manchester Police related almost entirely to an absurd misunderstanding. If the intention in removing me was to divert attention from Northern Ireland, then it was having entirely the opposite effect.

At that moment I had no idea what Kevin Taylor's part would be in all that was to happen later. I had not seen him at all that year. My last sight of him had been at a dinner dance at the Hotel Piccadilly in Manchester on 23 November 1985, which I had attended in an official capacity with the full knowledge and endorsement of my own Chief Constable. Kevin Taylor had told me at about that time that a police enquiry had been made of his bank by a detective I knew; I had told him that in view of this it would be professionally unwise of me to see him until the matter was resolved. He was hurt, but he understood and respected my position. I had also told him, before he thought to mention it, that if there were enquiries about him I would not ask my colleagues about them, even though I was entitled to do so, for fear it might be seen as unusual interest by a senior officer in a matter involving a friend. Those are the ground rules that must always apply, even to relatives and close family. The public expect it, and it is in any case common sense. Kevin Taylor's police investigation had been leaked to the *Manchester Evening News*, I would guess by someone close to the investigation, and the newspaper had approached him for comment about whether he could be the 'known criminal' referred to in the *Daily Mail*. They also asked James Anderton, who issued a bald and unhelpful press release that said:

Unless there are exceptional circumstances in a particular case, and it is thought necessary in the public interest, it is not ordinarily the Chief Constable's policy to comment on any police enquiry or investigation which may be in progress, or to confirm or deny the existence of any such investigation.

The story gathered momentum, and I was besieged even further by newsmen asking for comments about 'criminal contacts' and 'lavish hospitality'. There were even half-veiled suggestions by one of the tabloids that because Kevin Taylor and I had spent a short holiday together without our families, the West Yorkshire Police were investigating allegations of homosexuality. The situation had horrifying implications, but still there was absolutely no information from West Yorkshire Police or James Anderton. Matters were now extremely serious, as speculation and rumour raged unchecked. The volatile mixture of official silence and my own ignorance of what was being investigated meant the press could fly any kite they wished. All I could do was stand at my front door and repeatedly deny any misbehaviour, and keep on saying that I knew nothing of what the investigations were about.

I felt that this unfair and damaging situation could surely not be allowed to continue, and I searched for answers. The Police Committee Chairman, Councillor Norman Briggs, was stubbornly resisting all efforts by members of his own Committee to find out what he knew. He was being closely and professionally advised by a lawyer, Roger Rees, and I was being investigated not only by a Chief Constable, Colin Sampson, but by Assistant Chief Constable Shaw, who has a law degree. They were in turn supervised by the Chairman of the Police Complaints Authority, Sir Cecil Clothier, QC, who is a judge. There was a battery of legal guns on the other side of the trench, and I decided it was time to seek legal advice of my own. I needed a well-respected Manchester solicitor who would give me objective and honest advice and guidance through what had become a 24-hour-a-day nightmare. My Coventry friend was just too far away. Manchester is the biggest news centre outside London, with every national newspaper represented as well as the television studios of Granada, *TV-am* and the BBC. I desperately needed to make contact with someone who could understand and cope, on a daily basis, with the already enormous and expanding media investment in this story.

There are plenty of fine solicitors in Manchester, but not too many who are comfortable with extreme media pressures. I spoke to some trusted friends in legal circles and unanimously they referred me to Rodger Pannone of the Manchester firm of Goldberg, Blackburn and Howard. I had heard of him, but had never met him. I contacted him at his home and saw him there with another partner of the firm, Mr Peter Lakin. It was the single most sensible move I made, and I did it just in time. In later months I was criticized by some members of the Police Committee — especially its present Chairman, Councillor Stephen Murphy — and by some senior policemen, for seeking legal advice 'too soon'. Given that I was in a situation without precedent in police affairs in this country, and especially given the wild rumours and speculation about alleged criminal behaviour on my part, I cannot see that I had any alternative. If I had not done so I was jeopardizing not only my job, but more importantly my reputation and that of my family, and I could never allow that to happen. A powerful political and police machine, fully serviced legally, was busily grinding away behind closed doors as I waited outside, dealing with the real world at the expense of the health and strength of my family and myself. Rodger Pannone and Peter Lakin were to become an integral part of my life for many months to come. Without them I would undoubtedly have gone under.

After my meeting with Pannone and Lakin they acted quickly. We made a carefully considered decision to call a press conference for the following morning at their offices. It was professionally organized and was attended by every national newspaper and television company as well as regional and local press and broadcasting stations. About 150 people crushed into a conference room and they were given an entirely free rein to ask any questions they wished of me. The solicitors agreed with me that I should refuse to support the growing conviction that the whole business was a smear campaign to remove me from the Northern Ireland enquiry. I repeated my innocence of any wrongdoing and spoke freely of my family friendship with Kevin Taylor and of our holiday in America almost five years earlier. My solicitors, through the media, pressed for details of the allegations against me so that I could begin to defend myself. I made public, for the first time, the extent of public support and police messages of goodwill I had received since the Police Authority had issued their press release seven days earlier.

The press conference went well: I had laid myself open to examination, as I had done throughout the previous week, but with the important difference that it was properly co-ordinated by two solicitors of the highest stature and reputation. The pictures and stories filled the television screens and column inches that day, the following day and the next Sunday (8 June). It had the desired effect. The public pressures it created promptly resulted in the West Yorkshire investigating officers' arranging a secret meeting between Mr Sampson and me for the following Monday. So secret was it that my solicitors and I were not told of the venue until the last minute. Nevertheless, when we arrived in a taxi at the Police Training School at Sedgley Park, Prestwich, in a leafy north Manchester suburb, the television crews were already camped outside. This leaking of any newsworthy information about the progress of the enquiry became a wearisome feature. Details of whatever was planned, or whoever was to be seen, were insidiously leaked to media sources beforehand. The result was that I was always the last to know; newspaper reporters regularly told me what was to happen next, and they were invariably right.

The meeting at Sedgley Park was short. Mr Sampson gave me an official form under the provisions of the Police Discipline Regulations 1985 that simply stated:

Information has been received which indicates that during the past six years you have associated with persons in circumstances that are considered undesirable, and by such association you may have placed yourself under an obligation as a police officer to those persons.

That was all. The source of the information was never made known to me, and there were no names, times, dates or places. There was absolutely nothing I could even begin to build a defence against. The long-awaited form had two very significant words heavily crossed out, and Mr Sampson made it quite clear to me that no 'allegation' or 'complaint' had been made against me. The meeting was formal and professional. Mr Sampson emphasized his commitment to fairness and to maintaining his own reputation for integrity. My solicitors and I accepted his assurances but asked for more information. Who are the people I have associated with? What obligations have I placed myself under? No answers were forthcoming. Then, out of the blue, Assistant Chief Constable Shaw asked me to provide him with full details from my bank account, my credit cards and any other savings accounts I had had over the previous six years. I asked why he needed them and was politely told that I was under no legal obligation to provide them. The implication was obvious, however. If I refused, the assumption would be made that I had something to hide. This request was unprecedented in what was a purely disciplinary matter. Even in the most serious of criminal investigations a senior judge has to give permission for the police to examine bank accounts. If I refused they would have no power to obtain the information. Shaw also asked me to surrender my passport to him.

I asked for a few minutes to speak to Peter Lakin; he was as dumbfounded as I was. It had been announced publicly by the Police Committee that I was not the subject of any criminal suspicion whatsoever. I was not suspended and no complaint or allegation of any sort had been made against me, and yet my passport and finances were to be put under scrutiny. Why? My inclination was to refuse the request. I assured Peter Lakin that I did not fear any examination of my accounts; it was simply that I bitterly objected to the humiliation of it and could not see what possible relevance my financial affairs could have to a disciplinary charge. I was later to learn that it was nothing more than a 'fishing' expedition to see whether I had paid my way five years earlier on my holiday with Kevin Taylor. The bank account showed I had, but the request for six years' records conveniently opened up other avenues of inquiry.

I decided to allow them access, but reflecting now I wish I had not done so. It was the most signally humiliating task my wife and I have ever had to undertake in twenty-five years of married life, and the effect on her was profound. Had I denied access, no doubt comment would have been made in the report and my refusal would at some time have been leaked to the press. But with hindsight I think I would rather have coped with that. What I had not reckoned with was the sense of intrusion that the resulting questions aroused. Stella has always looked after our financial affairs, and I had to ask her to explain to West Yorkshire officers movements within our accounts, and our purchases and income for six years. Line by line, in the early hours of the morning, we tried to recall long-forgotten transactions. The bank could help only to a degree. It was clear that guesswork was unacceptable; we had to be accurate, otherwise the conclusion would be reached that my finances were suspect. We cried with anger, but we answered every single question put to us. The process of doing so drained us in a way I could not have imagined. I doubt if I can ever forget, or forgive, the half-disbelieving manner in which our explanations were eventually received.

After this short interview with Mr Sampson, Rodger Pannone advised me not to make a public issue of the continuing failure to give me any real information about the investigation. Pannone undertook to initiate no further statement for fourteen days unless Mr Sampson's enquiries were completed before then. Had we wanted to, we could have publicly condemned the inadequate, imprecise and quite unhelpful nature of the information given to me, which was

John Stalker as a police constable in 1961, when he was twenty-two.

John Stalker as a Detective Inspector in 1971, when he was thirty-two.

Greater Manchester Police Chief Officers group in 1985. (*Back row, left to right*) ACCs David Phillips, Bernard Divine, Dan Crompton, Paul Whitehouse, Robin Oake. (*Front row*) DCC John Stalker, Chief Constable James Anderton, ACC Ralph Lees.

Sir John Hermon, Chief Constable of the Royal Ulster Constabulary. (*Photo: Bryn Colton, Camera Press*)

The car in which Eugene Toman, Sean Burns and Gervaise McKerr were killed. (*Pacemaker Press Intl. Ltd.*)

Seventeen-year-old Michael Tighe.
(*Pacemaker Press Intl. Ltd.*)

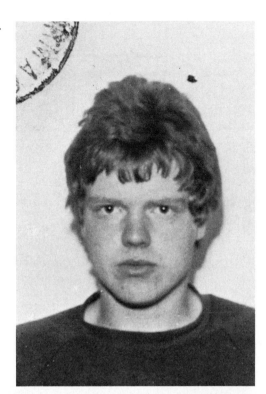

The hayshed in which Michael
Tighe was killed and Martin
McCauley was wounded.
(*Pacemaker Press Intl. Ltd.*)

The six copies of John Stalker's interim report into the RUC, which were delivered to the RUC on 18 September 1985.

John Stalker with Her Majesty the Queen and James Anderton at Police Headquarters, Manchester, on 21 March 1986. (*Manchester Evening News*)

Colin Sampson, Chief Constable, West Yorkshire Constabulary.

The first press conference, held in Rodger Pannone's office in June 1986. To Stalker's right is Pannone, and to his left, Peter Lakin. (*Photo: I. Featherstone/ Manchester Evening News*)

John Stalker and his family reading messages of goodwill during his suspension. (*Left to right*) Stella, Francine, Colette and John Stalker. (*Manchester Evening News*)

John Stalker at work on his smallholding during his suspension. (*Daily Express*)

The Stalker family moments after learning of the Police Authority's decision to reinstate Stalker (22 August 1986). (*Daily Express*)

John Stalker leaving for work on his first day back, Saturday, 23 August 1986. (*Left to right*) John, Theresa, Stella, father Jack and Colette. (*Manchester Evening News*)

James Anderton, Chief Constable of the Greater Manchester Police Force. (*Press Association*)

John Stalker with Her Royal Highness The Duchess of Gloucester in January 1987, following his return to work. This was to be his last official engagement. (*Photo: John Fox/ Manchester Evening News*)

John and Stella Stalker leaving Police Headquarters on his last day as a policeman, 13 March 1987. (*Daily Express*)

quite outside the spirit of the Police Discipline Regulations. These regulations demand that information be given to an accused officer in sufficient detail for him to be able to defend himself, and that the full name and address of the person making a complaint must be provided to him. Mr Sampson was clearly embarrassed by his inability to meet his statutory responsibility to me as an officer suspected of disciplinary breaches, but if he sensed my understanding and sympathy for his position he did not respond to it.

The press were clamouring for details as we left, and again later at my home, but I kept my promise and said nothing. That same afternoon a West Yorkshire 'Police spokesman' stated that 'Mr Stalker is now aware of the information in Mr Sampson's possession. That was his main criticism but he is now in the picture.' I was not aware of the information in Mr Sampson's possession, and I most certainly was not in the picture, but the press thought I was and began to interpret my silence as hiding a serious allegation. West Yorkshire Police, within hours of a delicate agreement being reached between me and their own Chief Constable, had again thrown the debate open for public scrutiny. The press expected me to respond. The following morning's newspapers carried the headlines 'STALKER TOLD AT LAST', or 'FULL DETAILS NOW GIVEN', or 'MYSTERY CHARGES NOW GIVEN TO POLICE CHIEF'. All, of course, quite untrue.

Local newspapers began to hint at the existence of a photograph with a 'known criminal' and myself on it. Again, no names or details were mentioned, but my journalist sources told me that the information was leaked from Manchester Police headquarters. Newspapermen were frantically trying to find out what they believed I knew, and for fourteen days I was powerless to tell them I still knew nothing. The Chairman of the Police Committee, Councillor Norman Briggs, the man who had called Mr Sampson in, issued a pathetically forlorn press release saying 'I do not know what Mr Stalker is alleged to have done. I have heard nothing since the announcement [of two weeks earlier!]'. This from the man who was supposed to be the public and independent spokesman for a group of forty-five Police Committee members who constituted my disciplinary bosses. It was increasingly clear that the Police Committee had lost control of a matter that was legally and morally theirs to oversee. The Chairman had decided to keep the rest of the Committee in the dark, and he in turn was starved of accurate information. As the picture slowly came into focus it seemed that Councillor Briggs had in the early stages been given incorrect information that had caused him to act in a way he would not otherwise have done; but at that stage neither he nor I knew this.

The Northern Ireland connection would not go away. As the lack of any real evidence against me became obvious, I was even more convinced that the roots of my problems were buried deeply over there. Unsolicited and vehement RUC denials regarding their involvement only fuelled that belief. They protested too much. Two weeks had now gone by since my removal from the investigation, and absolutely no justification for that dramatic action had been forthcoming. The evident need to remove me was obviously more pressing than having a reason for doing it. Nevertheless, the Deputy Chairman of the Police Complaints Authority, Roland Moyle QC, PC (who is a former Labour Minister in the Northern Ireland Office), publicly said on BBC radio that there were 'no links' between my predicament and Northern Ireland. In as classic a muddled statement as I have heard, he firmly said that 'the allegations [Mr Sampson had specifically indicated there were no allegations] did not come from Northern Ireland'. 'Where did they come from?' asked Sir Robin Day. 'I do not know who made them,' said Mr Moyle. His statement, not unnaturally, made matters worse; but even then he was not finished. When asked whether, at the moment he was asked to approve the appointment of Mr Sampson to conduct the enquiry into me, he had known of Mr Sampson's parallel appointment to take over in Northern Ireland, he admitted openly that he did *not* know. Sir Robin Day asked whether it was a good idea for Mr Sampson to undertake both enquiries, and Mr Moyle replied defensively, saying that his concern was to ensure that Mr Sampson was competent and had the resources to undertake the investigation into me. Nothing more. He had no interest in Northern Ireland other than to say he was absolutely sure there was no connection. The irony for me was painful as I witnessed the full legal weight and power of the Police Complaints Authority thrown behind a senior Chief Constable enquiring into unspecified disciplinary matters against me. I compared it with my struggles over the past two years to investigate, without any help whatsoever, six alleged murders by British policemen, as well as perjury and conspiracy offences. Mr Moyle's premature and disastrous radio interview did him little credit in the eyes of my family or many of the press I spoke to. The same day (10 June 1986) the Prime Minister, in the House of Commons, refused to comment about my 'suspension' or enquiry when questioned by Seamus Mallon MP, who was raising the matter for the second time.

On 11 June I had to face the pain of handing over my passport and records of six years' bank and credit card accounts to a man who would not say why he wanted them. My family finances are much the same as anyone else's. I had a salary that I pretty well lived to each month, I have a hefty mortgage, and in the years between 1980 and 1986 I had moved house once. The actual number of cheque transactions that a family such as ours makes in a six-year period is staggering. There were hundreds. Add to those our building-society deposits and withdrawals and credit-card transactions and things multiplied enormously. Assistant Chief Constable Shaw came to my home about noon that day. He was accompanied by someone new to me, Chief Superintendent Robinson of the West Yorkshire Police, and my good friend John Thorburn. With a heavy heart I handed to Robinson authorizations to examine my entire bank and credit-card accounts. Mr Shaw then asked, on behalf of Chief Constable Sampson, for me to hand to him any documents or records connected with my Northern Ireland investigation. I gave him all I had in my possession. I later found out that at about this time West Yorkshire officers had confronted my secretary and taken from her uncompleted typescripts of reports of mine that I had given her before I was taken off the investigation. The word processor was searched and cleared, and the disks taken to the headquarters of West Yorkshire Constabulary at Wakefield. The take-over of my Irish investigation was conducted as coolly as a raid on a criminal's home. Nothing was left to chance. A clampdown was imposed on all information and a wall of secrecy thrown up around the activities of the new investigators. I was totally and forever excluded from the enquiry that had taken up most of my waking hours for two years past. It was a sad day for me.

The press and broadcasting crews were part of our lives pretty well permanently, and the pressure did not diminish. The telephone rang constantly from early in the morning until past midnight, with calls either from friends or from reporters seeking details of the accusations against me. I kept my promise that I would not discuss the enquiry or the lack of details with the press. The intense frustration of not being able to gather together answers because I did not know the questions was eating at me. While I stayed at home waiting and praying for some information, I was reading newspaper accounts of West Yorkshire policemen hawking albums of photographs around Manchester asking for identifications of people on them who had been present at functions I myself had attended. News began to trickle in from my family and friends that they had been approached by the Sampson team, but no contact was made with me.

One occasion of acute interest was a fiftieth-birthday party given by Kevin Taylor almost five years earlier, which more than two hundred people attended. I remembered it well. Stella and I had attended for just over an hour, long enough only to deliver a birthday present and have a drink and a sandwich. My wife had been ill; indeed, had it not been for Stella's insistence that she felt well enough just to do that, we would not have gone at all. What I could not understand, if the stories about the photographs were true, was why this party had suddenly become important. It had been an innocuous affair, attended by many well-known people from the Manchester area. Present had been doctors, lawyers, councillors, at least one local Lord Mayor, and one Member of Parliament. I recalled seeing one or two *Coronation Street* stars, and hearing some wonderfully nostalgic piano music played by a fine musician I knew from many years ago. It had been a pleasant evening, and had Stella been feeling well we would have stayed and no doubt enjoyed ourselves. Nothing happened to which anyone could take exception or which could have embarrassed or compromised me in any way. Now, however, I found myself reading about this party in every newspaper; finally *The Sunday Times* and *Observer* of 15 June made full reference to it. All my information during those bleak days was gleaned in this way. Three weeks after my removal rumour, innuendo and gossip were still the base currency of the day. I continued to wait it out; I had no choice.

My mother had taken the pressures bravely, but eventually they had their effect. She had had an artificial heart valve fitted some years before, and now her doctor was worried. On 16 June she was taken ill and rushed into Manchester Royal Infirmary. Her physical strength had completely left her and she could not walk. She remained in intensive care for several days and my father, who is in his seventies, came to live with us. His pragmatic, down-to-earth, incisive style appealed to the many newsmen still coming to the house, and they enjoyed his company. I recall him in conversation with them, bitterly condemning *The Times* as an entirely inadequate newspaper because of the unreliability of its racing tips, and the *Daily Mirror* for never recovering from the departure of the columnist 'Cassandra' thirty years or so ago. For my father, real newspapers disappeared when the *Daily Herald* ceased trading.

Each day brought more and more cards and letters of encouragement from all parts of the country, mainly from people we had never met. They continued to come for many months, many of them hopefully addressed merely to John Stalker, Manchester. Stella and I, over the next six months, eventually answered every one of them personally. There were many callers at my house, and I answered the door one evening to a man who introduced himself as a spokesman for the workforce of a big employer in Manchester. He told me that his union colleagues, about three hundred of them, had asked him to present to me and my family their best wishes. He gave us a bouquet of flowers and a letter. He was hesitant and obviously unused to what he was doing, but his sincere words were those of someone who was unhappy about the way things were being handled. His sentiments were typical. The enormous swell of public support we were privileged to receive undoubtedly kept us going.

By now the Irish newspapers were very much in evidence, and fresh piles of letters began to arrive from Northern Ireland and the Irish Republic. There was a surge of renewed interest following a BBC *Panorama* programme entitled 'Stalker — Coincidence or Conspiracy?' written and presented by the reporter Peter Taylor. This posed questions about the connection of Northern Ireland with my predicament. The programme mentioned for the first time in public the MI5 bugging of the Hayshed and the death of Michael Justin Tighe. Suddenly a whole new area of discussion and speculation was opened up and the media glare was switched dramatically back onto Northern Ireland. For the moment I had to keep quiet: my undertaking to Mr Sampson to remain silent for fourteen days was honoured. But this silence was becoming increasingly difficult to maintain, given the constant demands of the press.

The *Manchester Evening News* was beginning to mention another function I had attended with Kevin Taylor and which was under investigation by Mr Sampson. This had been the Autumn Ball at Manchester's Hotel Piccadilly held on 23 November 1985, at which I had been an official guest, along with two Members of Parliament. About five hundred people had sat down to dinner, and the event was sponsored by the local Conservative party, of which Kevin Taylor had become a committee member. I had attended a similar function the year before, representing the police force. I had been to similar functions involving all political parties, and I simply regarded myself as a civic guest. My attendance in no way compromised my position as a police officer; indeed, I had told James Anderton I had been invited and would be attending. He said he also had received an invitation, but was unable to attend because of another commitment that evening. At no time had he indicated to me that he disapproved; in fact he expressed his support for my attendance. It was one of hundreds of similar evening functions a Chief Constable and his Deputy attend in Greater Manchester in the course of the year. It was an unremarkable, routine part of our job, and I could not imagine why Mr Sampson's officers should be interested in this particular evening. The only special factor was, of course, Kevin Taylor.

I was beginning to suspect strongly that the West Yorkshire investigation teams — and at times there were about two dozen of them — were dredging my official diaries, which I had handed to Mr Shaw, and back-tracking for six or seven years in order to find something to justify my removal from work. I knew there was nothing to find; but not finding it could take many months. I had had absolutely no contact with Mr Sampson since our meeting ten days before. As the Sampson team took apart my life, it was almost as if I did not exist. My mother was seriously ill, my wife and two daughters were caught up in a daily nightmare not of their making, and still the only certain fact was that I was being subjected only to an internal police disciplinary enquiry. If the investigation had been of a criminal nature the West Yorkshire Police would have been obliged to act much more responsibly, since my lawyers would have sought the intervention of the courts, or indeed the Police Complaints procedure. But a disciplinary investigation of this extraordinary nature offered no real protection to a man in my position.

Speculation about the nature of the allegations against me became even more gross in nature. There was insidious talk of Kevin Taylor's having links with organized crime in Manchester and having murky political ambitions. In the meantime, like some sort of giant lighthouse, the beam of emphasis switched this way and that across the Irish Sea. On 18 June 1986 the Northern Ireland Secretary, Tom King, mistakenly and damagingly told the Irish Foreign Minister, Mr Peter Barry, that I had fully completed my report *before* being taken off the investigation. This was absolutely untrue. The cover of every document in my report, delivered to Sir John Hermon in September 1985, was embossed in gold with the words 'INTERIM REPORT' — all sixteen volumes of it. If such an elementary mistake could be made in a highly important and sensitive political and diplomatic exchange, I had little confidence in the accuracy of what Mr King was being told about me.

Members of the Police Committee were privately enraged at the poor information they were being given, and they began publicly to complain. Councillor Briggs's position as Chairman was under threat. Councillor Edward Gallagher of the Committee publicly apologized to me for the treatment my family and I were receiving, and he declared the entire Committee to be as much in the dark as I was. Kevin Taylor, through his solicitor, publicly pleaded with James Anderton to let him know whether he was under any sort of investigation, and repeated again that he had never been in any trouble whatsoever in his life, and had never even been questioned by police about anything. The rumours and innuendo were destroying the lives of both our families, but arguably his immediate position was more desperate. He needed the life-blood of cash flow and bank and customer confidence in order to keep his business going, and these were drying up because of the rumours. I at least had only my sanity, my job and my good name to think of. The official silence from Manchester and West Yorkshire Police Headquarters was total, in direct contrast with the back door leaks to the press, which were becoming louder and more numerous. There seemed no end to the irresponsible flow of good and bad information about the investigation into me and into Kevin Taylor. The *Daily Telegraph* of 21 June 1986 carried a cheering headline that read 'STALKER ENQUIRY FAILS TO FIND EVIDENCE OF MISCONDUCT'. The story beneath it claimed that the matter was almost at an end. There was a brief flurry of intense speculation that smear campaigns and false accusations against me were inspired by powerful members of the Masonic Order in the Manchester Police and the RUC. The Masonic Order in the North West called a press conference to publicly deny any involvement of their secret craft in what was now universally referred to as the 'Stalker Affair'.

The *Manchester Evening News*, predictably perhaps, was the first newspaper to make progress and to throw some new light on what was going on. Their resourceful reporter Paul

Horrocks — who has excellent official sources, and who reported throughout with impeccable detachment and honesty — mentioned a former police officer, Stephen Hayes, as the 'known criminal' with whom I might have had contact. Hayes had worked for me fifteen years earlier as a young constable, but had left the police force shortly after that to set up a private-investigation business. He had prospered, and by 1986 he had established a firmly based commercial undertaking dealing in investigations and insurance work. In the early years after he left the Force he had been convicted of attempted bribery and had been given a suspended prison sentence. He had, so I later learned, picked himself up, split from his business partner and made his own way after that conviction. I knew of him, and had nodded to him and acknowledged his presence at the dinner dance at the Hotel Piccadilly in November 1985; but I had not spoken to him. He had taken a table for his guests, and so far as I was concerned he was merely one of five hundred people. I was aware that Kevin Taylor knew him, and I guessed that Taylor might have consulted his firm commercially; but so far as I was concerned Stephen Hayes was a face from the past. I was neither friendly nor hostile towards him because I do not really know him. As a former policeman he understood my position, and later said so publicly. As it turned out, the *Manchester Evening News* was absolutely right. Stephen Hayes was to become a central figure in Mr Sampson's subsequent interviews with me.

The two weeks of silence promised by Rodger Pannone to Colin Sampson were almost up, and the pressure from the media for me to break that silence became intense. The Sunday newspapers particularly were anxious to learn what I knew. I doubt if they would have believed me then if I had told them the truth — that officially I knew nothing, and unofficially I knew only what the newspapers had told me.

Eventually I received a call requesting me to see Mr Sampson again. This time he insisted I travel the sixty miles to

Wakefield with my solicitor for a meeting on the following Monday afternoon. This was an unnecessarily hurtful act, because the accepted routine is for such interviews to take place within the area of the host police force. It was quite wrong for us to be summoned to Wakefield for what was a Manchester enquiry. I was convinced, however, that any obstructiveness or lack of co-operation on my part would have been welcomed by some West Yorkshire officers. It would have given them breathing space and a reason for dragging their feet and blaming delays on me. They were under pressure to find something to hang a disciplinary charge on.

After talking to Peter Lakin I agreed to travel to Wakefield. The army of press and television reporters inevitably learned of the date and time of my appointment, and they besieged my home again throughout the weekend of 21 and 22 June. On the Sunday evening before the interview I managed to escape long enough to take my father to see my mother in hospital, and we called later at the home of a good and supportive friend. The three of us glumly watched Argentina — or more precisely Diego Maradona — beat — or cheat — England in the World Cup football match. The omens were not good.

The following morning television crews tailed me the fourteen miles to Peter Lakin's office, and onward to Wakefield, where we were greeted outside Police Headquarters by scores more. I found it remarkable, in view of what else was going on in the world, how great were the resources thrown into following my progress through the labyrinth of police discipline. The interview with Mr Sampson lasted several hours. Assistant Chief Constable Shaw wrote down in longhand every word uttered by his Chief Constable and myself. Chief Superintendent Robinson took a leading role, constantly feeding pieces of paper to Sampson and whispering to him questions to ask me. I could see that Mr Sampson was not particularly well prepared. Mr

Shaw, who had been the early investigator, kept his head down in embarrassment and made his notes. He did not ask a single question.

A series of names was put to me, some of which I recognized, others of which meant absolutely nothing to me. I was asked to account for credit card and cheque transactions from many years before, and because of Stella's memory and organization I was able to do so; the questions were random and without any apparent purpose. I was then shown six photographs, only one of which I appeared in. This was said to be a party snap of Stephen Hayes taken four years earlier at Kevin Taylor's fiftieth birthday party. There was an indistinct image of a man who might or might not have been me in the far background; I acknowledged my presence at the function, even though the photograph did not prove it. The other five photographs were of my wife talking to Kevin Taylor or his wife, Beryl, with other people close by. It was all totally innocuous. The interview was drawing to a close and it was clear that the four-year-old photograph with Hayes on it was the apparent sum total of evidence against me. I had been in the same room as a man who had been in trouble with the police.

Mr Sampson reeled off to me the names of five other people whom I had not heard of, or knowingly met. He then mentioned a further three people whom I do know, and told me they were criminals, handing me a typed list of their 'convictions'. I told him I had known these three men for many years and I knew of no convictions against them. What were they? I studied the paper I had been given. One had been convicted only once, eleven years earlier, for handling a stolen writing pad and a roll of Sellotape, valued at £2.00. This had happened two years before I first met him. The second person had one conviction for disposing of a small amount of scrap metal twelve years earlier — again before I met him. The real 'criminal' was reserved for last, however. One of the men at the birthday celebration, a respectable taxi proprietor, had been detained as a ten-year-old in 1944 for stealing two pounds of potatoes during a war-time blackout. I had been four years old at the time he had committed this one and only misdemeanour in an otherwise honourable life.

These solemn revelations should have been laughable; but I felt angry and sick. The enormous public expense, the international publicity, my removal from a multiple murder enquiry, the family heartbreaks, my mother's serious illness, everything seemed to have resulted from the fact that I had once delivered a birthday present and stayed for an hour in a group of over two hundred people. In that group had been three hardworking men, each of whom, once in his distant past, had made a never-to-be-repeated mistake. None of them had ever been in prison, and I knew nothing of their single misdemeanours of many years before. I was to discover later that even their wives and families did not know of them. They do now, however.

I felt anger rise as I looked at Mr Sampson's serious and unforgiving face. Here was a man whose reputation I had respected, one of the country's most senior and eminent Chief Constables, who was flanked by two other very senior officers and who was asking me to explain my presence in the same room as these three men. I reflected on the important work that none of us was doing, and on the monumental waste of the public's time and money. I kept my temper and told Mr Sampson that I knew these men to talk to, but that I had never been to their homes. I said that they were respected men in their fields, and that I knew absolutely nothing of these convictions, one of which had happened forty-two years ago when I was a toddler. Was he saying I should have known? Was he suggesting that senior policemen should misuse the police national computer in order to check out their friends and contacts? He did not answer. The interview was like a bad dream. I saw hard eyes and accusing words mouthed without any real conviction. It suddenly dawned on me, however, that I was not the only one under pressure. I realized that I sat across the table from two very apprehensive men, Sampson and Robinson. One, Sampson, was apprehensive because of his inability to obtain any evidence against me despite a massive and expensive trawl through my life using a small army of policemen. The other, Robinson, was apprehensive because his professional credibility seemed about to crumble. At the end of that interview it was they, not I, who were wearing a hunted look. They had failed to find what they had been told was there to be found, and they did not know whom to blame. I glimpsed a fleeting look of doubt in Mr Sampson's eyes.

I explained and proved my full payment to Kevin Taylor of my share of the cost of our stay in America five years earlier. There was a flurry of whispered conversation between Sampson and Robinson, and then peculiar mistakes began to happen. I was confidently asked by Mr Sampson about my return flight with Taylor from New York. I said we had flown home directly from Florida, fifteen hundred miles away. No, I was told, it was New York. I told them they were absolutely wrong and that we had never been to New York. I saw fear in the eyes of Chief Superintendent Robinson; he became flustered. He had made an unexplained and embarrassing mistake in front of his Chief Constable, who was clearly none too pleased. But more worryingly, he had totally confused important flight numbers, dates and airports. Was he talking about someone else? Perhaps a different Mr Taylor? He obviously did not know. I wondered how many more damaging mistakes of that magnitude had been made. The line of questioning relating to New York was immediately dropped, but strangely it was to surface again many months later.

Mr Sampson asked me about my use — on five occasions over a period of a year, for very short journeys — of a police

142

car. At this juncture, Sampson's interest was simply in my use of these vehicles. Later he was to broaden the scope of this question to include my carrying passengers who included my wife and Kevin Taylor. I told him that each of these journeys was authorized, and I explained the arrangements existing in the Greater Manchester Force. There are seven unmarked black Granada police cars that are designated for 'VIP use'. That use has included ferrying councillors, magistrates, judges, politicians and royal visitors around the county. Occasionally they are used by senior officers, but I had made it a rule on my appointment as Deputy Chief Constable that they were not to be taken by policemen for routine use. They were available only for journeys outside the county or for civic or official occasions. I had very rarely made use of one — fewer than a dozen times in two years — but Mr Sampson had diligently traced those few occasions and wished to talk to me about them. I told him that all of these journeys were connected with official business. Four of them had been to evening functions after my day's work, which I attended as the Deputy Chief Constable representing the Force. One of them had been a two-mile trip to a luncheon meeting at which James Anderton had been speaking. Mr Anderton uses an official car and police driver on a daily basis, quite properly, and is collected from his home each morning and returned each night. A Jaguar car and driver is legitimately allocated for this purpose and for evening functions involving his wife and himself.

I asked why I was being singled out for examination on these few occasions during a nine-month period. I was not answered. I told Mr Sampson that I used my own car more than any other Deputy or Assistant Chief Constable I have known in the Greater Manchester Police Force. I preferred it that way because I liked the flexibility it gave me; but more importantly, I did not like tying up a policeman or a civilian driver on such duties. Mr Anderton was generally well aware of my use of a car on these few occasions, and I told Mr Sampson so. I told him something else: that during my Northern Ireland enquiry, in February 1985, I had received information from Manchester Special Branch, who had been given it by an absolutely reliable source, that I had been targeted by a terrorist group. I had been given the name and description of a man who had been sent to this country to catalogue my movements in the smallest detail. It was a careful operation, well financed, and I was advised to treat it seriously, which I did. I regularly travelled backward and forward to Northern Ireland using false names and documents in order to protect myself, and changed my routine pattern of life. All this Mr Anderton knew; indeed, he had of his own volition approached the Chairman of the Police Committee, who had agreed to the installation, at public expense, of a burglar alarm at my house shortly after I moved into it. Mr Anderton had even asked me whether I wished to have a permanently armed police officer with me at all times and an unmarked car and a police driver with proper radio communications. I had decided against this because of the extreme concern such high activity would cause my wife and family.

I had accepted the offer of an intruder alarm, and thanked Mr Anderton for his concern and suggestions. But I told him that I would try to lead as normal a life as possible. The one other concession I would make would be, on some occasions, and with his authority, to use a car and driver for official evening functions rather than to leave my own car vulnerable in a public place. Mr Anderton was clearly worried about my safety, and agreed without hesitation. As Deputy Chief Constable it was obviously within my discretion to judge when to do this, and that was totally accepted by the Chief Constable, who acted helpfully and positively towards me throughout that stressful time. I could not understand why Mr Sampson was now raising, in a disciplinary context, my use of a car on those few occasions. I knew that I had not employed a police car for wrongful private use, and I explained to Mr Sampson the terrorist threat and the sensible precautions I had agreed with my own Chief Constable. I told him about the burglar alarm at my home and of the reliable source of the information regarding my being targeted by terrorists. I provided him with the name of the Special Branch officer who had received it.

I did not expect to hear any more about this handful of journeys involving no more than eighty miles, which I had openly and justifiably made many months earlier. I thought that Mr Sampson would check my explanations and speak to Mr Anderton and the Special Branch officer, both of whom would confirm the truth of what I had said. I was wrong again. Mr Sampson, it seems, did not ask Mr Anderton, and he certainly did not approach the Manchester Special Branch officer. I left the Wakefield Police Headquarters and gave an unavoidable press conference on the steps to the dozens of waiting newsmen. I told them the truth, that the interview with Mr Sampson had been mainly concerned with Mr Taylor and that a number of names had been put to me, some of which I recognized but the majority of which meant nothing to me. I told them I had discussed the use of police cars in my official duties, and that I had heard nothing from Mr Sampson that, in my view, would prevent my early return to work. As I left Wakefield I felt more relaxed and happier than I had done at any time since I had first received the fateful call four weeks earlier. It had taken twenty-seven days for me to be given any detail of what had led to my removal from duty, but at last I knew something positive. It was all grotesquely out of proportion, in its triviality, to the matters I had been investigating, but at least it was out in the open and I was able to tackle it.

That same day the Conservative Member of Parliament for Barrow-in-Furness, Mr Cecil Franks, who is also a

Manchester solicitor, said 'a number of people, including half a dozen MPs, have been sucked into the Stalker affair, and none of us have been told what it is about. The whole thing is bizarre. We are all being tainted with innuendo.' He, it seemed, had also been asked whether he knew any of the people at the birthday party that Mr Sampson had asked me about. He said, 'There were over 150 people there. How on earth can I be expected to know them? It is absurd. The police carrying out this investigation are quite obviously groping in the dark without factual evidence to go on.' He echoed the feelings of dozens of people who had told me of their interviews with the West Yorkshire officers. The investigation was continuing even as I was at Wakefield. Efforts were made to trace and interview all five hundred guests at the Hotel Piccadilly ball, and those seen were asked only two real questions. They were: 'Did you see Mr Taylor buy Mr Stalker a drink?' and 'Who did Mr Stalker talk to?' The questions must have had some purpose, but the result of them was to convince many respectable and honest people in Manchester that the police were intent on wasting their valuable time. Most of them did not even know Mr Taylor or me. I learned, for example, that a Detective Chief Inspector and a sergeant had interviewed the directors of Manchester City Football Club to ask whether I had taken complimentary sausage rolls or a free cup of tea in the course of my official attendances at the ground during the course of a season. The same thing happened at Manchester United. The heavy-handed manner of some West Yorkshire investigators, and the supreme irrelevance of it all to the hundreds of people they saw, probably brought the police force generally into more disrepute in Manchester than anything I was alleged to have done. It became a sour joke that social status in the city depended on whether or not you had been interviewed by the Sampson team. Tee-shirts and bumper-stickers appeared with the slogan 'I never met John Stalker' or 'Kevin Who?'

Local politicians were now stirring into action. The Chairman of the Police Committee, Councillor Briggs, was under attack from his Labour colleagues for his secretive handling of the affair. In response to criticisms he said, 'Each day something fresh has cropped up. If I had tried to respond to everything it would have been impossible to keep abreast of the situation.' His decision had been, therefore, to respond to nothing, and politically the matter roared out of control as individual members of the Committee, starved of information by their Chairman, Mr Sampson and the Police Complaints Authority, speculated publicly on what might be happening. The man who should have been doing the talking, Councillor Briggs, remained sadly quiet. He tried to put things right on 30 June, when he presented a written report to a special meeting of the Committee, but details it contained were inaccurate and incomplete in important areas, and it was badly received. His efforts did not help him either politically or emotionally. The whole Stalker affair was slipping from his grasp, and yet the statutory responsibility lay squarely with him. He ignored reality in that Committee Report when he limply said, 'It would be quite unfair and improper for me to comment further or to anticipate the findings of the investigation.' Unfair to whom? He had entirely misread the situation. It was precisely because of unbounded speculation that the situation had become as bad as it was. I had been told nothing, his Committee had been told nothing, and he had been told very little. The people who kept so much from him placed a great deal of unnecessary pressure on an honest man. He carried alone a burden of responsibility that should have been shared.

The enormous public interest did not diminish following the interview in Wakefield, and my home remained under siege. Four weeks' continual attention had not diminished the interest of the story to journalists, who were now contacting me from all over the world, expecially America and Australia.

My brother, who was on business in Singapore at the time, read a full account of it in the local newspaper there. On his return he wryly reflected that he could never have expected to read in a Far Eastern newspaper that the Prime Minister of Great Britain was denying knowing anything about his brother.

Rodger Pannone now called a second properly organized press conference at his offices for 25 June. He gave out prepared details of the interview with Mr Sampson, and repeated that there had still been no 'allegation or complaint' made against me. Indeed, these two words had again been deliberately crossed out by Mr Sampson on the official form handed to me two days earlier at Wakefield. In answer to questions about Kevin Taylor's friends, I said that I had never knowingly associated with criminals, but that at big functions, private or public, which hundreds of people attended, I could not be expected to know of their presence. I had a simple golden rule, which was that I would never compromise my police ethic for anyone — criminals or otherwise. I asked for no favours and I gave none in return. My family pay their own parking tickets and I pay full price for everything I buy, even including private 'phone calls from my office telephone. There is no such thing as a free lunch for a policeman, and I had kept my integrity and reputation for thirty years by never forgetting that. I also told the assembled journalists that I had been subjected to the most rigorous of MI5 vetting checks on three occasions in the last ten years, two of them in the last five, and all of them during my friendship with Kevin Taylor. If there had been the slightest question mark over my financial position, my private or professional integrity, I would have failed those checks. I was the only one of my team in Northern Ireland to have security clearance to the highest possible level. How on earth could these smear stories now gaining currency ever be true, given that sort of official check? This hitherto overlooked information about regular vetting checks had a significant impact. It made people ask what was really happening.

The press conference was a highly charged affair. I put my neck on the block for forty-five minutes, and honestly answered all the questions put to me except those relating to Northern Ireland, which I did not answer at all. At its conclusion, Mr Pannone again made it clear that Mr Sampson had given no details of any allegations or complaints against me, and he made a request on my behalf for me to be allowed to return to work. It seemed a fair request: desperate police enquiries by at least sixteen policemen, conducted night and day for five weeks, had failed to find anything of any substance, and I was still in the limbo of 'extended annual leave'. It was clear that this pantomime could not be allowed to go on for much longer.

The Police Complaints Authority were angry about my press conference. Indeed, all of the official bodies connected with the matter — the Police Committee, the Home Office, the Royal Ulster Constabulary, the Inspectorate and especially the Chief Constables of West Yorkshire and Greater Manchester — would have preferred that I stay at home behind drawn curtains and keep quiet, since the more I said the more political and public pressure was exerted to hasten the enquiry. But for all this, my position was not significantly different from that five weeks earlier. I still knew of no allegations against me, nor had any complaint apparently been made. I had merely been presented by Mr Sampson with verbal accounts of social occasions involving the presence of Kevin Taylor, which I was being tacitly invited to regard as having possible disciplinary offences inherent within them. Nothing was actually put to me as a breach of discipline, nothing was unequivocal. I had been placed in a position where I was invited to read the mind of the interviewer and make assumptions about what he might want to know. There was always a hidden agenda.

The Police Complaints Authority trained their guns on my solicitors and issued a news release the following day sternly demanding 'that the matter should be investigated and adjudicated upon in accordance with the statutory disciplinary procedures and not through the public media'. That said, they promptly closed their own doors and diverted the telephones. Rodger Pannone and I wish we could have done that ourselves. With my family I did my best to deal civilly with the unremitting media barrage. I became an expert in newspaper and television deadline times, and realized that these spread over an eighteen-hour period. The newsmen, with only one or two exceptions, were unfailingly courteous, but their numbers and persistence were driving Stella and me to despair. My daughters took some pressure from us, and Colette — my twenty-year-old elder girl — spoke to the hundreds of callers. Every evening, as I visited my mother in Manchester Royal Infirmary, I would be met at the Nelson Street entrance by newsmen wanting to know how she was. She was in fact very ill, but I would not say so, and indeed she would not allow me to. Her fierce pride was shared by all the family, and we refused to allow her illness to become a feature of the affair. The press interest in the story had not faded after five weeks, but some of the newspapers were looking for some human interest to freshen it up. I would not allow my mother to fulfil that role. In the event it was Stella who provided it, the day after the press conference.

We were both weary of the incessant telephone and doorbell interruptions, and we decided to lock up the house for a day and drive the thirty miles to the pleasant Victorian seaside town of Southport. Half-heartedly we looked in shop windows in Lord Street. Neither of us had much enthusiasm, and I had completely failed to reckon with the power of press and television. In a couple of weeks Stella and I had become nationally recognized faces, and every few yards we were stopped by well-wishers. It was heartwarming, and we were grateful; but I was doing my best to have as normal a day as possible, and it was obviously not working out. I told Stella so, and we began to walk back to the car; across the road hurried a well-dressed middle-aged man with a young Alsatian dog on a lead. He came directly to me and began to pump my hand and say how sorry he was about the situation we were in. Suddenly his dog lunged at Stella and sank its teeth deep into her left hand. It just would not let go, and I had to prise open its jaws. The dog had bitten through a gold ring, which saved her little finger from being severed, but there was a gaping wound along the side of her hand. The man offered sincere and abject apologies, but Stella collapsed with fear and shock. I took her to hospital in a taxi and the wound was stitched and dressed; but it was all too much for her. She had stoically and courageously dealt with a situation in our lives that was not of her making, or understanding. Apart from hospital visits we had not left our house together for five weeks, and on the day we did she was savaged by a dog. Pent-up emotions were now released as the combination of shock, pain, blood, disbelief and, I suppose, injustice, made its impact. We both wept. As I write this I have before me the bloodstained *Manchester Evening News* she had just bought, and had been carrying as the dog bit her. Symbolically, perhaps, the worst of the staining is across the front page headline, which says 'STALKER — JUSTICE AND TRUTH'.

# 5

## *Suspension*

We came home that evening to a growing story that I was about to be formally suspended from duty the following Monday. Labour members of the Police Committee had met to discuss the matter, and were reported to have decided that they had to do something to force the hand of the Police Complaints Authority and the official investigation; the act of suspension might achieve that. There were reported leaks of a remark by Councillor Briggs that a boat belonging to Kevin Taylor 'had been under surveillance by American Security Agencies'. This was a complete lie, as the Americans later confirmed, but the damage to me was done. I had once sailed on that boat, during the holiday in Florida. Councillor Briggs had received this wholly inaccurate information from the police and had, in good faith, passed it on to his Labour colleagues. I am absolutely certain that it was this information that hardened the attitude of some members of the Committee towards me. Even among sceptical councillors there still persists a feeling that information provided by a senior policeman, in confidence to one of their members, must be true. With some otherwise shrewd members of Police Committees, it is almost an act of faith always to believe the police unless it can be shown that they are wrong. There can be no smoke without fire, they say. In this case there was. It was poor Councillor Norman Briggs who again unwittingly carried the false message to his colleagues.

The strengthening rumours of impending suspension brought hundreds of press calls seeking comment from me. My solicitor, Rodger Pannone, dealt with them, but still the reporters came to me for a personal comment about the possibility of suspension. I said that it would bring enormous distress to my family and me, and repeated again my innocence of wrongdoing. Rodger Pannone responded to the speculation by asking how much longer the investigation would continue, and criticized the Police Complaints Authority for their public statement condemning the involvement of the media. He said that the Police Complaints Authority is not the only independent public representative having an interest in the truth: the press can equally be regarded as having an impartial public role.

The Sunday newspapers of 29 June brought new disclosures. We learned that, according to one paper, co-ordinated Masonic influences in the RUC, Orange Order and the Greater Manchester Police were at the heart of my troubles. Another newspaper told us that a West Yorkshire police enquiry team had asked at our favourite Chinese restaurant whether I paid for my meals by cash or by credit card, or whether I paid at all. I had provided six years of my financial records to avoid this sort of deeply humiliating enquiry, but still Mr Sampson's police trampled through my life without regard for any of it. Had they taken the trouble to look at my American Express records for the previous twelve, let alone six, years, they would have seen that I always settled the cost of meals in this restaurant by that method. But they paid heavy-handed visits to this and other restaurants, and then someone told the press, who followed the investigation one close step behind.

By this time I did not believe that my family or I could be hurt any more. It seemed I could expect no sensitivity, or even basic courtesy, from the investigating police officers or the Police Complaints Authority. My own Police Committee had not contacted me for five weeks, and yet I was now reading of their intention to hold a special meeting on Monday 30 June 1986 to discuss my future. I offered to attend that meeting and to answer any questions whatsoever about any aspect of my life, including — so far as I could — my enquiry in Northern Ireland. The request was put to them by my solicitors, but the Police Committee did not take up the offer; they did not even acknowledge it.

On Monday 30 June I went to my solicitors' office, hoping for some confirmation of the suspension stories in the newspapers, and seeking a response to my request to attend the special meeting of the Police Committee. We could not even confirm that there was a meeting, even though every reporter interested in the story had been given information about it. I returned home bewildered and emotionally empty. I could not understand why no one would tell me what was going on. This was my life they were dealing with, and it was crumbling around me. My wife, children and family were beside themselves with worry and fear. Their respect for the police was rapidly evaporating, and although they love me as a husband and a father, their pride in me as a policeman was dying. They began to believe that the organization whose ethos I had defended was in fact vindictive and crassly inefficient. They looked at me with accusing eyes. How could I continue to say that apparently vengeful policemen and others 'were only doing their job'? I tried to keep faith. The way in which the investigation into me was being conducted bore no resemblance to any police enquiry I have ever been associated with. It seemed wasteful in resources, and insensitive in operation. In my opinion it was over-staffed, under-worked and badly briefed, and I had to keep reminding myself that Mr Sampson was investigating only a possible internal police disciplinary matter. The word 'serious' had never been used, and there was absolutely no criminal aspect to it.

I heard the news of my suspension from the television news. Expected as it was, it still struck me like a knife in my back. A newspaper reporter was with with me when it came, and he saw the effect it had on my wife and me. For a policeman, suspension from duty is the ultimate indignity, apart from imprisonment. It usually heralds criminal proceedings, and the disgrace of it is awful. To make matters worse, Councillor Norman Briggs had given a press conference that afternoon, and again he spoke words that were not his. He told a packed and knowledgeable gathering of the press that I had been given details of the 'complaint' against me; that Mr Sampson on the very first day had told me of my 'undesirable associations with known criminals'; and that on 23 June I had been given a formal notice containing the 'detailed allegations'. All of this was quite untrue, and the newsmen knew it and told Briggs so. He replied, 'I simply cannot understand why Mr Stalker says he doesn't know.' He had simply been fed a false story. The hapless Councillor went on to express the Police Committee's concern over the Home Office's handling of the matter and the appointment of Mr Sampson to head both investigations. He sensibly called for another investigating officer to be appointed before Mr Sampson began his work in Northern Ireland. But his plea was ignored: Mr Sampson continued to undertake his dual role. Councillor Briggs, as Chairman of the Police Committee, had been given a golden chance to put the record straight and admit the mistakes he had made, but he did not take it. Naively, he still placed his trust in what he was being told, and I had to publicly say, through my solicitor, that he was again misleadingly and damagingly wrong.

Norman Briggs continued to soak up the pressures. I cannot understand or excuse, however, his not telephoning either me or my solicitors to tell me of my official suspension before announcing it to the world. That was his duty, and he failed in it. It was also, I believe, the duty of James Anderton to make sure that Briggs did so, or perhaps more compassionately, to do it himself. Neither of them did so, nor did Colin Sampson, and the result was that I heard it with my family at the same time as ten million viewers of the ITN early evening news. The Police Complaints Authority's plea to keep the issue out of the media had been ignored within forty-eight hours by Councillor Briggs and his advisers, and the matter was again firmly in the public arena.

We waited that evening in the forlorn hope of some official contact from someone. None came, and for Stella it was the final insult. I had asked her, and indeed all of my family, not to speak publicly. I did not want to cloud the issue with family anguish or anger. But she was prepared to be silent no longer. The public announcement of my suspension had uncorked her fury and she gave a number of lengthy press and television interviews. She was still in severe pain from the dog-bite, but her quiet, controlled anger, mixed with obvious sincerity and bewilderment, brought the human interest the press had been looking for into sharp focus. She had never spoken to a pressman or faced a television camera in her life before these events, but she was superb. The two years of living with my job in Northern Ireland, the five weeks of waiting for details, and above all twenty-four years of being a policeman's wife, welled to the surface. I saw her on a special Granada television interview filmed in my front garden, as she nursed her bandaged hand. She spoke honestly and eloquently from the heart, and I wept for her.

Two days after the decision to suspend me I received a letter signed by Roger Rees, the solicitor acting for the Police Committee, formally telling me of my suspension from duty and demanding I deliver up my identification card. I did not have it at home — it was in my office — but if I had, I would have insisted that he come personally to collect it.

Stella's anguished interviews touched a public nerve, and the result was an enormous groundswell of sympathy for her, my daughters and my mother. They were individually flooded with letters, cards, flowers and calls from around the world. Stella had said in a radio interview that 'John is not the only one with the name Stalker. We all share it and our name, not just his, will be cleared.' The strength and fortitude she had quietly shown to me were now public property, and I was proud of her. It had been her decision to talk openly to the cameras; she had not asked for my advice because she knew that I would have asked her not to do it. She did not do so again; she did not have to.

Meanwhile, political pressure mounted. A group of eight North West MPs raised questions in Parliament, as did the Shadow spokesman for Northern Ireland, Peter Archer. The Solicitor General (now Attorney General), Sir Patrick Mayhew, told the House of Commons that the investigations into me were 'quite separate' from those into Mr Taylor. My own Member of Parliament, Sir Fergus Montgomery, who was a determined and perceptive supporter of my family and me throughout, asked for a speedy end to the affair. He complained in Parliament of the decision to make my suspension public 'before they had the courtesy to tell Mr Stalker'. The Secretary of State for Northern Ireland, Tom King, made it clear in the Commons that his main wish was for my RUC enquiry, under Mr Sampson, to proceed 'as expeditiously as possible'. On 3 July 1986 he said, 'I am anxious to see the RUC enquiry completed at the earliest possible moment. I wish to see no further delay and the matter must be pressed on with, with no hold-up. My concern is that this matter now be pursued as vigorously as possible, the facts established, and if charges are to be brought, they should be brought at the earliest possible date. At the moment we have innuendo and rumour affecting matters that happened in 1982, four years ago, and this is undoubtedly doing damage to a police force of outstandingly brave men who are seeking to uphold law and order in Northern Ireland.' As I write this (in November 1987), almost nineteen months after Mr King's powerful statement to the House, there have still been no public developments, neither have charges been brought or publicly commented on.

Try as they undoubtedly did, official spokesmen of the Home Office and the Northern Ireland Office never managed to separate in the public mind the RUC enquiry and the investigation into my conduct. The disastrous decision to appoint Colin Sampson to both jobs did enormous damage to the earnest claims that the two matters were not connected. The Parliamentary summer recess was imminent, and pressure grew for Mr Sampson to finish his investigations before then. On 9 July an all-party delegation of councillors, led by Councillor Briggs, travelled to the Home Office to urge the removal of Mr Sampson from the RUC investigation. Typically, Norman Briggs was trying to act honestly and fairly in his efforts to bring some sort of credibility to both investigations. His efforts failed, and the position remained unchanged.

During the week of that meeting in London, Kevin Taylor told the newspapers that James Anderton was a personal friend of his and that he had been to a number of functions with him, at which I had not been present, including one at Police Headquarters when I was in Northern Ireland. The Police Committee Chairman acted promptly. The Chief Constable, very properly and constitutionally, was summoned by Councillor Briggs to his office and asked to explain his contact with Kevin Taylor, which it seems he did. A press conference followed at which Councillor Briggs said that 'full details of his limited contacts with Mr Taylor have been given to me by the Chief Constable. Mr Anderton has explained he is not a friend of Mr Taylor.' Briggs's rapid reaction certainly indicated that he had learned quickly from the débacle of my situation. If Councillor Briggs had given me that same facility he granted to James Anderton, and which is provided for under the law, the public trial of my family and the police force could have been avoided. I believe that with each twist of the story, Norman Briggs realized the mistakes he had made earlier, and so the pressure on him inexorably grew.

This pressure was added to by much-publicized claims made by a Salford constituent of his, a man awaiting trial for fraud, that two detective officers — one with strong RUC connections — had visited him in prison and had promised him leniency in return for his co-operation in discrediting me. The deal had apparently been that the police would bring him to my home, where he would walk to my front door and be photographed, by concealed detectives, handing me an unsolicited packet; otherwise, he would meet me by contrived accident in some other public place where the same thing would happen. The man concerned, William McPhee, approached the *Guardian* newspaper, who took from him a signed affidavit in which he named the two police officers, and which was given by the newspaper to my solicitors. In it McPhee makes it clear that he had rejected the police approach, and that he was not seeking any money or any advantage for his story. On the face of it he had nothing materially to gain, and my solicitor passed the information, the names of the officers, the signed affidavit and the man's full details to the Police Authority for action. Inexplicably, they passed them to Mr Sampson for investigation. I have heard nothing about it since.

On 11 July, in answer to growing media claims of a morale crisis in the force, James Anderton called together his thirty or so top commanders and confidently assured them that the enquiry being conducted by Mr Sampson had nothing whatsoever to do with the RUC. Mr Anderton went on to say, with some emotion, 'I want to see John Stalker walk back

159

through that door with his reputation unblemished. Nothing would make me happier.' I read of his remarks and I could not understand why he had not picked up the phone to me or my wife. I had known him and worked with him for almost thirty years, and I do not think he would have compromised himself by doing so. Had he done so, it would have gone a long way towards restoring his reputation with me and my family. To the same meeting, and in typical style, he explained his initial actions thus: 'Gentlemen — please believe me. Duty, that stern mistress of the soul, demanded I do no less than what I did in relation to my Deputy Chief Constable.' His statement, I am told, was received in total silence.

An important move was made on 13 July 1986: the Chief Constable of the Royal Ulster Constabulary, Sir John Hermon, fifteen months after I had requested it, formally suspended from duty the two senior Special Branch officers who had been involved in the formulation of false cover stories following the fatal shootings. Mr Sampson is reported to have requested that my fifteen-month-old letter of April 1985 be acted on. It was a bitter irony for my family that, by contrast, I had been suspended on the basis only of rumour, and before any enquiries whatsoever had been made. They compared the two sets of suspensions with some sadness.

At about that time I was immensely cheered by the return home of my mother after her three-week stay in hospital. My father had been helpful to us at my home in looking after the farm animals while Stella and I were busy between 'phone calls, solicitors' offices and the hospital. My mother was not fully recovered, but she was getting better, and it was good to see her in her own home again. The hospital authorities at Manchester Royal Infirmary had been magnificent; not just in their professional care for her, but also in their sensitivity to her position. They had jealously guarded her from pressmen, and had made sure that she was kept informed of developments during the day-time when we were not there.

The nurses and doctors acted as news couriers for her as soon as she was well enough to receive information. Even in a public ward, they managed to find her an extra television set to watch news bulletins and interviews. I shall be forever grateful to them all. But six weeks of worry and concern had visibly taken their toll, probably more on her than on anyone. She had changed in that short period from a sprightly, fit lady into an old woman. But the spirit of trust and pride in her sons shone just as brightly in her eyes, and within a day of returning home she wrote to her Member of Parliament, Michael Meacher, who took up my matter with the Government. Her return home gave all of us renewed strength. My three brothers and I are at our closest when she is the binding force, and her absence in hospital had been our overriding concern. My temporary troubles were as nothing compared with her safe return from hospital: her illness put everything else in perspective. Now she was back and the team was complete.

The letters of support and encouragement continued to flow in. The routes they took were sometimes circuitous, but still they came. The local postman had become accustomed to the filming of his morning visits by television crews, and the bundles he delivered always had their share of letters addressed 'John Stalker, Manchester' or 'John Stalker, Police Chief, England'. Telephone calls and messages from America increased as influential newspapers in New York and Boston took up the story of my suspension from duty, and the reasons they believed lay behind it. In a powerful article in the *New York Times*, William Safire asked blunt questions of the British government. He ended by saying quite unequivocally that although terrorists may endanger lives, toleration of the cop who deliberately kills a suspect threatens our way of life. He said exactly what I had tried to impress on my team two years earlier. The quickening American interest raised the temperature yet again, and the newspapers here kept the story prominent. The Prime Minister was asked in Parliament by the Liberal Home Affairs spokesman, Alex Carlile, for 'urgent answers to this extraordinary mystery'. Mr Carlile also wrote to Mr Tom King at the Northern Ireland Office, but no public comment was made.

From the early part of July onward I had been receiving information from trusted colleagues that my home telephone was being intercepted by police. At least one of my sources is highly placed and would be in a position to know. At first I regarded it as highly unlikely. I was not suspected of any criminal offences, and I know enough about Home Office 'intercept' warrants to be sure that police discipline would never be sufficient reason for granting one. But I also knew that there are less official ways of listening to people's telephone conversations. I kept the information to myself and carried on as normal. Occasionally, however, when my solicitors or family phoned me, I was genuinely uneasy and I asked them not to say too much. Eventually I learned that my solicitors believed that their office telephones were also being listened to. They also believed that their offices in Deansgate, Manchester, were under police surveillance from another building, from an observation point that I later discovered not only exists, but was the scene of some strange and unexplained activity at that time. We had no proof, of course. Nevertheless, we complained. Our complaints brought forth carefully worded and very specific statements from James Anderton in which he said, 'Neither Mr Stalker's nor Mr Lakin's telephones have been tapped under any authority granted or obtained by me.' The matter of the surveillance of their offices was never denied. Peter Lakin accepted these assurances about his own telephone, but my suspicions remained that unauthorized procedures were taking place without the knowledge or authority of Mr Anderton. My sources have never changed their story in this regard.

In mid-July 1986 I was asked to travel again to Wakefield to see Mr Sampson. The time and place of the meeting had, as usual, been leaked and the press were waiting. I think that by this time some journalists realized that the affair was burning itself out. No new information was finding its way to the media. I recall a respected journalist from a Sunday newspaper calling at my home on his way to return his hire car to Manchester Airport before leaving the story altogether. He told me that I had been through a process deeper and more searching than anything MI5 or Special Branch could undertake. Newspaper cheque books had been waved and every stone turned over. 'You have', he said, 'survived the Fleet Street vetting machine. We are satisfied there is nothing for us to find and the circus is beginning to move on. You have nothing else to worry about. Good luck.'

I went with Peter Lakin to Wakefield Police Headquarters on 17 July. The style of interview was the same. I was handed an official form that yet again specifically made it very clear that still no complaint or allegation was being made against me. There was nothing new to answer except a series of statements relating to further use, on three occasions, of a police car under circumstances that Mr Sampson regarded as unauthorized. I emphatically disagreed with him, and again explained why I believed him to be wrong. Mr Sampson seemed hardly to listen. It was obvious he had not taken up my request at the last interview for him to check my very infrequent use of this facility against the daily use made of official cars by the Chief Constable and other senior officers in the past. I told him that his enquiries into this triviality were unfairly selective against me, and that, based on past practice, I had every reason to believe that Mr Anderton knew of the use of cars for evening functions and accepted it as being perfectly in order, both for me and for himself. I mentioned again the security consideration, and asked finally that if he felt it was his duty to regard my use of a car as a disciplinary matter, then in fairness to me he review the identical, but infinitely more frequent, use by other senior officers over the previous few years. I was away from work, suspended, and obviously could not examine the records myself. It seemed to me that new rules had been formulated against me alone, and were being retroactively applied. Mr Sampson pursed his lips and looked hard at me. I suspected that he had no intention of doing what I had asked him to do, and later information showed that I was right. It seemed that his interest lay in finding disciplinary offences against me, and neither my explanations nor my plea for enquiries to corroborate them were ever acted upon.

Peter Lakin and I left and spoke to the waiting newsmen on the steps of the police station. I told them that nothing new had been discussed, and that I saw no reason why I should not be allowed to return to work very soon. Peter Lakin emphasized that once again, during this fourth lengthy and formal interview, no complaints, allegations or charges of any kind had been made against me. I returned home and began the long wait for news. Unless something fresh surfaced, or a point needed to be clarified, that was probably it. I had been seven weeks away from work and it was time to take stock. I still had no real information other than a string of disconnected events and names spread over a period of six years. The common denominator was Kevin Taylor, a man I had known for many years but actually saw only on four or five occasions each year. My professional integrity was being questioned because of the people *he* knew, although he himself was a man of unblemished character. Based on my interviews with Mr Sampson, it was obvious that all that existed evidentially against me was dross. The supposed misuse of police cars, even had it been true, was trivial. I had idly worked out that the cars had used about £6 worth of petrol if all the journeys were added together.

I knew that there is not a single police chief in the country who could not have been in my position. It is just not possible for a policeman to live a normal life among the public we are supposed to serve without knowing someone who may have been in trouble. In Greater Manchester alone, every year over fifty thousand people are arrested by the police — most of them for the first and only time. If any senior policemen, including James Anderton, Colin Sampson or anyone else, were to say to me that they knew the pedigree and history of every one of their friends, contacts and acquaintances — and in turn, of *their* friends and associates — I would tell them that they are either not telling the truth or they are misusing the police criminal record computer. It is impossible to know these things, and it is right that it should be so. We are a civilian police force. Senior policemen are not privileged beings; we have no more right to live in a pure and rarefied world than anyone else.

My family and I had done all we could. I had co-operated with Mr Sampson's enquiry to a far greater extent that I was obliged to. My future, and the value of thirty years as an honest policeman, were in the hands of Colin Sampson and the forty-five members of the Greater Manchester Police Committee. The trouble was, only Mr Sampson knew what it was all about. The Committee was still in turmoil because of the lack of information given to them.

In the House of Commons on 18 July 1986 the Prime Minister declined again to answer questions or comment while the investigation continued. Two days later the Secretary of State for Northern Ireland, Tom King, revealed in a letter to his Opposition counterpart, Peter Archer, that it had been Sir John Hermon who had statutorily approved my removal from the enquiry into his Force, after consultation with the Attorney General and Her Majesty's Chief Inspector of Constabulary, Sir Laurence Byford. This was the first official acknowledgement of the role played by Sir John in events surrounding my removal. Tom King also made it clear that the appointment of Colin Sampson to replace me as investigator was also made by the Chief Constable of the

RUC. Mr King carefully emphasized that he personally had played no part in the decision to appoint Mr Sampson to the Northern Ireland investigation. He said again, very forcibly, that 'The Irish Government naturally is taking an interest in this enquiry, which has a clear bearing on relations between the RUC and the minority community. They share my concern to see that all issues are resolved as quickly as possible.'

I had thought that the Wakefield interviews were at an end, but I was suddenly asked to return again to see Mr Sampson on 29 July. He did not say what he wanted, and I could not imagine. He had seemingly exhausted all his questions at the last meeting. We made the wearisome journey to Wakefield to be told that Mr Sampson merely wished to clear up one or two points about the use of police cars — something I thought I had done at earlier meetings. He hardly mentioned Kevin Taylor; indeed, Taylor had become a peripheral issue. Mr Sampson and his intense lieutenant, Chief Superintendent Robinson, seemed obsessed by this handful of journeys in a police car. They were like dogs with a single bone. Mr Sampson asked me whether I regarded myself on these occasions as representing the Chief Constable. I told him that I attended as the Deputy Chief Constable representing the Greater Manchester Police. Mr Sampson's view of the role of a Deputy was obviously very different from Mr Anderton's. Sampson clearly took the line that official functions should be attended by the Chief Constable, and by his Deputy only on those occasions when he himself was unable to attend. James Anderton and his successive deputies, including me, have had a very different perception for the last ten years. In Manchester the Deputy Chief Constable, and indeed the Assistant Chief Constables, are regarded as individuals in their own right and are directly invited to official functions. There are just too many for the Chief Constable to attend, and over the years a practice has evolved of the DCC and ACCs representing the Force, often at functions to which the Chief Constable has not been invited. I took it as an important part of my job to be seen by, and to talk to, as many of the citizens of Greater Manchester as I could. I valued pursuing an active programme of involvement with the community at all levels, and I knew that Mr Anderton encouraged that philosophy among his senior officers. I am a man of Manchester and it was no hardship for me to do so. Colin Sampson's deputy clearly does not have this wider role, and I found it increasingly difficult to talk to Sampson with any degree of common understanding. He, I and James Anderton are three very different people, off and on duty, and as policemen were worlds apart in the way we viewed our jobs.

Sampson's close and disproportionate interest in the minor issue of police cars convinced me that he was anxiously aware that the initial disciplinary aspects involving 'undesirable associations' were fast fading. I knew there was no substance in them, and it looked to me as if Mr Sampson was at last realizing it. The question of the use of police cars was a makeweight, and I suspect we both knew it.

I left Wakefield Police Headquarters for what was to be the last time, and spoke to the still waiting pressmen, whose continued interest astounded me. I returned home and we began the long wait until the unknown date in the future when decisions would be made. Mr Sampson had finished with me; my bank accounts and credit-card records had been returned to me. Although I had never been accused of anything, I had gathered from the line of questioning that I was suspected of bringing discredit upon the Force by associating with Kevin Taylor, who was a man rumoured to be under police suspicion. During that thirteen-year friendship I had attended four functions at which men with criminal convictions had been present, although this was not known to me. One of the functions had been organized by a political party, and this was obviously frowned on by Mr Sampson. Finally, over a period

167

of two years, I had made eight short trips on duty in a police car in circumstances that Mr Sampson clearly felt to be unauthorized. On four of these journeys I had given a lift, without diverting, to an 'unauthorised passenger' — one of them my wife; one of them Kevin Taylor and colleague of his; one of them a man who that same evening had presented to Mr Anderton an official gift of a snooker table and equipment for the use of policemen at Police Headquarters; and one of them a local magistrate.

I had answered all of Sampson's questions, and I was quite convinced there were no grounds for taking the matter further. The deliberations would now be for the Police Committee: they were the body whose decision it would be either to return me to work or to refer the entire matter to a legal tribunal. The Chairman of the Committee, Councillor Norman Briggs, had still not confided in his Committee colleagues the extent of what he knew, and he had been subjected to unremitting pressure for almost nine weeks. He left for a short holiday in Cheltenham, where on 2 August 1986 he died of a heart attack. He was a good man, and I knew him fairly well. Stella and I were very much saddened by the news of his death. I had spoken to him at almost every Manchester United home game in the previous five years. He was a keen fan, and sat near me with his close friend Stan Orme, the Member of Parliament for Salford. We used also to recommend to each other various theatrical productions in the city. He had been thrust into a situation not of his making within a few weeks of his appointment as Chairman of a new Police Committee, following the dissolution of the Greater Manchester Council. He had been obliged to shoulder an awesome burden, and then had piled upon himself an even greater burden. The decision to effectively suspend from duty the Deputy Chief Constable should not have been his alone, neither should the pressures that followed. Finally he was accused, wrongly, of being part of a Masonic conspiracy to discredit me. Norman Briggs was not a Freemason. I felt his death deeply. Salford had lost a good councillor, and the community had lost an honest servant. Despite everything, I would have trusted him to be fair and of independent mind when the report about me was placed before him.

Now that he was dead, his opinion had died with him, and Police Committee business was in chaos. The Vice Chairman was a magistrate, Mrs Audrey Walsh, voted there by a combination vote of Liberals, Conservatives and magistrates. But the ruling Labour group would not endorse her elevation to the Chair, despite her vast knowledge, over many years, of Police Committee affairs. A hurried meeting resulted in the appointment of a back-bench Labour member of the Committee, Councillor David Moffat, as Acting Chairman. He too was new to the Police Committee and he was pitchforked into the chaos left by Norman Briggs's death. The Committee was still fragmented, and individual councillors spoke daily to the press and on television. The northern headquarters of the Freemasons' Society threw open their doors for a press conference to say that 'to the best of their knowledge' there had been no Masonic conspiracy in the Stalker affair. Their spokesman invited the public to test the openness of Masons about their membership. 'Ask them', he said, 'they will tell you. We are not ashamed of being Masons.' Two days later, on 8 August, Sir Philip Myers was bluntly asked by a Police Committee member whether he was a Mason. He replied, 'Some time ago I was sent a questionnaire [by Stephen Knight, author of the book *The Brotherhood*] asking the same question. I threw it in the wastepaper basket, and I propose to do the same with your question.' He is reported not to have responded to an appeal for him to investigate links between police Masons in Manchester and Belfast.

I mention these matters not to suggest that Sir Philip is a Freemason — if he is, he is entitled to be so — or that there were any Masonic links. I just do not know. I am not a Freemason but I know many good and efficient policemen who are. It is merely illustrative of the twists and turns of events surrounding the Stalker affair, all of which served to keep the matter in the national headlines. There was no respite, for me or for my family, even after nine weeks, from speculation and conjecture.

On 9 August I read in an article written by the shrewd Peter Murtagh, of the *Guardian*, the good news that the enquiry into me was at an end, and that the report was due to be presented by Mr Sampson to the Police Complaints Authority the following week. Peter Murtagh had been consistently ahead of other national daily newspapers correspondents in his information, and I felt a lot happier. (He was later to win the Journalist of the Year award for his coverage of the story.) I had ceased to regard as unusual the fact that my contact with the investigation was through the newspapers. For ten weeks they had told me everything, and this latest *Guardian* story proved to be absolutely accurate.

At home my daughter Colette's twenty-first birthday came and went in a sadly subdued way. The weather was good, and I tried to throw off the mood of depression that had settled on my daughters and my wife by organizing an impromptu party for friends and family. I was heartened to see several policemen arrive, bringing cards and good wishes. But the spirit was not there, and what should have been a happy day died a quiet death. The press cameras at my gate were there to record it.

On 10 August *The Sunday Times* carried a story headlined 'STALKER CLEARED'. It said I would return to my job later in the month, and that the West Yorkshire Police had failed to find evidence that substantiated claims made against me. Their information was accurate, and had been obtained many days before the report had been delivered either to the Police Complaints Authority or to the Police Committee. The newspaper also said, inaccurately, that I had been told unofficially of the results of the investigation. The daily newspapers consequently asked me for comment. Of course I knew nothing, and Rodger Pannone again took on the job of protecting me from the onslaught. The pendulum began to swing away from me towards the end of the week as other newspapers were leaked information that the report *had* found 'evidence' of wrongdoing. *The Sunday Telegraph* of 17 August ran a major article headlined 'STALKER TO FACE A TRIBUNAL'. We were in despair: if this were true it would mean a further long delay, for a hearing before a senior Queen's Counsel and two other eminent laypersons, who would conduct a form of court hearing at which evidence from witnesses would be called. A full typed transcript would be prepared — a long and expensive job — and this would be presented eventually to the Police Committee for their decision. Reading the *Sunday Telegraph* I felt myself to be at the lowest point since the first day. I knew that a tribunal would be fair and objective, but I also knew that the procedure could easily take another twelve months, during which time I would remain suspended. I knew that my family — especially my mother — would find it impossibly hard to cope with. The pressures were building again, and I prayed I would have the strength to resist them.

By the beginning of the week beginning 18 August it became obvious that Mr Sampson's report had been leaked in its entirety to some members of the press. There had been deliberate and insidious leaking of its contents for some time, but reporters were now quoting chunks verbatim from what was obviously the official report. Paragraph and page numbers were referred to, and I was in no doubt that the whole massive document, not just portions of it, was in the hands of the press.

Events had run their predictable course. Either a policeman, a councillor or someone at the Police Complaints

Authority — whether through mischievousness or for money I do not know — had deliberately handed to a newspaper a complete copy of a highly confidential document. This was a document that had been transported and delivered under strict controls by a firm of private security operators to the Police Committee and its members. I now read in full in my newspaper what Mr Sampson had said about me, and his recommendation that I should be placed before a tribunal. It was dislocated world I was in. I knew that the newspaper reports were accurate, but I could not believe that Mr Sampson could possibly have arrived at such a conclusion. I began to rationalize what might have happened. Perhaps the press had been deliberately leaked a false or dummy report in order to find a dishonest policeman or to derail the information express. Perhaps they had obtained a draft report, prepared weeks ago and now altered. Perhaps it was a cruel joke. Perhaps, maybe, what if, supposing — everything we discussed in the occasional quiet of our home was prefaced with one of these words.

The certainties of my life were no longer in place, and I was beginning to lose my grip. Rodger Pannone saw this happening and took control. He spoke firstly to me and then privately to the Police Committee. Through a press statement he said publicly to the Committee: 'Basic humanity and natural justice indicate that the pressure on Mr Stalker and his family of these allegations should be brought to an end as quickly as possible. Mr Stalker has a complete explanation for each point made by Mr Sampson, and the Police Committee are invited to ask him about each and every one. If they are not satisfied, they could then refer him to a tribunal.' I publicly pleaded that if judgment were to be passed on me, then it be made by my Police Committee, all of them people of Greater Manchester, and not by way of some bureaucratic and drawn-out procedure. I also said that I would have resigned from the police force at the outset of this investigation had I anything to hide or had I done something to be ashamed of. I had again, because of leaks, been forced to defend myself — through Rodger Pannone — in the glare of the media spotlight. Mr Sampson's 'points' were in the nation's newspapers and on its television screens before I had had a chance to answer them. I could see how innocent people, without the love of family and the support of a good solicitor, might give up. There is a point when even belief in oneself is not enough, and when the blows become too hard to take. I found myself, for those few months, outside the processes of justice, and even though this was only a disciplinary matter, I saw how they can be abused. I do not know who the leakers were, but I suspect there was more than one. At no time, to my knowledge, was this leakage ever publicly condemned by either Mr Sampson, Mr Anderton or the Police Complaints Authority.

On 19 August a second *Panorama* programme by the reporter who had made the previous programme, Peter Taylor, disclosed that a boat owned by Kevin Taylor, which I had been on in America five years earlier, had subsequently been sold in Spain to a man who was suspected — a long time later — of using it to ship cannabis. The programme very fairly stressed that Kevin Taylor had no connection whatsoever with the criminal use of a boat he had once owned, and emphasized again that he was a man of good reputation. The aim of the programme seemed to be to say that my friendship with Mr Taylor meant that I had to be removed from the Northern Ireland enquiry in order to maintain its purity, that I was taken off in order not to discredit what I had already found. It was a convoluted argument that convinced very few people — especially as the programme at no time mentioned the entirely different perspective of the first *Panorama* programme of only seven weeks earlier, which had dealt with the bugging of the Hayshed, and which subsequently won a television prize as a piece of outstanding investigative television journalism. It was not the fact that the second programme completely contradicted the first that disappointed us, for there is nothing wrong with an honest reappraisal and change of stance; but the lack of any explanation why it had done so confounded me. The two programmes were quite separate, and the viewer of the second was never invited to consider the first. It was as if it did not exist. The effect of this was, if anything, to strengthen the belief that the first programme was the closest to the truth. If my removal was intended to protect the integrity of my own enquiry then it failed miserably. The way to safeguard it would have been to wait until I was actually shown to have done something wrong before replacing me. The taking of such premature action discredited the motives of those responsible for it and damaged the report far more than any unconfirmed rumours circulating about me could ever have done. I found this rationalizing of the reasons for removing me from my enquiry during the last few weeks of my two-year enquiry faintly insulting. It was clever but not convincing.

My plea to be allowed to attend the Police Committee was about to be turned down, but even that refusal was given to the newspapers rather than to me. Eleven weeks after Mr Sampson had, in the name of the Police Committee, sent me home, the Committee finally reached the point at which they had real authority returned to their hands. I was bewildered by the leaked decision to exclude me from their deliberations — it seemed out of step with the fair and independent line they had tried to take as individuals. It was clear that they were acting on legal advice, and my solicitors were not permitted to challenge this decision. According to the leaks, the clerk to the Committee, Roger Rees, had told them that they had three options. The first was to take no action whatsoever on the report; the second was to adjourn matters for a disciplinary hearing of their own; and the third was to opt for an independent tribunal under the aegis of the then Lord

Chancellor, Lord Hailsham. Mr Sampson said that the evidence 'demanded' that it be sent to a tribunal. The Police Complaints Authority issued a public statement to the effect that the investigation had been completed to their satisfaction, saying that the resulting report ran to 1,500 pages, with written statements from 154 witnesses.

The press and television crews were once again clustered around my house looking for comment. The handing over of the Sampson report — all 30,000 words of it, not including written statements — to the press had resulted in a chorus of calls to me to respond to the hundreds of comments it contained. But while individual reporters had read the report, I had not. Of course, I could not respond; but the constant refusals were wearying. I said only this: 'I have nothing to fear from any tribunal, but I would be sorry and would regret such a move because of the extra burden and strain such a very expensive and complex procedure would place on my family. I do not think such a step is necessary. If I am to be accused of bringing discredit on the Greater Manchester Police, and of misusing vehicles, then I should be judged by the people of Greater Manchester, the members of the Police Committee.' The press stayed outside my home until after midnight on the eve of the meeting of the Police Committee. I took the telephone off the hook, and with my wife and daughters spoke about the following day. I told them that whatever happened we would be in the public arena all day, and that I could not avoid it. I was still hoping against hope that the leaks were wrong and that I would be given permission to attend the meeting of the Police Committee, but Mr Rees had not yet officially replied to my request. If my plea to be listened to was turned down, then I intended to spend the day at my solicitors' office in case they changed their minds. We spent a sleepless night. Tomorrow would be either the end of a nightmare or the beginning of a new and much longer one. The date of the meeting, 22 August, had a particular poignancy for me.

Exactly twelve months earlier, at a few minutes after seven in the morning, fifty-five people had died at Manchester Airport as a charter flight Boeing burst into flames. I had been quickly on the scene and had commanded all police operations at the Airport on that harrowing day, and as I moved about my house I thought of the painful memories that loved ones and friends would be experiencing at that very moment. My heartache was not important compared with their losses. One or two morning newspapers mentioned the links between me and the first anniversary of the tragic air crash.

The *Daily Mail*, however, again twisted the knife. It told me in large letters that an informer lay at the heart of my troubles: according to them he had supposedly given information six years earlier about Kevin Taylor, but had since died in prison (in fact he had been dead for over twelve months). The *Mail* named the dead informer as David Burton, or Bertelstein, and said that his information was the spark that lit the fire of suspicion. It was another crazy spasm in the story, but it confirmed for me that, if it were true, there had been some desperate grasping at straws to find reasons to remove me from Northern Ireland. Events since then have shown that Burton was a well-known criminal and pathological liar, and that everything he had said about Kevin Taylor was absolutely untrue; but he was now conveniently dead and the story could not easily be discredited. It was a classic smear story, and I was suspicious of the reasons for its appearing in the *Mail* (reported by Margaret Henfield) on the very day my future was to be decided by the Police Committee. The malicious leakers had been at work again.

The four of us prepared as dozens of press and television crews circled my house. I spoke to Rodger Pannone and arranged to go to his offices to await news of whether I was to be allowed to speak to the Committee. It was clear that the day's proceedings would last for many hours, and I telephoned in advance to a police station about two hundred yards away from my solicitors' office confirming that I would be needing my parking space for the day. Ten minutes later the Chief Constable's secretary telephoned Stella to say that Mr Anderton had given personal instructions that I was not to be allowed to park my car in the police station. It was an act of supreme pettiness, and the pressmen present in the room witnessed it at first hand. There was genuine surprise that a man of perceived stature and Christian values did not have either the courage or courtesy to telephone personally a man who was his deputy and who had been a professional colleague for nearly thirty years. It surprised many, but not my family, although the cruelty of it reduced my wife to angry tears.

A BBC television crew drove us to Rodger Pannone's offices, where we stayed for the next twelve hours. The Police Committee formally refused my request to be present. I was not to be allowed to speak; they did not wish to see me. I read all the morning's papers and was confronted again with fresh extracts from the confidential Sampson report. Many members of the Committee had broken ranks, including some magistrates, and were giving comment and interviews to lunchtime television and radio news bulletins. The whole affair had become a bizarre forum of opinion and lobbying; indeed, the only voice not contributing to the day's debate was mine. The day wore on and nerves began to jangle. Rodger Pannone kept me protected, but the isolation was as hard to bear as the exposure. Stella and my daughters, Colette and Francine, remained with me all day in the same room, but I can remember little of those blurred afternoon hours. Early evening came, and with it word of an adjournment. The television news told of the secret questioning of Chief Constable Sampson over a lengthy period and of the exclusion of James Anderton from the Committee Room and proceedings.

It was late evening before the telephone call came. I spoke to the Acting Chairman, Councillor David Moffat, who told me that by an overwhelming vote — thirty-six to six, with no abstentions — the Committee had decided *not* to send the matter to a tribunal. 'You are now restored,' he said, 'to your position as Deputy Chief Constable of the Greater Manchester Police.' I thanked him and told him I would return to my desk the following day. I went back to the crowded room, now filling up with newsmen, and told them of the marvellous decision. My family and I embraced each other. It was the end of the worst three months of my professional life, and I felt the welling up of a strange mix of happiness and anger. I was happy to be back, but angry at the sheer ineptitude of it all. The contrivance had been so transparent and I was sick at heart with the hypocrisy involved. It had all been so unnecessary.

If, as I suspected, the objective had been to take me out of Northern Ireland, then today's deliberations were of little consequence to the people who had wished for that. I was back at my desk at Manchester, but I would never complete my work in relation to the death of Michael Justin Tighe. I learned that evening that the Police Committee had added a rider to their decision to reinstate me: it said that in view of my high office I should be more circumspect in my associations in the future. The Committee, in fact, had no right to do this; their sole legal responsibility had been to accept or reject Sampson's recommendation to send me to a tribunal. Nothing more and nothing less. They had, in fact, found a fourth option to the three given to them by their legal adviser, Roger Rees. Comment such as that, which indicated a degree of opinion or 'verdict', was an option open to them only *after* either an informal or formal hearing, at which they would have been obliged to listen to me. They had made a value judgment having heard only the 'prosecution' evidence of Mr Sampson. It was largely hearsay and conjecture, and I had not been allowed to challenge it. But I was worn out, and decided to let the mistake pass; my family's relief and joy were too important to spoil by legal pedantry, and I knew that any complaint on my part would inevitably lead to the delay of a tribunal. The Committee had been fair and honest, and my going back to work was all-important to me. But nevertheless this fundamental mistake was indicative of their collective inexperience and lack of knowledge of their powers and authority. Individually they are sensible and shrewd people and I respect most of them greatly — indeed, they perform a difficult job well — but I think they would agree that, as a body, they made many avoidable mistakes in those three months.

The night belonged to me, however, and my family and friends. I telephoned my parents and then went home. There I learned from a number of people of the chaos that had reigned as Councillor Moffat had tried to contact me to courteously tell me of the Committee's decision before I learned of it through the media. My solicitors had carefully told Roger Rees that I would be at their offices awaiting the Committee's decision. That message did not get through to the Chairman, however. James Anderton, who knew I was at the solicitors because he had refused my request to park my car close by, stayed silent, but in answer to a question said he 'did not know' my home telephone number. For over half an hour after the meeting ended, Councillor Moffat had valiantly tried to track me down by phoning my home and Rodger Pannone's home, finally tracing me to the telephone I had sat by for the previous twelve hours. It had been another shambles.

I talked with Stella until the early hours, enjoying the release from anxiety and confusion, and we thought about my return to work. I was confident of my position; my integrity had not been tarnished in the eyes of either the Force or the public, and I had honestly answered press questions about my anticipated future relationship with James Anderton by saying that I saw no insurmountable problems. I had emphasized that we were both professionals, and that our duty was to the public and to the police force. I had received overwhelming support and I had no doubts that I could pick up the reins of my job very quickly. Life was good again, and I looked forward to the coming years with the enthusiasm I have always had for a job I enjoyed in a city I love. Sadly, it did not turn out that way. I did not realize it then, but my career as a policeman was entering its last few months.

# 6

## *Reinstatement*

I returned to the job I loved on Saturday 23 August 1986, attended, as usual, by dozens of press and television crews, who had been at my home from very early morning. I was a policeman again. This was not the time for the recriminations that many newsmen would have liked me to voice; first I needed to see how I was received back. My parents, without saying they were coming, made the long early-morning journey from their home to mine, and there was happiness in my mother's eyes as I drove away. Her words of 28 May came back to me. 'Don't worry, you will return with your integrity intact,' she had said. I had taken careful and honest stock of myself; I was under no self-delusion. My life had been publicly laid bare; but my certain knowledge that there was nothing there to be ashamed of had sustained me. I do not mean that I was the perfect policeman; there are very few of those about. I have cut plenty of corners and made some hefty mistakes and questionable decisions; but I have never sold the public or myself short either in endeavour or in honesty. The immense public and police support had continued unabated throughout the past three months, and as I drove to Police Headquarters I knew that I had lost nothing in reputation as a policeman.

I arrived at Police Headquarters to find that since I had last been there in late May a completely new one-way road system had been introduced, and, feeling extremely foolish, I could not at first find a way in. One newsman cracked, 'Do you think James Anderton has changed the locks as well?' His joke was to prove not very far off the mark.

I worked at my desk all day. Saturday is a quietish day in Police Headquarters, and I spent it reading my way through what had been happening during my absence. My secretary, Linda, had obviously never doubted I would return. Each day she had watered the plants, and changed the calendar, and copies of police correspondence were all neatly piled in date order on my desk awaiting me. My office was clean and fresh. She had had faith, and that meant a great deal to me. The morning papers reported political comment about my reinstatement. Cecil Franks MP and Tony Lloyd MP called for a judicial enquiry into the entire investigation into me, and Stuart Bell MP, a Shadow Spokesman on Northern Ireland, demanded my immediate reinstatement to the enquiry in Northern Ireland. His was a brave but futile call: I had been forever removed by Sir John Hermon, and I knew I would never be reappointed. Sir John, by burying his apparent personal antipathy towards me, could have done much to allay public suspicion about the reasons for my removal by returning to the position that had existed eleven weeks earlier. Colin Sampson had not begun to take over; obviously he had been too busy in Manchester. Meanwhile, my team were ready for me to pick up where I had left off. But I never thought for a moment that Sir John would take this course, and I was not mistaken. If he had done, this long and seriously damaging saga might have been ended, and the public would have promptly forgotten it. But instead, the whole business inevitably rumbled on and suspicions remained.

I received many hundreds of calls on that first Saturday at my desk, from ordinary members of the public, dozens of policemen, friends, members of the Police Committee and even strangers. I did not, however, receive a call from the man I most expected to ring me. I had no communication whatsoever from James Anderton. He knew I was going back to my desk that day, but he did not telephone. I learned, from various newsmen, that he was away from the Force area on his annual leave; he had, however, been in Manchester until late the previous evening at the Police Committee meeting that voted to reinstate me. In his absence I was in charge of the Force, but I had no idea where he was or how I could contact him. The following day, Sunday, came and went without any contact either from him to me or from his wife to mine. Stella and my daughters regarded Joan Anderton as a friend, and had not really understood why she had not made contact throughout the previous eleven weeks. I spent some time telephoning around and eventually confirmed, through another senior officer, that the Chief Constable was indeed on holiday; but we did not know when he intended to return.

Monday 25 August was a Bank Holiday, and a very busy day in Manchester. I had still heard absolutely nothing over the weekend from James Anderton, and by now it had become very embarrassing. The dozens of newsmen who telephoned me merely wished to hear that the Chief Constable and I had begun to heal the wounds and that he had welcomed me back to work, or at least made contact with me. I tried to hedge my answers with possible explanations, but I had to tell the truth, which was that although it was now almost three days since I had been reinstated to duty, and to acting command of the 7,000 policemen and 3,000 support staff of the Force, I had heard absolutely nothing from the Chief Constable. The newsmen drew an understandable conclusion, and reports of his 'snub' appeared in every newspaper. At the time I attempted to be diplomatic and to make excuses in order to try to maintain the confidence of the Force in their two most senior officers. I do not have to do that now, and I can say that his four-day silence after my reinstatement seemed to me another indication of childish discourtesy. But much worse, in my view it was unprofessional and showed a disregard for the efficiency of the Force. As his Deputy, whether he welcomed me back or not, I was entitled to know where he was. There is a variety of instructions and orders that can, by law, only be given by a Chief Constable, or in his absence his Deputy. I saw this as an ominous indication that he did not really welcome my return and had no intention of easing my re-entry into the work of the Force. The weeks that followed sadly proved my intuition to be right.

The following day was a normal working day, and I arrived at Police Headquarters at about half-past eight. As usual, press and television cameras were waiting there. What should have been by now a dead story had been kept very much alive by the suggestion of a rift between James Anderton and myself. I am not certain what they expected to see — a punch-up in the car-park, perhaps — but they were there in force. Some of them had even gained access to the entrance of the secure underground car-park, where they managed to film the arrival of the Chief Constable, driving himself in an anonymous Japanese car rather than being driven in his official Jaguar. He had obviously given the press who were waiting at his home the slip by changing his routine. I went to my office, and about two minutes later I heard him enter his office and close the door. I waited for some indication that he wished to speak to me, and it came exactly one hour later. He came into my office — which adjoins his, and is separated only by the secretaries' office — and said, 'We have much to talk about. We must do it now.' There was no warmth, no handshake and no words of welcome. He turned and walked into his own office and I followed him.

He spoke in a torrent of words. I said very little. He said that he had had no alternative but to act as he did, and that one day he would tell his own story, of the pressures he had been under for the last ten weeks. He did not expand on this, but seemed to be referring to the presence of the press at his home and at his Lake District weekend cottage, which had distressed his wife. His words were those of a man who felt very sorry for himself, and he kept saying that he had 'had no alternative'. He made no mention of the damage caused to the Northern Ireland enquiry and the crucial Anglo-Irish agreement, of the enormous public expense of the wholly unnecessary train of events, of Councillor Briggs's tragic and premature death, or of the pain caused to my family and me. There were no regrets, no apologies and not a hint of having made even the slightest misjudgment. He said to me that all actions taken by his officers in relation to me had been with his full knowledge and authority, and he warned me about bearing grudges against anyone. I thought he protested too much.

It was now my turn to speak, and I told him that in my view, based on the very reliable information I had received and my own extensive experience, he had acted hastily and ill-advisedly on unchecked and incorrect information. I was disappointed and angry at the way in which the affair had brought the senior echelons of three major police forces into public disrepute: Greater Manchester, the RUC and West Yorkshire. I was particularly critical of the role of others, including members of the Home Office Inspectorate, and said I intended to submit a detailed report to the Home Secretary about what I sincerely believed to have been a badly handled and extremely damaging episode in the history of the British Police. I also made it clear to him that properly, and within my sphere of responsibility as Deputy Chief Constable of the Force, I intended to give the CID the benefit of my experience. My Northern Ireland investigation had for two years or more kept me from many important duties within Greater Manchester. But now I was back, and I would begin immediately to involve myself in the work of the Force. I told him that in my view there were some elements at senior level in the Criminal Investigation Department who were inexperienced, unsure of themselves and dangerously narrow in their views. Such a combination would almost certainly mean future problems for him, and I told him I would do my best to try to bring home with me the lessons I had learned in Northern Ireland.

There were in fact two particularly pressing matters I wished to discuss with Mr Anderton, and I was anxious to see for myself what his reactions would be when I raised them. I said that in September 1985 Kevin Taylor had told me that a Manchester detective, Inspector Anthony Stephenson, was making enquiries about him at his (Taylor's) bank. When I learned of this I had decided immediately to sever contact with Kevin Taylor except for the one official attendance at the Hotel Piccadilly in November, which I had discussed with Mr Anderton before I went (and to which, I reminded him, he had raised no objections). Soon after that conversation with Kevin Taylor, in October, I had spoken to Inspector Stephenson's senior officer (a Superintendent) and had told him that although I did not wish to know what the investigations into Taylor were, it would be useful to me to be told whether they were sufficiently serious to prevent me from inviting Kevin Taylor and his wife to a forthcoming Christmas police function. The Superintendent had said he knew nothing but had gone away and then reported back to me to say quite emphatically that there were no police enquiries whatsoever going on into Taylor. There was an investigation into one of his tenants in a warehouse he lets, but this was not, I had been assured, connected with Kevin Taylor. I now told Mr Anderton that it seemed that this Superintendent had either told me deliberate lies, on instructions, or had told me the truth, which was that Taylor was not in fact under investigation in October 1985. Which was it?

I also told Mr Anderton that in April 1986, about five weeks before I was removed from the Northern Ireland enquiry, an Assistant Chief Constable of the Force had told me of a 'big squad of secret-surveillance police that had been set up in the last few days to investigate a policeman'. I knew nothing about it, though as Deputy Chief Constable I should have done, if it were true. I had sent firstly for Assistant Chief Constable Bernard Divine, the head of the Complaints and Discipline Department, who knew nothing. I had then sent for Assistant Chief Constable Ralph Lees, the head of Crime Investigation, and he too flatly denied that any such squad existed. Was this, I now asked the Chief Constable, a squad set up to investigate me at exactly the same time as I was recommencing my investigations in Northern Ireland, and had either of the two Assistant Chief Constables lied to me? It was important for me to know if I was to function properly for the next eight years or so as the Deputy Chief Constable.

I asked Mr Anderton directly where the truth lay. His answers, in my opinion, form the two most important sentences in the millions of words written about the Stalker affair. They convinced me that the true reason for my removal from duty was wholly connected with my investigations in Northern Ireland, and that the questions of friendship with Kevin Taylor and journeys in police cars were exactly what I suspected they were — contrivances intended to distract attention from my shoot–to–kill investigation and to further delay submission of the final report into what happened in the Hayshed. Flustered and red in the face, Mr Anderton said, 'No enquiries had properly been started into your friend Taylor in October. And no police officer [obviously meaning me] was under investigation in April.' He was cold, defensive and very clearly furious at having to answer such questions. Those few blurted words confirmed for me, however, all that I suspected: that investigations into Kevin Taylor did not truly begin until *after* I had delivered my report into the RUC to Belfast on 18 September 1985, and that enquiries into me did not begin until after I had been given clearance in March 1986

187

to have access to the tape and to see Sir John Hermon and his Deputy. The police raid on Kevin Taylor's house on 9 May 1986 — two weeks before I was removed from the enquiry — had been the first serious action taken by police against him, and that had happened only after I had made it clear I was returning to Northern Ireland to discuss the possible suspensions or removal from duty of the Chief Constable and/or his Deputy.

Mr Anderton realized the significance of what he had told me. I told him I was considering the preparation of a further report for the Association of Chief Police Officers (ACPO) about his role in the matter. He was at that time Vice-President of the Assocation, and the following month was appointed President. He would surely be worried that my report might affect his Presidency and he was angered by my intentions, but he made no comment. He countered by criticizing the television and radio interviews I had given in the course of defending myself, and said that he too would be submitting a report to the Home Office about the matter. The conversation was white-hot with barely controlled anger on both sides. After having known him for almost thirty years, I know that Anderton does not like argument that lasts beyond an initial disagreement and then acceptance of his authority. Indeed, he rarely experiences it. He is a decisive man and an effective leader, but the reverse side of those qualities are moods of sudden impatience and argument by assertion. He had the last word. 'You are forbidden', he said, 'to see the Taylor file.' I told him, as coolly as I could, that I had no intention of asking to see it because I had no need to do so, but that I resented the obvious implication that he felt I could not be trusted with it.

I tried to discuss several official civic and social events that were in my diary for the rest of the month and the remainder of the year, and to enquire whether he agreed with Mr Sampson about the role of the Deputy Chief Constable at social functions such as these; but he obviously did not wish to advise me. Our conversation was quite clearly at an end: he looked down at his papers and waved his hand for me to leave. The fact that the overwhelming majority of the British public, press and police officers thought that an awful mess had been made did not seem to have touched him at all. He was extremely angry, and it showed. As I turned to leave his office he said, 'There are many press and cameramen at the front door asking for pictures of you and I shaking hands. If you wish we will give them their pictures. It might be what is needed now.' I refused. I now knew exactly where I stood with him. He was concerned only with one thing — the public's perception of him and his relationship with me. He was trying to put right the 'snub' stories of the past four days. I told him I was prepared to say publicly that there was no rift between us but I could not face the hypocrisy of smiling and acting out lies for the benefit of the cameras, especially not on my first official working day after the traumas of the past three months. I agreed to a conciliatory press release but not to photographs. 'So be it,' he said, and I left him. The press was told that 'John Stalker and I have always worked very well together in the public interest and for the good of the Force, and there is no reason why we cannot do so again. A police force without a Deputy Chief Constable is certainly not fully effective, and I am glad to have John Stalker back on duty.' I was asked by the press to respond, and said, 'I am very anxious now that the two of us get on with re-establishing our relationship, which has always been professionally very good in the past. There is no rift between us, but of course we have not spoken to each other for the past three months.'

We both got down to our respective jobs, and it took me only a day or so to pick up the reins of what had been happening operationally within the Force. I received the best possible welcome and co-operation from the twenty-odd Chief Superintendents, all of whom I spoke to or called on within the course of the next few days. But there was still too much disconcertingly unresolved business between James Anderton and me, too many words left unsaid.

On Thursday of the week of my return I spoke to him again. I had decided that it was vitally important for the Force and myself that I speak at the earliest opportunity in a full and open way with the acting Chairman of the Police Committee and his senior colleagues, but I did not wish to do this behind the Chief Constable's back. I needed to clear the air with them and to talk on a man-to-man basis rather than with legal intermediaries present, and trammelled by Committee procedures. I particularly wished to discuss with them some philosophical questions of the nature of a senior policeman's job, how they saw it and how I saw it. I had been back at work for almost a week and everything seemed to be exactly as before. I was still, for example, expected to make judgments about the use of police cars on exactly the same basis as hitherto; there were no guidelines either for the six Assistant Chief Constables or myself about such use, and Mr Anderton seemed not to wish to address the issue. Yet I knew that Mr Sampson had recommended disciplinary proceedings against me on nine charges, eight of them relating to the use of a motor-car. I had no idea upon what basis he had arrived at that conclusion, and I felt that the Assistant Chief Constables and I were entitled to know what Mr Anderton and the Police Committee thought about this matter; otherwise, I felt, it was very possible that I could find myself in trouble again. The situation was entirely unsatisfactory: I had never been formally told by anyone what I was accused of; the Police Committee meeting to discuss me had been held in private; I had not been asked by the Committee for any explanations or given the opportunity to speak; yet I had been returned to work following a Committee resolution to 'take no action' about the use of the cars. Did this mean that my use of them was totally justified, or that the Committee frowned on it but decided it was too trivial a matter to pursue?

Mr Anderton was no better informed about what the Committee expected of me than I was — or so it seemed — and it was almost as if the last three months had never happened. The issues that had brought my family to its knees and the Greater Manchester Police to the headlines were still being ignored, clearly in the hope they would go away and that life could continue as before. I spoke to Anderton during the mid-morning of 28 August and told him that I had made an appointment to see two senior members of the Police Committee, Councillors Moffat and McCardell. I spoke in general terms about my confusion over Sampson's apparent obsession with the relatively trivial matter of short journeys made by me in police cars. James Anderton seemed friendly and helpful, possibly because of my obvious determination to pursue matters with his new Committee Chairman, Councillor Moffat, who had been openly supportive of me before and since my reinstatement.

As I spoke to Anderton it became clear that my earlier suspicions regarding this matter had been correct. Sampson, before recommending proceedings against me in relation to the cars, had apparently not contacted either Mr Anderton or Sir Philip Myers to ask them specifically about the terrorist threat to me. I reminded Mr Anderton of the identity of the man who he knew had been sent to this country from the Republic of Ireland to target me, and spoke of our detailed conversations about personal security measures I should take, including the eventual installation of a burglar alarm at my new home at police expense. Mr Anderton recalled the matter clearly and said that Mr Sampson should have checked my story with him but did not. I had already confirmed for myself that the Special Branch detective sergeant who was in possession of all the information regarding terrorist interest in

191

me had never been seen by Sampson. I wondered what other superficialities the Sampson report contained. I told Mr Anderton that I believed the Police Committee had been badly misinformed about many aspects of the affair, and that when granted the opportunity I intended to give them the explanations they had been denied. I said that I would start by telling them that one of the people to whom I had given an 'unauthorized lift' had that evening presented to the Chief Constable himself an expensive gift (a new snooker table) for the use of shift workers at Police Headquarters. The benefactor was surely entitled to be brought at police expense to the Chief Constable to perform this pleasant task. Mr Anderton remained absolutely silent: he had clearly forgotten about this aspect of it.

The newspapers were apportioning blame, and even those sections of the press usually supportive of Mr Anderton were firmly laying it on his shoulders. The *Sunday Telegraph* said in bold headlines 'ANDERTON GETS THE BLAME FOR STALKER FIASCO'. The government, it seems, were not pleased, and neither was the Greater Manchester Police Committee, which on 30 August announced its intention to call the Chief Constable to account for his behaviour both in and outside of office. The death of Norman Briggs, and the consequent loss of his individual authority, had again made pertinent the Chief Constable's already discussed relationships with several businessmen, including Kevin Taylor, and his own use of his police car and driver for trips to race meetings and Rugby League games outside the county. At senior level the Force was still very much in turmoil, and the buffetings showed no signs of diminishing. Everything either Mr Anderton or I did was news. When I privately asked the Complaints and Discipline Department to review their procedures for suspending police officers from duty, and called for a report, the newspapers learned of it immediately. When John Thorburn, my number two in the Northern

Ireland enquiry, was moved to number three as Mr Sampson brought in Assistant Chief Constable Donald Shaw of his own Force, the press made much of it.

Pressure was mounting on Anderton to make some sort of public response to the growing complaints over his alleged ineptitude, and he spent the best part of the day of 1 September drafting and redrafting a long press release. Although this mentioned me several times, and clearly I was central to it, I did not know he was preparing it. He did not speak to me about it, or indeed give me a copy of it even after he had issued it to the press. Part of it said, 'I wish to make it absolutely clear that there was no conspiracy attached to the case. As far as I am concerned the investigation into John Stalker was justified, necessary and properly conducted. I am also satisfied that all the action was taken in good faith according to the authorised procedures. I did no more, nor any less than my duty.' I arrived home about 7.00 p.m. that day and throughout the rest of the evening received dozens of calls from the press asking for a response to this very important statement by the Chief Constable. I knew nothing about it until they informed me and I was embarrassed and disappointed that he had not seen fit to tell me of it himself. The press, of course, were quick to spot that I had not known.

I confronted Anderton the next morning, but he looked straight at me without comment. Questions of poor morale in the Force were the subject of much comment, and they were affecting Anderton deeply. He sees himself (not without justification) as a charismatic, natural leader of men with an ability to weld them together for a common purpose. He is very uncomfortable if he suspects his staff are in any way equivocal in their loyalty or support. The local Police Federation representative, Police Constable Ian Westwood, said, 'Mr Stalker's suspension had a devastating effect on morale, but since he has returned to duty things have improved'. Anderton did not like this: he resented the implication that my absence, through his actions, had 'devastated morale'. Nevertheless, I believe that experienced street policemen and detectives knew that steps had been taken by inexperienced supervisors that were premature and ill judged. As the story unfolded the ordinary policeman asked himself one question: 'If the Chief Constable can deal with his own Deputy in this way, what chance do the rest of us have?'

The Committee was in ferment; a split began to appear between those who wished to get to the bottom of the affair and those who wished to forget the mistakes and start again with a clean sheet. Some wanted to question the Chief Constable about his private life or his use of his official car, others did not. The *Guardian* newspaper mentioned an (unnamed) 'senior police officer' as having privately met key members of the Committee to discuss with them both the Chief Constable and me. At seven o'clock in the morning of 3 September I received a strong complaint at home from the Chairman of the Police Authority about this unconstitutional activity by the unnamed officer. That morning I asked the Chief Constable whether this officer was acting officially with the knowledge of Mr Anderton. I knew nothing of his activities and said I did not enjoy reading about this sort of police intervention in political caucuses in the newspapers, or receiving telephone complaints at seven o'clock in the morning. Anderton had clearly been embarrassed by the leak to the *Guardian* and to the Chairman. I asked him if he knew and approved of this officer's behind-the-scenes moves. He did not give me a straight answer, but it was clear that he knew of them. I had not considered taking the Chairman's complaint further in any formal sense, but Anderton clearly thought I had and he said, 'I forbid you to chastise anybody for these meetings. I will speak to Councillor Moffat. Everybody is leaking and I am sick of it.' He was obviously worried about the *Guardian* story, written by Peter Murtagh, and the Chairman's early-morning call to me rather than to him.

Anderton locked himself away in his office for the rest of the day. I think he was concerned that Councillor Moffat and other influential members of the Police Committee were beginning to establish a comfortable working relationship with me. They had displayed an easy acceptance of my return to work, and I was busily making up the ground I had lost in the previous three months. The Police Committee and the Force were settling their differences for the first time since the Spring, and I genuinely felt that things were on the move again. For the second successive day Anderton spent the afternoon preparing another long press release, one that again crucially affected me, but which he issued without either telling me or giving me a copy. His statement seemed not to relate to anything in particular, and certainly nothing that had happened in the last few days; the unexpectedness of it made a particular impact. It referred to his impending installation as President of the Association of Chief Police Officers. This is a national appointment, and usually involves a great deal of absence from the Force both in London and abroad. This unsolicited statement of Mr Anderton's said:

To remove any doubts and false impressions I wish to inform all concerned that the anticipated duties of President of ACPO will make no material difference whatsoever to my role and function as Chief Constable of the Force which will continue to be effectively under my personal direction and control. Such minor adjustments as may be necessary from time to time to accommodate my additional work and responsibilities specifically within the ambit of President will definitely not impinge to any great degree upon the command and structure of the Force and no problems are envisaged in that respect.

In short therefore I shall be still very much in charge. The Chief Constable also seeks to reassure the public that morale in the Force is strong.

It was all rather pompously silly and unnecessary but it indicated, I think, his insecurity and desire to put me firmly in my place and to remind the Police Committee that they should deal with him and not me. Again, sadly, the Force had become a public football in one man's private game. The jokes began immediately — cartoons of Jim 'Bruce Forsyth' Anderton appeared on notice boards. 'I'm in charge,' they said. 'Good game, good game!'

Requests from the press for my response began before I left the office that day. Anderton had issued the release to the world and had passed my door to do so but had not told me. He was attempting to put out the fire of press attention on the Force by pouring petrol on it. I issued a simple press release that said 'It would not be proper for me to comment on what is the Chief Constable's press statement.' Heaven knows what the police Press Office thought about what was going on on the eleventh floor. I went that evening to see the acting Chairman of the Police Committee, Councillor Moffat, and Councillor Tony McCardell. They were amazed and annoyed at the new banner headlines in the evening papers and on television, and at the renewed clamour from the press for a political reaction to Mr Anderton's 'I'm in charge' statement. They asked me what on earth was going on: why had the Chief Constable done this at this time? I could not, of course, answer them; I too had learned of it for the first time in the newspapers. The three of us spoke for over two hours about the Sampson report, and I explained fully the specific security circumstances under which I had used police cars on those few occasions. I gave them details of the very real terrorist threat and they were glad to know of them. If they had allowed me to speak to them earlier, if Mr Sampson had told them the details of matters that in fact he did not inquire into, or if the Police Complaints Authority had done a more thorough job of supervising his investigation, then most of Mr Sampson's mammoth report could have been reduced to a few pages. In two hours I satisfied Moffat and McCardell that the eight charges made against me relating to cars were quite groundless and should never have been pursued to the lengths they were. We parted agreeing not to speak to the newspapers about our meeting. I found both councillors to be mature and perceptive men, with their feet very firmly on the streets of Greater Manchester. I felt deep frustration that I had not been allowed to meet face to face with them and their Police Committee colleagues three months before.

But still the headlines continued. It was quite uncanny how even small events made big news. The following day James Anderton was in London and I was in charge of the Force. I learned, about lunchtime, that a group of senior police officers from Chile was scheduled to make an official visit to a sensitive computerized department of the Force that afternoon. The equipment-suppliers, a commercial concern, were hoping to sell similar equipment to Chile. I asked who had authorized the visit and was told that 'it had been mentioned' to an Assistant Chief Constable who was also in London that day. I reflected on the political row that might ensue if a Labour-controlled Police Committee learned of its police force entertaining senior police representatives of a repressive military dictatorship. Neither the Chief Constable nor I, nor the local politicians, had been told of the visit. I therefore cancelled it. I told the Assistant Chief Constable in charge of community relations of my decision, and he whole-heartedly agreed with it. I had been to Chile two years earlier on an official government visit; I had met their police and had spoken at great length to most of the members of the military government including President Pinochet. I expected my decision to be gladly endorsed by the Chief Constable the following day. In the event he was extremely angry; he said I had made a political issue out of an operational police visit. The politics of Chile were immaterial, he said; they were fellow-policemen on a fact-finding visit and I had treated them discourteously. I disagreed with him, but told him that if he considered I had acted wrongly then the Chilean police party was still in Manchester and I would, if he wished, apologize to them on his behalf and extend the invitation once more for them to visit that day. Did he wish me to do so? He did not know what to do and abruptly dropped the subject; but he did not reverse my decision.

# 7

# *The Sampson Report*

On 6 September 1986 David Leigh of the *Observer* came to
my home and offered the opportunity of reading a copy of the
Sampson report on me that he had obtained. I read it from
cover to cover and made notes before handing it back. I do not
know whence the newspaper obtained it, but I recall that it
was a photocopy. My solicitors had also been handed a copy,
which apparently came from a different source. Even at a
glance I saw that the report was inaccurate in material and
important areas. The cover itself used the words SUBJECT:
ALLEGATIONS OF MISCONDUCT AGAINST DEPUTY
CHIEF CONSTABLE JOHN STALKER. Mr Sampson had
of course always made it absolutely clear that there were no
allegations against me; nevertheless, that was the word he
used on the cover of his report. The document was repetitive
and superficial, but worst of all it contained within it many
selective and damaging arguments about my conduct that I
had never been given the opportunity to answer. It was
imprecise and one-sided and made a number of false
assumptions. It was a report that the writer clearly thought I
would never see, and in my view it was probably the most
subjective file of papers I have ever seen submitted by a senior
police officer.

I was appalled; my first thought was how on earth had this

disjointed, inaccurate and poorly detailed report ever been endorsed by the Police Complaints Authority as having been 'completed to their satisfaction'? It certainly fell a long way below the standard I would accept from even a very junior officer. I paused before I read it again, but on second reading it was even worse. The inaccuracies were more worryingly fundamental. For example, it referred to my 'investigating the deaths of three men in Northern Ireland'. I had from the outset investigated the deaths of *six* men. And this was from the man who was now conducting the Northern Ireland enquiry. I could not believe that Colin Sampson, a man for whom I have had great respect, had signed his name to such a shoddily put-together document. I understood what a Police Committee councillor had meant two weeks earlier when he described it as a 'Mickey Mouse effort': it scampered up culs-de-sac, sniffing and nibbling at rumours before running away from them and squeaking from a distance. It was so seriously and damagingly inaccurate in a number of areas that I would undoubtedly have considered taking action for defamation had the report not been protected by legal privilege. My solicitors informed me that because of the leak, any course of legal action would proceed not against Colin Sampson, who had written it, but against the person who handed it to the *Observer*; I have no idea who he or she may be.

The Sampson report was a hefty document, impressive to look at but containing nothing of real substance. The bulk of it concentrated on building up a picture of Kevin Taylor and people he knew, several of whom had been in trouble with the police in the past, but most of them many years before. It attempted to link him with a group of men known locally as the 'Quality Street Gang' – a jokey name attached to half a dozen criminals who had taken it themselves from a television advertisement for Quality Street confectionery that depicted men in big cars and dark glasses ostentatiously buying chocolates. It had all been many years ago and the group no longer exists — they have moved into legitimate prosperity or bought villas in the sun. Kevin Taylor does know some of them, and he readily admits it; he has bought parcels of inner-city land from them and played cards with them. But I have never met any of them, and I had told Sampson so. The West Yorkshire team had traced and interviewed most of them and they too said they knew Kevin Taylor but did not know me.

Sampson's report emphasized that Kevin Taylor has no convictions, but went on to try to establish him in the eyes of the reader as a man who is a criminal in everything but name. This the report does by stringing together lists of people who knew other people, some of whom had met Kevin Taylor. It reminded me of those trendy board games that can emphatically prove that Joan Collins is linked to the Archbishop of Canterbury, or Terry Wogan to Rasputin. If you do it for long enough, no doubt it could be shown that everyone is linked to everyone else. It just needs time and determination. The report showed without doubt that Kevin Taylor had met a number of people I was glad not to have met, but that is all it showed. It then went on to assert that as a senior policeman I should have made secret and periodic checks on Taylor, and this would have meant regularly using police criminal and intelligence computer records to check not just on him, but on his contacts. All this for a man I met about six times a year. If senior policemen *were* to do that (and it is, after all, illegal to use police records for that purpose) for each of their friends and contacts, they would probably have little time to do anything else.

The report confirmed for me what I already knew: that Mr Sampson had not checked many of the explanations I had given him. He wrongly referred to the interest of terrorist groups in me as not being direct, and to my having brought it to the attention of Mr Anderton in February 1986 instead of the true date of February 1985. This fundamental error meant that my use of police cars was regarded by Mr Sampson as having taken place on dates *before* rather than after my being told of the threat.

One of the report's two most important revelations related to the source of the information whence the poisoned story about me had flowed. In paragraph 396 Sampson says this: 'The person who could be regarded as being principally responsible for the 'allegations' [sic] against Deputy Chief Constable Stalker is now dead. David Burton (alias Bertelstein) was a professional criminal who was a regular informant to the police *and other bodies* [my emphasis]'. Burton was a man who had been actively involved with terrorist groups in fraud and arson in Belfast, and who was well known to the RUC. I have been told by an impeccable police source that he was an informant who worked closely with the RUC. I can only speculate about who the 'other bodies' may be, but it is not unreasonable to assume that they may include the military and MI5. Burton, significantly, began to become important only a week or so after I had started to suspect the existence of the MI5 tape recording of events at the Hayshed and the death of Michael Justin Tighe. I began the task of seeking out the tape in February 1985, and the Sampson report told me that later that same month, and again in March 1985, quite unknown to me or my Northern Ireland team, Burton was interviewed in prison on four occasions by two detective inspectors from a special unit of the Manchester Police. The report does not tell us why he was interviewed, or what prompted police interest in him at that very significant time. Indeed, Mr Sampson specifically refuses (in paragraph 184) to say what is on the tape recording that the two officers made of those four interviews with Burton. It is, he says 'extremely sensitive, and confidentiality is absolutely essential'.

The second jarring surprise was that Mr Anderton's assurance to me of only a few days before, that Kevin Taylor had not been under investigation in October 1985, was contradicted by Mr Sampson, who in paragraph 19 says that a special squad was investigating Kevin Taylor for at least twelve months before that, from mid-1984. The report does not, however, say that Mr Anderton knew of the existence or the activities of his squad before January 1986. I assumed that either Mr Anderton misinformed me in our conversation of a few days earlier or, more likely, he had not known of the activities of a special squad of his officers, reporting to a Detective Chief Superintendent, who, for eighteen months or more, were investigating a friend of his own Deputy Chief Constable.

I was deeply affected and disappointed by the Sampson report. It bore the stamp of a commissioned and rushed work, and it had little cohesiveness or clarity. I understood the pressure that Sampson had been under to complete it quickly — indeed, Rodger Pannone and I had been instrumental in keeping that pressure up — but the way he had approached the issue of the use of police cars had distracted him from undertaking a thorough attempt to show links between Kevin Taylor's friends and me. The finished result was in my view a hugely indigestible chunk of speculative writing that left the reader wondering what he was expected to think. The wheel had turned full circle: the rumours, speculation and gossip mentioned to me by Mr Sampson on 28 May were still no more than that. Mr Sampson, in his final paragraph, had appeared to dodge ultimate responsibility for the mess by suggesting that a tribunal would be the best way to sort it out.

The Police Committee, thankfully, had seen this report for the contrivance it was, even if the Police Complaints Authority had not. I closed the report for the second time with a sense of real foreboding. I hoped that Mr Sampson would tackle the infinitely more complex and important issue of the Hayshed tape in a different and more concise way than he had his investigation into me.

The national papers would not let go of the idea that I should be allowed to resume my work in Northern Ireland. The point they made was a sensible one: the talk of conspiracy to remove me because I was doing 'too good a job' was continuing to cause enormous damage to the RUC and government. The way to scotch that belief would be to return me to Belfast and to the question of the tape. I knew there was absolutely no prospect of that and had said so often, but I stuck to my official statement that 'I regret not being allowed to finish the enquiry. I would go back if I was asked, and I am sure that Mr Sampson will do a thorough and professional job over there.' I believe that even those in the press who doubted the 'conspiracy theory' idea began to wonder what lay behind the decision not to allow me back. There was, after all, no reason not to do so. I knew it, and so did those whose decision it had been to take me off the enquiry, who included Sir Laurence Byford, Her Majesty's Chief Inspector of Constabulary, Sir Philip Myers, Sir John Hermon and James Anderton: a very powerful police quartet.

On 12 September, Mr Anderton was installed as the new President of the Association of Chief Police Officers. This is a most prestigious position, and is deservedly seen as a career pinnacle for a Chief Constable. It is achieved only by eminent police chiefs, and its function is that of spokesman and focal point for the views of the Association. The President, during the year of his tenure, meets regularly with the Home Secretary and his officials and represents the Association at home and abroad at conferences and national events. The installation is a formal affair, traditionally carried out at the ACPO Autumn Conference, which takes place, usually in late September. This is preceded by a big press conference attended by the retiring and the incoming Presidents.

The September 1986 installation and press conference at Preston was attended by just about every newspaper and television and radio station in Great Britain and Ireland, but they wished to ask Mr Anderton only questions about his handling of the issues affecting me. They were not interested in his already well-known views on policing policy and practice. The retiring President, Sir Stanley Bailey, valiantly tried to direct questions to the work of the Association, but the presence of Mr Anderton — who had been uncharacteristically elusive — was too good a chance for the press to miss. He was bombarded with dozens of questions, which he steadfastly refused to answer until eventually he lost some control. Brushing Sir Stanley Bailey aside he said, 'I am not aware of any other comparable case of any enquiry concerning a police officer where any figure central to that enquiry, particularly a Chief Constable such as myself, should be harassed and hounded day after day by the media to answer questions supposedly arising from widespread public concern. I think plainly it is outrageous and no individual, let alone a Chief Constable, should be subjected to that kind of treatment or be expected to respond.' This earnest plea from a powerful and articulate Chief Constable to be treated more sympathetically than anyone else who attends an open press conference fell largely on deaf ears; but very few members of the police, press or public missed the implication that a Chief Constable should somehow be regarded as having greater privileges than other individuals. I did not attend the Preston conference, and I am glad I was not able to do so.

On 12 September 1986, in an exclusive profile, Paul Horrocks of the *Manchester Evening News* revealed Mr Anderton's desire to convert to Catholicism and quoted him as saying that it was the will of God that he be the Chief Constable of Greater Manchester. The Presidency of ACPO, public utterances about divine influence in Anderton's work, and the seemingly never-ending ripples of the Stalker affair, meant that the Greater Manchester Police Force was obviously not going to enjoy any respite from the media spotlight.

A number of good investigative journalists, notably David Leigh and Jonathan Foster of the *Observer* and Peter Murtagh of the *Guardian*, were now going back over the Sampson report and interviewing key figures mentioned in it. They were discovering that many witnesses vehemently denied having said what Mr Sampson reported they had said. Cecil Franks MP described Mr Sampson's interpretation of his statement as 'a travesty of the truth'. Other professional people, including senior policemen, said that what they had been quoted as saying was totally untrue. My fears for the report were being realized by others, quite independently of me. It was indeed a misleading document, and the newspapers were rapidly exposing it as such. Mr Sampson, sensibly, refused to respond, saying it was a matter for the Police Complaints Authority. Mr Roland Moyle of the PCA did not rise to that bait, and also stayed silent.

Mr Anderton returned to his office from the ACPO conference on 16 September and I spoke to him at about 5.00 p.m. that day. I told him that I had seen a copy of the Sampson report. He was shocked and taken completely by surprise. He said, 'You must say nothing. The correctness of your having it is questionable, but if you have it, so be it.' I did not allow too much time for discussion. I told him of a number of serious inaccuracies and stressed that although I could not seek legal redress through the courts I intended to put the record straight with people who needed to know, and to make a record of it. I had begun this process with the acting Chairman of the Police Committee, Councillor Moffatt, and there were a number of similar aspects that now needed to be discussed with him. I mentioned a wholly inaccurate suggestion in the Sampson report, based on an anonymous phone call, that I had wrongfully interfered thirteen years earlier in the prosecution of a theft charge. Mr Sampson had never asked me about this, and had I not read this report I would not have known about it; and yet he speculated on it in his report, leaving the matter unresolved. As it stood there was a strong suspicion that I might have acted unlawfully. Had Sampson done his job and asked me about it, I would have been able to show him that everything had been done absolutely properly and that the case had been heard by a court. I would also have been able to tell him that the reason why he had failed to resolve the matter was that he had been examining the records of the wrong police force and the wrong courts.

Mr Anderton was clearly appalled by this basic and elementary omission by a fellow Chief Constable. He saw, I think, a looming shadow over the credibility of the efforts of the West Yorkshire Police during the past few months. He looked at me and said, I believe honestly and sincerely, 'You cannot allow that to rest as it is. You will have to take it further.' I spoke to him again about the use of cars both in the past and now that I was back at work. His manner towards me was warm, and for the first time in four months I felt an effort on his part to renew the bonds of trust necessary between a Chief Constable and his Deputy. I spoke frankly to him of my confusion about what was now expected of me in my job as Deputy Chief Constable. I told him of my hurt and disappointment that he had not spoken up when Sampson was making a major disciplinary issue out of a handful of journeys in a police car. Mr Anderton said that he had not initiated those investigations, that it had been entirely Mr Sampson's decision. 'Had I been asked,' he said, 'I would have said that permission would have been given to you.' I asked whether by that he meant in answer to a question from Mr Sampson or from a tribunal; but he did not reply. My impression, however, was that he would have cleared me entirely of unauthorized use of cars and would have endorsed my authority to decide to carry a passenger, but only before a tribunal; he had obviously distanced himself from Sampson and the questions Sampson was asking of me. Mr Anderton's answers strengthened my suspicion that the whole episode was a 'time-buying' exercise. A tribunal would have ensured that I remain suspended and ultimately forgotten. At that moment, in September 1986, I had yet to form my conclusions about who stood to benefit most from that. I am now much clearer about it.

We ended our conversation amicably. 'Life should go on as before,' he said. 'We both have to make our judgments.' I told him that I had always made my own judgments, but that the events of the past months had almost crippled me and my family. I was now unsure of what he meant about 'life going on as before'. Did that include attending official functions, going to football matches, retirement functions and so on? What if I accepted a free sausage roll and a cup of tea at Maine Road or Old Trafford football ground? Would Mr Sampson be making the trek to Manchester to resume his investigations into me? I was not being facetious — such things had been seriously questioned by Sampson, who had delved deep into their legitimacy. Until I knew clearly what Mr Anderton approved of, I felt disinclined to take on any official engagements. Mr Anderton said that there was nothing whatsoever wrong with continuing to do any of the things we had done before or had just discussed. 'It would be intolerable if either you or I were prevented from doing so,' he said. I left his office feeling even more bewildered by his silence during those weeks when I had needed his support. He knew the type of investigation being made by Sampson, and had not intervened. He had never, it seemed, wanted me back. But why?

At that time, in September 1986, the Social Democratic Party Conference was taking place in Harrogate, and delegates spent a half-day discussing the Stalker affair. There were calls for my return to Northern Ireland and for a judicial enquiry; the Conference carried the motions without opposition. A Manchester councillor, Chris Muir, who is also a director of Manchester City Football Club, said, 'This must never happen again. The former Chairman of the Police Committee, Norman Briggs, has died from worry and harassment, Mr Stalker has aged ten years and Mr Anderton has lost his "bottle". The sufferers are the people of Manchester.'

Back in Manchester the Police Committee responded at a meeting by calling upon the Home Secretary to ban newspapers from reporting any aspects of disciplinary proceedings against senior police officers until the outcome had been decided. It was a strange move, coming as it did from a Labour-controlled Committee, particularly one that had in the past issued press releases with unseemly haste. It was a gesture, nothing more. To introduce that sort of ban would have meant changing the law so as to do the same for criminal investigations and for all police discipline matters, not only those against senior officers. It would have stifled free debate and discussion. I suspect that the argument had not been fully thought through; in the event, it was rejected many months later by the Home Secretary, Douglas Hurd. That same meeting also saw the farewell of the acting Chairman, Councillor David Moffatt, as he too became a political casualty of the affair. The Committee decided it wanted a fresh start with another Chairman, and Councillor Stephen Murphy, a Lancashire National Union of Mineworkers official, was voted in. The new era was heralded by a decision not to ask Mr Anderton any questions about his off-duty friends or his alleged misuse of his Jaguar police car. More importantly, it decided not to seek any explanation from him about his initial handling of matters affecting me. 'A majority of Labour members want to try and build bridges with the police force and the Stalker affair has detracted from these aims,' said Councillor Murphy. It looked as though a new page had been turned, and I hoped to be allowed to do my job without further fuss. What I found extremely surprising, however, was the attitude of the Police Committee when I asked them to help me resolve some of the effects of their mistakes. Chief among these was my legal bill.

I had made a decision to employ good solicitors, and I will never regret that decision. I believe the precipitate actions of the Police Committee and their use of a lawyer as their spokesman had left me with no alternative but to do likewise after a week of handling matters myself. Their decision to name me in a public statement had provided the ignition for the media explosion that followed, and I felt the Committee should at least contribute to my solicitor's fees. It seemed a fair request because had the Committee decided to refer me to a tribunal rather than return me to work, then *all* my legal bills would have been paid at public expense, even if I had been found guilty and dismissed from the Force. Common justice demanded, it seemed to me, that they should not allow me to be unduly penalized financially because I had been found not guilty at an earlier stage. I did not know what my final bill would be, but I guessed it would be substantial, and I mentioned it to James Anderton. He said, 'I am sure the Committee will take a benevolent view. I shall discuss it with the new Chairman and Mr Rees when you receive your account.' He was seemingly sympathetic, but again he was interposing himself between me and the Committee. It was obvious he did not wish me to speak to them direct or begin to build up any close relationship with them. I told my solicitors of his promising response and hoped that he meant it. I could not face the prospect of another protracted legal wrangle with the Police Committee. I put it to the back of my mind and got on with my job.

Thursday, 18 September, was a significant date: it was exactly twelve months since I had delivered my interim report to Sir John Hermon. Twelve months in which absolutely nothing seemed to have happened in relation to the content of the Hayshed tape. That morning I sent for Assistant Chief

Constable Ralph Lees, the head of the CID. I had not been able to see him since my return to work because he had been on holiday. I suspected that what I had been told in April was untrue, when I had asked him about the formation of a special squad tasked to investigate a policeman. I also wished to check whether it was correct that I was not under investigation in April, as I had been told. I told him that in my view either he or his officers had given the Chief Constable an over-inflated story that had not stood up to scrutiny; that he had made the cardinal error for a detective of rushing in without checking his facts. Burton, the informant, had given him a tissue of lies, and he had believed them. Every rookie detective is told such a story at some time in his life, and it is then that he learns to be sceptical.

Lees reacted very weakly. He seemed genuinely sorry about the course of events and said that none of it was his fault. He blamed it entirely on other officers, and said that the Chief Constable's personal interest in the Taylor case justified his own lack of supervision over it. I asked him whether he knew Burton was an RUC informant — had he even asked? 'No, I didn't,' he said. I asked him whether he had thought to ask me what stage my enquiries were at in Northern Ireland before sending two detectives to see Burton on four occasions. Did it not occur to him that there might have been some connection? He remained silent. I said that I doubted very much whether any enquiries were made about me before everything was passed over to Mr Sampson. 'You are right,' he said. 'Nothing was done, no checks were made until Mr Sampson made them.'

I was now completely satisfied that the decision taken in Scarborough on 19 May 1986 by Sir Laurence Byford, Sir Philip Myers and James Anderton to remove me from the Northern Ireland investigation was made without any real enquiries having been started. Lees confirmed for me that anything of any significance done in relation to Kevin Taylor had happened after I had delivered my Interim Report to Belfast in September 1985, and that I was of no interest until after I had begun to prepare to return to Northern Ireland to interview the Chief Constable and obtain access to the Hayshed tape. Lees said, without being asked, 'I am not part of any conspiracy against you, you know, and I am not a Mason.' Ralph Lees is a man who is uncomfortable as head of CID. He is a good and effective uniformed policeman and administrator, and has done these jobs all his professional life with great distinction; but he has never, not even for a few months, been in the CID. He has not arrested anyone for over a quarter of a century. To be thrust into the job of heading a thousand detectives without even basic detective knowledge was not fair to him, and indeed I had made that point to James Anderton in late 1984 when this move was made. I had become even more concerned when almost immediately he had brought in as his number two a Chief Superintendent, Peter Topping, who was also markedly deficient in senior supervisory CID experience. I knew Peter Topping to be a useful man in many ways, but he was not in my view ready to head the operational arm of such a big CID. The man for that job was John Thorburn, who was working in Northern Ireland with me, and while we were busy in Lurgan and Armagh decisions on CID appointments were made in Manchester that I would have strenuously argued against.

I sent for Chief Superintendent Topping on 26 September. I told him that he had presented an over-inflated story to the Chief Constable, who had acted on it to the extreme detriment of the Force, himself, and me and my family. Topping said, 'I did not. I was only doing my job. I referred everything to Assistant Chief Constable Lees. He did the rest. It was not my fault.' I asked him whether the press reports were true, that since his appointment to the CID, the Drugs Squad and the Fraud Squad had all come to be members of Masonic lodges. I made it clear that I was not being critical — I merely wished to know. He said, 'They are there on ability. I emphatically deny any wrongful influences.' I said to him that I was not suggesting there were any, but that some people might see it as unhealthy. He said, 'I would welcome any scrutiny of their activities. I choose people on their ability — nothing else — and I resent any inference that I do not.' I asked him whether he would always exercise a preference for a fellow-Mason, all other things being equal. Topping replied, 'Yes, I would, and I do: and I see nothing wrong with that. In sensitive departments I need to know I can trust my officers. The ones I have chosen are all there on personal merit. I *know* without doubt I can trust them; others I only think I can trust.' I discussed with him his lack of experience, especially of murder investigation, and he replied, 'I am a good detective. I know I have never conducted a murder enquiry, but that is not an important issue. I could if I wished to. Anyway I have been too busy with the Taylor enquiry to take on that sort of a job.'

I told Topping that I would be paying a fair amount of attention to his department now that I was back, particularly the massive increase in manpower and resources allocated to the Surveillance Squad and Crime Intelligence Departments. I was anxious to satisfy myself that they were acting legally and being properly supervised and directed. The same thing would apply to the Special Branch and other sensitive departments, of all of which I had a great deal of experience. I told him, as I had the Chief Constable, that my interest would be constructive and advisory, but that my experience was now available to be tapped in a way not previously possible because of my absence from the Force. He clearly did not like what he was hearing, but he could do very little about it. Such was the level of paranoia at Police Headquarters at that time that before he left my office he offered to allow me to search him to show he was not equipped with a concealed tape recorder. It had never occurred to me that he might be, and I refused.

The question of the activities of David Burton (alias Bertelstein) as an RUC informer was raised in the House of Commons by Cecil Franks MP, who asked the Home Secretary for a statement. Mr Franks said he 'found it incredible and inconceivable that the connection had not been picked up by Mr Sampson, who had dismissed any Northern Ireland connection. His report is, in many ways, tendentious.' He added his name to those of the Police Committee, Amnesty International, the SDP Conference and many Members of Parliament in calling for a judicial enquiry. A week later the Labour Party Conference also agreed to press for a judicial review, but their requests were refused by the Home Office.

# 8

## *Last Days*

Towards the end of September the legal bill for my defence arrived from the solicitors. It was for £21,980. This represented many hundreds of hours of work by Rodger Pannone and Peter Lakin, often at weekends and deep into the night. The four long and unnecessary trips to Wakefield, and the time spent while Mr Shaw painstakingly recorded every word that was said, in longhand, was a significant factor in the hourly total of the bill. It had been mentioned in Parliament the week before by Cecil Franks that the cost to the ratepayers of the investigation into me would be about £250,000, and the solicitors' fees represented even more expense. As a family we had known that the bill would be substantial, and I had responded to anticipatory press questions by saying, 'Restoring a good name does not come cheaply. I do not know how much the final bill will be, but it will be paid. If necessary I will borrow the money.' I was never more determined about anything in my life. Whatever the costs for the services of Rodger Pannone and Peter Lakin, they were worth it. They had protected our sanity as well as my job and reputation.

I had not mentioned it in any detail to Stella, since she had enough on her plate, but I had secretly resolved to myself that if necessary I would sell our home to pay the bill. We had moved in only twelve months earlier and we had taken out a big mortgage. Most of our spare cash we had used to fit a new kitchen and buy carpets and curtains, and I had only a small amount in the bank, which was earmarked to replace furniture we had had since we were married. I had not discussed the escalating costs with Rodger Pannone: as I have said, there are some things in life that are priceless, and my reputation for honesty was one of them. The solicitors made it clear to me that they would not press me for early payment, but Rodger Pannone felt very strongly that the Police Committee should pay the bill. Like me, he took the view that if a guilty man taken to a tribunal has the right to have his legal bills paid by the Police Committee, then an innocent man dealt with at an earlier stage should be entitled to at least the same treatment. He wrote as much to Roger Rees, and the request was considered by the Police Committee on 9 October 1986. They resolved:

> that no contribution be made towards Mr Stalker's costs;
> that Mr Stalker be advised to contact the Association of Chief Police Officers;
> that a letter be sent to Mr Stalker explaining that the above decision is based on the principle of the case.

I was informed of the Committee's decision by a press reporter in my office at Police Headquarters. I had not seen or spoken to the Chief Constable for two weeks and did not know his view of my predicament. The press headlines were again full of the Stalker affair. The hopes of us all, especially the Police Committee, that the Force be spared more publicity were again in tatters. Their decision was widely reported in newspapers and on television, and for the first time I had seriously to talk to Stella about the distinct possibility that we would have to sell up. The only alternative would be to resign and convert my pension into a lump sum, but I was reluctant to do that after almost thirty years as a policeman, and after the traumas involved in getting my job back. The decision not to pay me anything was due for formal ratification by the full Committee on the afternoon of 17 October. I knew it would almost certainly be a formality, but I asked for permission to speak to them before they finally rubber-stamped it. I had a concern that they were not always fully briefed individually about the options open to them, and of course I was familiar with the police discipline regulations in very fine detail. I was refused permission to speak, as was my solicitor. James Anderton said to me, 'I would prefer you not to attend the Committee at all this afternoon. There will be press embarrassment if you do, and the new Chairman is very anxious to keep away from any more controversy.'

At 1.00 p.m., an hour before the meeting began, Peter Lakin telephoned me with good news. A councillor well known to both of us had rung him to say, 'I have just left the meeting. Tell John Stalker not to worry. It's all settled. The Committee will pay seventy per cent and he will be asked to pay thirty.' I immediately phoned Stella, who was tremendously relieved. Without doubt £6,600 is a lot of money, but it was easier to find than £22,000: it meant the house was safe, and I was very pleased to be able to tell her so. I sat through the afternoon at my desk waiting for news. I got it, as usual, from the press. Mike Unger, the editor of the *Manchester Evening News*, rang me and said that the original decision was to stand. The Police Committee had decided they would pay 'not a penny' towards the bill. I rang Stella, who was waiting by the telephone. 'Not a penny,' I said. 'I'm sorry.' She remained absolutely silent and put down the phone. I went home right away. Stella was devastated; she knew that we had no hope of paying the bill unless I sold the house or left the Force. I had been living with this possibility and had to some extent conditioned myself to it. She had not realized how serious it was until the last few days, however, when the reality had begun to sink in.

I turned on the early evening television news to see the Chairman of the Police Committee, Councillor Stephen Murphy, giving a surprise press conference in which he defended the decision not to contribute to my legal bill by saying that to do so 'would be a dangerous precedent'. He showed in his comments that he had misunderstood, or been misinformed about, the position of the Police Committee in matters such as this, because he went on to say that it would 'open the floodgates for junior ranks to claim their legal bills'. The statutory responsibility of the Police Committee extends only to the Chief Constable, the Deputy Chief Constable and the six Assistant Chief Constables — eight people in all. The remaining members of the Force (about seven thousand) are of no relevance whatsoever to the Police Committee in any disciplinary sense and are in any case fully legally protected by their Staff Associations in disciplinary matters.

Councillor Murphy then strongly criticized me for 'picking the best legal brains in the country' in response only 'to newspapers that don't always tell the truth'. He went on to say, 'If Mr Stalker felt he had to go along and take legal advice because of that, then he is not the kind of person I believe he is.' He defended the decision by blaming deficiencies in the discipline regulations. He was then asked about the unfair anomaly of payment of my fees from the public purse had I been sent to a tribunal. He replied, 'Well, it didn't go to a tribunal. This Authority is not penalizing Mr Stalker. He has to answer for the decision to seek legal advice himself. If a motorist is pulled up for speeding, he doesn't run off and seek legal advice until he receives a summons.' He was uncompromisingly unsympathetic (which of course he was entitled to be), but he had not grasped the essentials of what was at issue. His analogy was plainly naive. Speeding motorists have to be told why they have been stopped, they are not pulled in to the side of the road by a lawyer who then names them publicly, nor are they sent home indefinitely. Councillor Murphy was the third Chairman of the Police Committee to hold his position in six weeks, and his sketchy knowledge of matters was evident. I believe that he felt there had been enough shilly-shallying in months gone by, and was determined to display his new resolve and personal strength of character to his Labour colleagues, who were still very much divided. Quite unequivocally, he said, 'There is no question whatsoever of this Committee giving any further consideration to Mr Stalker's bill. We have made a decision and that decision will stand.'

The original Committee decision had raised some press interest but this major, and quite unexpected, press conference again resulted in renewed national press and television involvement. For a Committee that professed to wish to avoid the media spotlight, its successive chairmen were uncommonly fond of calling press conferences. The trouble was they seemed to expect that this should be the end of the matter. In the real world of radio, newspapers and television it does not, of course, work like that. Frank speaking by Councillor Murphy immediately prompted comment by other pundits, and the newsmen deluged my home once again. We were in turmoil, and it was becoming harder and harder to cope with it. What was it about this case that resulted in me and my family having to hear virtually everything from newsmen? Why on earth had I again not been allowed to speak to the Committee, or at least to be present when they made their awesome decisions affecting my life and that of my family? I could accept the sincerity of their views, but found it impossible to understand why they did not feel it necessary to ask me anything before arriving at them. Of the three chairmen only Councillor Moffat had ever made any effort to contact me before calling press conferences, and now it seemed we were back on the familiar tracks. My immediate job was to begin to ease my family into the stark realization of considering the sale of our house, while at the same time reminding them that if this were indeed to happen then it had all been worth it.

I stayed in all evening, but there was no call from Mr Anderton. Although he had told me not to attend the meeting, he did not tell me the result of it. I received no telephone call from him during the weekend, which I spent handling dozens of callers and visits from pressmen. My wife became ill with the worry of it all, and I stayed home with her on the Monday. I still received no call from Mr Anderton. I went in to work on Tuesday 21 October, to find letters and telephone calls for me pledging financial help. They were from people I did not know, not all of them local, and one of them was for the substantial amount of a thousand pounds. I was at a complete loss to know what to do; the situation was wholly unprecedented. I had not asked anyone for anything and yet already cheques and postal orders were arriving from members of the public.

The same day a police constable telephoned the Chief Constable's secretary and then sent in a letter asking for permission to arrange a collection from the members of the Force to assist me. He said that there was a great deal of support from ordinary policemen on the streets and many of them had expressed a wish to contribute. I discussed these developments with Mr Anderton. They were wonderfully kind and positive gestures, but I could not do anything about them without the Chief Constable's authority. Mr Anderton promised early advice, and said he would speak to Sir Philip Myers and the Home Secretary. In the meantime donations were arriving at Police Headquarters, at my solicitors' office and at the offices of the *Manchester Evening News*. The editor of the *News*, Mike Unger, offered, as an individual, to act as a trustee of the donations so far received, and to use his office to receive the amounts on my behalf until it was decided whether I could accept them. This was an enormous kindness. He opened a holding account that day at a local bank, and an amount in excess of two thousand pounds was paid in.

The axe fell on the fund the following day. Mr Anderton issued a press release aimed at the *Manchester Evening News* spelling out the disciplinary offence that would be committed by me if I accepted any contribution from a member of the public without permission. At that moment, he said, permission had not been granted, but he was seeking advice. His press statement effectively stemmed the flow of donations: members of the public were told in effect that they could place me in renewed trouble if they tried to help. It seemed to me that whatever happened now, even if permission were granted, I could hardly expect the public to respond again. I resigned myself to that which I had always intended, to paying the bill myself by my own efforts. I was not angry at Mr Anderton's intervention, although to the public and my family it seemed to be just another spiteful and petty act. He was, of course, safeguarding his own position as well as mine, and I cannot blame him for that. I still doubt, however, whether he needed to issue a press release: a letter to Mike Unger explaining that donations might have to be returned would have served the same purpose.

The days went by, and then two weeks, without any decision from the Home Office or Sir Philip Myers about whether or not the fund was legally acceptable. On 6 November Mr Anderton told me that the Home Office now had no objections to my receiving public donations, but that the decision of approval was not theirs to give. The Police Committee was the proper authority. Not for the first time I felt like a pinball in a penny arcade. It seemed that for well over two years, in Northern Ireland, in MI5, and now in my own police force and the Home Office, decisions has been constantly delayed, discussed behind closed doors, altered, amended, shaped and then passed to someone else to endorse them. In the meantime the clock had ticked away and the seasons had come and gone. I had not sought any donations from the public or from policemen. I was immensely grateful for the warmth and goodwill such acts demonstrated, but I could neither solicit nor discourage them. Again, I was in the hands of the Police Committee, and Mr Anderton expressed the view that 'the new Chairman will be the stumbling block' because of his desire to put the Stalker affair behind him. I told Mr Anderton that whatever the decision I wished it to be quick and final. My wife was rapidly heading for a breakdown, and he would have to accept much responsibility for that situation because of the way he had handled matters. He was apologetic for the delays and seemed sincere in his wish that the fund be allowed to go ahead, but for my part I was sceptical and would not allow my hopes to rise. The responsibility for paying the solicitor's bill was mine, and I did not intend to look to the public for help. I knew that Rodger Pannone would not press me for immediate settlement, but he and Peter Lakin had worked tremendously hard night and day for many months, and it was right that they should be paid.

The Police Committee considered the matter on 17 November. It seemed a simple enough matter of either giving, or not giving, authority for the fund, but true to form, it proved not to be so simple. They agreed that 'the Deputy Chief Constable can receive donations from individual members of the public, but *such consent is conditional on all such payments being administered by the Association of Chief Police Officers* [my emphasis]'. I had already written to my Staff Association, ACPO — of which, of course, Mr Anderton was the new President — asking for some contribution to my bill. They responded quickly to the proviso imposed by the Police Committee that they should administer the fund, and in a press release they flatly refused either to make any contribution to my bill or to administer any donations from members of the public. They said, 'This is not a matter for

ACPO ... the handling of any donation is entirely a matter for the Greater Manchester Police Authority.' In the same week Mr Douglas Hurd, the Home Secretary, in a private letter to a Conservative Member of Parliament said, 'The Home Office played no part in the enquiry into Mr Stalker and there is no basis on which the Department might pay his costs. I shall consider whether there are any lessons to be learned for future investigations of this type.' A few days earlier, by a savage irony, the Home Office had circulated draft advice to Police Committees and Chief Constables that specifically dealt in great depth with the question of financial assistance to police officers in legal proceedings. Had this been in existence two months earlier I would have been in a much better-protected position. This advice was sent to Mr Anderton on 29 September and he circulated it to his Chief Constable colleagues on 31 October. In paragraph 2, it says quite unequivocally that 'where a Police Committee considers a police officer has acted in good faith in pursuance of his duties, it will normally be proper for them to ensure that he should be given the services of a lawyer and he should not be out of pocket.' In paragraph 3 it goes on to say, 'A police officer seeking financial assistance shall submit a report to his Police Committee. The Committee *should normally give the officer an opportunity to make oral representations to them if he wishes to do so* [my emphasis]'. So, the two points I had unswervingly maintained — firstly that I had throughout acted in good faith and that the turn of events demanded I employ a lawyer, and secondly my request to speak to the Committee — were, from September, recognized by the Home Office as absolutely proper. But it had all come a month too late, and no one had told the Committee because the circular was in draft form. It was eventually published unchanged and is now the criterion for handling matters of this type.

The decision by ACPO and the Home Secretary not to

contribute to my costs came as no surprise. This had always been a matter entirely between the Police Committee and me, but the refusal of ACPO even to administer the fund took everything back to the starting line. It was again a mess, and neither the public, the trustees, nor I knew where we stood. The Police Committee attacked the ACPO decision as 'disgraceful' and 'outrageous', but by now this was of little consequence to me or my family. I was exhausted, and so was Stella. I just could not face going in to work. The return to duty in August had been easy, my relationships within the Force were fine, and I felt no pressures other than those always inherent in such a responsible job. Then the setting up and closing down and setting up again of the legal fund was for the moment, however, one blow too many. I could not sleep, I could not concentrate, and I felt tired and defeated. The family doctor ordered us both to rest for two weeks, which we tried to do. It was the first absence I had taken from my job for reasons of sickness in twenty-six years, and it saddened me to reflect on the causes of it. Rodger Pannone learned of my absence from work, and on 5 December he made a public statement condemning ill-informed comments about my seeking legal advice too soon; he also made it clear that his firm would not be seeking an amount in settlement of their bill if such payment were to oblige me to sell my house. He had recognized the stress we were under and, yet again, his firm had acted swiftly, decisively and compassionately.

The Police Committee now amended their resolution requiring ACPO to administer the fund and gave permission to independent trustees to do so under the supervision of the editor of the *Manchester Evening News*. The public were now free to donate, but many weeks had gone by and the fund was effectively moribund. It stood at about £3,000, almost £19,000 short of the original bill, and donations had stopped. Then the *Observer* newspaper mentioned the matter, very briefly, and the result was unbelievable. Hundreds, and then thousands, of donations came either to me or to the *Manchester Evening News*. I cannot describe the tears I shed inside for the generosity shown by those thousands of people. It was, frankly, the most humbling experience of my whole life to read these letters and cards from people I will never meet, many of them anonymous, enclosing in some cases a postal order or a coin taped inside a Christmas card. The thread that ran through them all was one of sorrow and anger at the manner in which things had been handled, and of sympathy for my wife and parents. This swell of support from ordinary folk — most of them, I am certain, much worse off than me, was simply the most remarkable act of faith I have ever witnessed. I felt unworthy of it, and it should not have happened, but I was powerless to stop it. All I could do was to ask myself why? My belief is that the events of those middle months of 1986 touched some sort of a deep public nerve that neither I nor anyone else will ever fully understand. It had something to do with my investigations in Northern Ireland and the burgeoning public awareness of them, of course. But I believe it had much more to do with the stripping down, in the glare of newspaper and television attention, of a remote and powerful police figure — a Deputy Chief Constable — to an ordinary man with an ordinary family, elderly parents and a mortgage. It was a spontaneous mixture of public comradeship, half-understood anger, disquiet, a sense of injustice and, yes, charity. Within a few weeks of the *Observer*'s mentioning the existence of the fund, it had reached £15,000, most of it in donations of a pound or two. The final figure was reached following a theatre concert organized and performed in February 1987 by showbusiness people in Manchester including several stars from the television series *Coronation Street*. Early in the new year the full amount of £21,980 was reached and the fund was closed with an excess that went to a local children's cancer hospital.

On 3 December I was visited at home by about two dozen

newspaper and television reporters, who all essentially told me the same story. They said that there had been leaks from a very senior source 'on the eleventh floor of Police Headquarters' (the offices of the Chief Constable, Deputy and Assistant Chief Constables, and their support staff) that 'the Deputy Chief Constable is very ill and will not be returning to duty'. At least two of the pressmen had obviously seen my sick-note and knew the name of my doctor. I had handed the note, in a sealed envelope, to Mr Anderton on 24 November, and it was quite apparent that someone had leaked the fact that I was off work to the press and given details from the confidential doctor's note. On 5 December, on my return, I prepared a written complaint about this that I handed to Mr Anderton. He said he would 'sleep on it over the weekend' and would 'probably' fully investigate it 'although it would mean more bad publicity for the Force'. I do not know whether he did investigate it, for he has never mentioned it again. He is normally a thorough policeman, and I must presume that the reason he apparently made no enquiries was indeed to avoid bad publicity.

Relations between the Chief Constable and me were clearly never going to revert to what they had been before 29 May. I had returned to my desk hoping to quickly re-establish a basis for a competent, professional approach to our jobs, but this was now proving impossible. Mr Anderton was secretive where before he had kept me informed of his plans and his thinking. His public face in respect of our relationship was friendly and warm, especially at conferences or when any of the Assistant Chief Constables saw us together, but when we were back in our adjoining offices the curtain was lowered between us. His door remained firmly closed, his telephones diverted, and where before he would wander in, sit down and share problems and ideas, now he did not. He disappeared for days on end without telling me, and I had no way of contacting him without asking his police constable aide or his secretary. I remember on 13 November he physically locked himself in his office for several hours. I could not get to him — no one could. He was in, but would not speak to anyone. His staff said he 'was listening to tapes and must not be disturbed'. I stepped in to chair the daily morning conference of senior officers, but could not explain his absence to them. In the afternoon he had still not emerged, and I kept an appointment for him with a policeman he had arranged to see who was retiring after thirty years. A few days later, on 17 November, I saw him briefly in the morning and he mentioned some minor matters. An hour or so later I wished to speak to him and asked his staff where he was. 'It is all hush hush,' I was told. 'He has gone off to the security services [MI5]. We don't know when he will be back.' The next time I saw him he made absolutely no mention of his visit to MI5.

There were several other incidents that were deeply embarrassing because of my lack of knowledge of his whereabouts. I became quickly aware that some selected police officers were using another door to his office while the one near mine remained closed. When I learned of this I spoke to the officers concerned, who said disingenuously, 'The Chief Constable had sent for me' or 'I presumed he would tell you of our conversation.' On one occasion I asked him what was going on and told him that I felt he was encouraging, or at least not discouraging, a second line of communication that effectively bypassed me and left me unaware of important matters within the Force. I asked him bluntly whether he was trying to isolate me. He replied, 'I shall get my information from wherever it lies. You must do the same.' He was alternately very cold — hostile, even — and welcoming and smiling. He was, in the last few weeks of 1986, a man under extreme stress, and it showed. The tiniest of misfortunes within the Force was met with a towering display of fury that spent itself out as quickly as it took fire. He was a quite different Jim Anderton from the one I thought I knew.

On 11 December he spoke to me briefly before he left to travel to open a conference on AIDS and Hepatitis at the Police Training Centre. He was aglow with excitement, like a child who was anticipating a party. He said that at breakfast that morning he had been moved by the Spirit of God to speak out at the conference against modern immorality, which he felt had resulted in the scourge of AIDS. I asked him how the message had manifested itself, and he answered me in an almost detached, distant manner. He said that he could describe it best by asking me to imagine an invisible finger writing out for him on the breakfast table what the Lord wished him to say. I asked him whether the press would be present at the conference, and he sharply replied, 'I neither know nor care. I shall say what I must say to one man or to a million. I am an instrument of the Lord and I have no choice in these matters.'

Anderton was driven to the conference accompanied by Assistant Chief Constable Paul Whitehouse, and during the journey he scribbled down what he intended to say. He spoke his now-famous words about moral degenerates 'swirling around in a cesspit of their own making' and of 'homosexuals who freely engage in sodomy and other obnoxious practices'. His speech was very widely reported, and the pressure from politicians, press and other groups for him to retract what he had said was immense. He did not do so, and as he publicly said a few days later, 'I was moved by the Spirit of God to say exactly what I did. I felt compelled to speak as I did that day and I will not retract a single word I uttered that morning. I have never felt such peace of mind in my life before. I was completely calm. I was completely contented. I have no regrets at all.' That is exactly how he had seemed to me before he spoke at the conference. He was a man under some spiritual compulsion. Arguments about whether he, as a police chief, should have made such judgments and utterances missed the point. James Anderton can never separate the man from the police chief. He believes that the Lord has given him the authority of his position and the audience it commands *precisely* in order to speak out about issues that concern him as a man.

The Force was in absolute disarray over this. Policemen on the streets became the butt of jokes: huge newspaper posters appeared featuring his bearded face and the words 'HALO, HALO, HALO'. Cartoonists, comedians and raconteurs had struck a rich seam. It was the most newsworthy and bizarre statement made by a British police chief in the thirty years I had been a policeman, and again the Greater Manchester Force was bathed in a media spotlight it desperately needed to be spared. On 12 December, at a Police Carol Service at a city centre church, Anderton met my wife and daughters for the first time since before May. During the service a prayer was offered for my mother's continued recovery from her long illness. We saw him after the proceedings were over, but still he asked no questions of any of us and quite deliberately ignored my wife. By now I certainly did not feel I was part of his long-term plans for the Force.

John Thorburn had by this time left the police force to take a job in the private sector. In February 1986 he had asked for an interview with the Chief Constable to discuss personally with him certain matters within the CID about which he was very unhappy. He was never granted that interview; his report lay in Mr Anderton's in-tray for nine months and was still there in November when John Thorburn walked out for the last time. My Northern Ireland team was not taken back in its entirety to help Mr Sampson complete the job. At least two of its six remaining members were never again to be involved with it. The Home Secretary, Douglas Hurd, in a letter to the Leader of the Labour Party, Neil Kinnock, said, 'Mr Sampson had found no evidence that the police informer (David Burton) had ever acted for the RUC.' This was not the case. Burton, alias Bertelstein, was an RUC informant. The Home

Secretary also said, very obliquely, that he had 'been warned
that any enquiry into the source of the allegations against Mr
Stalker could prejudice the Northern Ireland enquiry now
nearing completion under Mr Sampson.' He explained this
further. 'The Attorney General takes the view that any further
enquiry *at this stage* (my emphasis) could be prejudicial to any
criminal proceedings which might follow from Mr Sampson's
investigations in Northern Ireland. These enquiries, which
have been under way since May 1984, and under the
supervision of Mr Sampson since June 1986, are into
allegations of considerable gravity.'

That letter from the Home Secretary was sent to Mr
Kinnock in October 1986. As I write this in November 1987
there have still been no decisions made, nor has there been any
explanation about how an investigation into the source of
Burton's lies about me could possibly jeopardize prosecutions
against policemen in Northern Ireland. It makes no sense to
say such a thing while at the same time denying any
connection between Burton and Northern Ireland. Of all the
Home Office statements this was by far the most puzzling,
and over twelve months on, it is even more so. What did
Douglas Hurd mean? A few days later the Northern Ireland
Secretary, Mr Tom King, assured Parliament that he would
make a 'statement to the House at the earliest opportunity' on
aspects of Mr Sampson's report concerning the management
of the RUC. Mr King also made it absolutely clear that there
would be no publication either of my interim report or of Mr
Sampson's continuation of it. I had kept abreast of matters
affecting the Northern Ireland investigation from newspapers
in exactly the same way as other members of the public, since
neither Mr Sampson nor his assistant, Mr Shaw, had ever
contacted me regarding any aspect of my Northern Ireland
enquiry.

At the end of October Mr King said that Mr Sampson had
delivered his report on the Hayshed shooting, and the tape

recording of it, to the Director of Public Prosecutions on 23 October 1986. It was, he assured Parliament, complete. Almost two months later, on 15 December, Assistant Chief Constable Shaw made his first contact with me and asked urgently, within forty-eight hours, for my official account of my attempts to obtain the tape and in particular about my series of meetings with Sir John Hermon and MI5 representatives. I wondered how much information about those efforts over eighteen months had been provided to Tom King before he made his October statement in the House of Commons assuring his colleagues that enquiries by Mr Sampson were completed. It certainly did not appear that they had been completed when, seven weeks after that statement, Mr Shaw earnestly asked for my account of events; nor, indeed, three months after that in March 1987, when Mr Shaw came to see me again to discuss the Hayshed tapes. It was a continuing feature of these Parliamentary announcements that they always seemed to me to be premature and hurried despite the certainty of the language invariably used.

On the same day, 15 December, that I was first asked for my official account of the quest for the Hayshed tapes, I spoke several times to Mr Anderton. He was preoccupied and distant; he had just chaired the usual morning conference when matters affecting the Force are discussed around his table. I had been present, as well as three Assistant Chief Constables, including Ralph Lees, head of Crime Investigation and, on the day, in charge also of uniformed operations. The usual crop of overnight incidents and crimes were mentioned, but nothing else. I saw Mr Anderton during the afternoon, and as I left the office to return home that evening he told me he would be in London the following day — 16 December — and would see me the day after that. He did not say where in London he could be contacted. I went home, and in the late evening I received a call from Rob

McLoughlin, a reporter from the Granada Television news team. He asked me for a comment on rumours that the Moors murderess Myra Hindley was about to be returned to the scenes of her crimes amid intense security. I told him I knew nothing of it and said his information was obviously incorrect. I did not comment further; I was entirely satisfied that he was quite wrong. Before he rang off he told me that another police source had indicated that four hundred policemen were to be mustered for a special operation well before dawn. It was, I thought, yet another bizarre press story about the Moors murders. These surfaced regularly, and invariably the latest one was even more unlikely than the last. In the twenty-two years since I had been a member of the original Moors murder investigation team I had grown accustomed to them. Nevertheless, in view of the leaked rumour of a big police operation, I telephoned the Duty Inspector in the Communications Room, who told me he had no knowledge of any such activity. I accepted what he told me and went to bed.

I woke up the next morning to hear the early news bulletins telling me that Myra Hindley was indeed on her way at that very moment from Cookham Wood Prison in Kent to the Saddleworth Moor above Manchester, and that 'over four hundred policemen are believed to be involved in the massive security operation'. I drove to work. There was no note from the Chief Constable, no briefing, no information whatsoever. Lees said that he had discussed it with the Chief Constable, and presumed the latter would have told me. I spent the remainder of the day in interminable phone conversations with the Home Office, other Chief Constables and senior policemen, and local politicians, trying to explain the reasons behind the dramatic move, even though I had no idea what they were. The press were frantic for comment, but were receiving none from the officer in charge of the case, Chief Superintendent Peter Topping. They knew that I was one of the very few remaining police officers who had worked on the original Moors murder investigation, and were looking for a comment. I avoided them all day but drove home to meet hordes of them at my front door.

I can now look back on this with a certain amount of detachment, and I suppose that this was the day I crossed the Rubicon. I sat in my home and reflected on events. I had been in sole operational charge of the Greater Manchester Police on a day of immense importance, the day the Moors murders were reopened after twenty-two years. It was a day of tears for relatives, of massive importance to the people of Manchester, and of enormous press interest. Emotionally, financially, operationally and politically it was a very important milestone in the history of the Force. Four hundred constables and almost every pressman in the country knew about it before I did. James Anderton had seen me leave the building to go home, knowing full well that I did not know and that he would be away from it all the following day, the day I would be in charge of his Police Force. It was, I suppose, the cruellest and most obvious insult it was possible to deliver to a Deputy Chief Constable. Worse still was the downright inefficiency of the decision not to tell me. I suffered very little, except inside; the Greater Manchester Police suffered a great deal from apparent lack of leadership and of information. It was, not to put too fine a point on it, an absolute disaster in terms of public perception, and I, the one man who might have saved it — because of my long and intimate personal knowledge of the case — was obliged to keep quiet.

I got rid of the last of the persistent pressmen late into the evening and talked matters over with my wife and daughters. I waited for a phone call from Anderton, but it did not come. As a family we talked honestly and frankly to each other. We are a close family and care about and respect each other's views. The three of them opened their hearts to me, and the strength of their feelings took my breath away. They were increasingly ashamed of my association with the police service; they wanted me to leave while they still respected me. They had understood my long and painful stand to clear our name and to return to work, but their pride in me was being eaten away by my apparent readiness to work for a Chief Constable in whom they no longer had any confidence. I saw with total clarity that their continued respect for me and the job I love depended entirely on my leaving it. It was not the men and women of the Greater Manchester Police they despised, it was simply the Chief Constable who headed them.

My family's reaction was raw and one-sided, but it was honest. They saw things very clearly from their position, and Stella put it finally to me. She said, 'If you stay, after today, you will be doing it for yourself and to pay the bills. You will not be a policeman because we want you to be.' That said it all. For all our married life I had been a good professional policeman; when Colette was born I had been a Detective Sergeant in the City Centre division, and when Francine was born I had been a Detective Inspector in Salford. We were a police family, and I had always shared my troubles and triumphs with them. They had stoically, and without complaint, put up with two years of my life away in Northern Ireland; they had loved and supported me through eleven weeks of suspension. They had kept me going, as I had them, during the blackest days of our lives, and neither their strength nor their unquestioning belief in me had ever wavered. I now saw tears of frustration and anger. My family were about to turn their backs forever on the second most important aspect of my life: my job. They wanted me to leave, and deep in my heart I knew they were right; but I needed time to think and to decide for myself. Stella, Colette and Francine had done their deciding and had told me what they thought, and I knew they would never mention it again.

I grappled with my thoughts long into the night and looked honestly at myself. I was forty-seven years old and had been a policeman all my working life. I knew that I could sit out the difficulties at work and continue as the Deputy Chief Constable on a high salary. I could begin, and probably in the long term win, a guerrilla war of sniping and scoring against a Chief Constable for whom as a man I had lost respect, although I still recognized his qualities as a policeman. I was well placed to create unease within the Force and to subvert, or even destroy, him if I so decided. I knew, of course, that I was never likely to replace him. His political and professional enemies, both locally and nationally, were already sidling up to me, looking for me to hand them ammunition to fire at him. He was extremely vulnerable because of his long absences from the Force on ACPO and other business. I also knew I had a strong power base within the Force, particularly with the influential middle and senior ranks, who, if I gave the message, would realize that I was intending to remain as number two in the Force for many years to come. Mr Anderton is eight years older than me and had often expressed his intention to retire either when he received a knighthood or in late 1988, at the end of his Past Presidential year. He has been consistent in his openly expressed resolve not to accept a post of Inspector of Constabulary even were it offered. In short, he was still the Chief Constable but his authority was no longer unquestioned, and the shrewder and more ambitious members of the Force recognized this.

The question I had to ask myself was whether I wished to stay. I still had a great deal to offer, and my affection for and commitment to the public and the Force was stronger than it had ever been. They had demonstrated their support for me, and I would perhaps be seen as letting them down if I resigned now. I looked at my financial position; could I afford to leave? I was entitled to a lump sum if I accepted a reduced pension, but that would be eaten entirely away in paying off my mortgage. I thought of what work I might do in the future, after I left, and realized that the world would not be beating a path to the door of a retired policeman with few skills other than those learned in the school of hard knocks. Common sense indicated that I should weather the storm and stay on. But I also knew that my effectiveness and whole-hearted effort as a policeman was dependent on the trust and pride of my family in the police ethos, and that this trust and pride was all but forfeited. I had always been a happy and enthusiastic man, and I feared that sourness or disillusionment would set in if I remained. I could never enjoy being the instrument of division within the police force. The trappings of privilege have never meant a great deal to me; pomp and ceremony, salutes and sycophancy are a seductive mistress for a very senior officer, and they can become addictive. I had always been contemptous of senior policemen who believed that those trappings meant something and who stayed on to enjoy the soft life, and I had no wish to become one of them. The choice was simple; stay and settle for safety, security and probably sourness, or go and try something new. What that might be I had no idea.

I slept on it and went in to work the following day. The pressure was still intense over the renewed Moors search, yet still I knew nothing of the rationale for resuming it at such an inappropriate time of the year. It was mid-December, the moors were bleak, hard and snow-covered, but policemen were digging away up there with their bare hands, and there was rampant rumour and conjecture following the visit of Myra Hindley to the scenes of her infamous crimes. Despite what he had said, the Chief Constable was not at his desk at all that day, nor the following day. I continued to give bland assurances to the many callers about his probable views on Hindley's visit, but the truth was I did not know where he was and he neither told me nor contacted me during those days. On Thursday 18 December he arrived in his office shortly after me at 8.30 a.m. and firmly closed his office door behind him. He did not come in to mention the world-wide interest that the Force had aroused during the three days he had been away, nor did he comment on my handling of it. At 9.30 a.m. he called his customary conference and we discussed relatively minor matters. The overriding reason for the dramatic return to the moors of Myra Hindley and an army of police and pressmen was never mentioned. It was the talking point in probably every house and police station in Manchester. But not at the Chief Constable's conference at Manchester Police Headquarters.

I spoke to Mr Anderton on his own after the other officers had left. He looked defiantly and directly at me, clearly expecting me angrily to raise the matter; but I had already decided not to do so. He knew perfectly well the disarray that the Force had been in for the three days he had been away, and the position in which he had left me. By not mentioning it he had made my decision for me. I told him that I had thought very carefully about it with my family, and had decided to ask the Police Committee to allow me to leave the police force. He looked at me coolly and said, 'I will raise the matter with Mr Rees; I am seeing him this afternoon.' He asked me for no explanations and made no comment. The Police Committee have the absolute right to refuse such a request — indeed, a number of Committees have in the past done so. A policeman of my rank, unlike Chief Superintendents and below, has no automatic right to leave until he is fifty-five years old, which in my case was a further eight years away. I did not know what their reaction might be, especially following the immensely expensive Sampson investigation, their overwhelming decision to return me to work, and the warmth of their support since then. I told Mr Anderton that I hoped for an early decision, whichever way it went, and wished to give three months' notice to leave the Force in March 1987. I expected he would mention it to Mr Rees and that my request would be placed, as is customary, before the next meeting of the Personnel Committee, which was to meet in mid-January

1987. I left his office and did not see him for the rest of the day. As usual since my return, his door remained closed. I drove to London the following day to attend the wedding of my youngest brother, Paul. Neither my mother nor my father was well enough to travel, but my brothers Michael and Tony and I made the trip from different corners of the country. Late in the afternoon I telephoned home to learn that a public announcement had been made of my leaving the Force, and that a press conference had been given by the Chief Constable and the Chairman of the Police Committee. My solicitor and friend, Rodger Pannone, was speaking to hundreds of press callers, who all wished to hear something from me.

I had not expected such a public issue to be made of the affair quite so soon. I had merely made a private request of Mr Anderton to sound out the Chairman informally before taking it further. Apparently Councillor Murphy had immediately and formally placed my request on the agenda for the Committee Meeting that afternoon, and they had given me the necessary clearance to leave the Force, as I had requested, in March 1987. I travelled home that evening and faced yet another big press conference the following day. Questions were asked and I gave truthful, but not complete, answers. I said that my family had asked me to leave and that I was not departing a bitter man. I refused to discuss the renewed police activity on the moors, nor would I talk about my relations with Mr Anderton. The Chairman of the Police Committee, Councillor Stephen Murphy, said to the press, 'I am sad to learn of Mr Stalker's plans to retire. He was able to clear his name after living under a black cloud, and I have looked forward to a long and mutually respectful relationship with someone I consider to be a fine policeman.' James Anderton said, 'I am saddened by Mr Stalker's decision to resign. However, there are many fine officers always available, and I am sure we will find a suitable replacement.'

The story quickly became a political issue, and because of

the speed with which my request had been processed, I was not really as well prepared for the flood of comment as I might have been. Martin Flannery MP, Chairman of the Labour Party's influential Northern Ireland Committee, said, 'It is now increasingly clear that Mr Stalker has been frozen out by an establishment which fears the result of his enquiry into the shoot-to-kill policy in Northern Ireland. Lingering in the background is the government, who fear Mr Stalker's findings as much as they fear the Peter Wright book'. [*Spycatcher,* by Peter Wright, a former MI5 officer, is at the time of writing banned throughout the United Kingdom and the British Commonwealth but has been published in the United States of America].

I had made the right decision; I intuitively knew it, and so did my family. In three months I would leave the police force and enter a new world that had not at that time taken any shape. But that did not matter; what did matter was the cohesion of a close family and my self-respect. I wished to leave the Force quickly, with no more harmful publicity and speculation. For myself I wanted only a Christmas at peace with ourselves, and for my mother's strength to continue to return. The new year would look after itself.

On 20 December 1986, amid a great deal of media attention and comment, the short-lived search of the Moors was called off because of the terrible weather conditions. I do not believe that the search of the Moors should have been reopened in the manner it was. To begin with, it was the wrong time of the year. If Myra Hindley was to be of any help she needed quietly and discreetly to be taken there at the time of year when she and Ian Brady had buried those children and when things looked familiar to her; she needed time for careful reflection. There was even press speculation that a reason for taking her there at that time was to remove public and media attention from the troubles besetting the Force. There was not the slightest chance of success once winter closed in, but nevertheless plans went ahead. As we now know, when the police operation was recommenced after the winter was over the sad remains of a further Moors murder victim, Pauline Reade, were discovered. The police officers involved in that tragic and difficult search deserved congratulations, and I whole-heartedly and sincerely paid my tributes at the time the body was discovered in July 1987; but I still believe that the decision to announce the reinvestigation, in the bitter winter months of 1986, was premature. I was later told by a colleague that I was not asked for my opinion about it at the time because it was known what I would say. Mr Anderton had approved it and no doubt he did not wish to be seen to be in disagreement with me again. The public reaction to the renewed digging was not favourable, indeed it was hostile, and this merely added to the difficulties the Force was experiencing. It was an unfortunate final act in what had been a disastrous year for the Greater Manchester Police.

Interest flared again in Northern Ireland on 20 December as a new political and religious dimension emerged. On the same day as the temporary abandonment of the Moors search, and amid much media speculation and comment, the Catholic Primate of All Ireland, Cardinal Tomas O'Fiaich, said in his Christmas message that Catholics could not be encouraged to join the RUC. 'They still believe', he said, 'that John Stalker had been suspended from duty because of an alleged RUC shoot-to-kill policy towards suspects." The RUC issued a statement expressing resentment at the Cardinal's 'unhelpful, hurtful and unconstructive' remarks.

As a family we had the Christmas we dearly wanted, free from pressures and especially enjoying the quickening return to health and strength of my mother. She had said nothing to me about my decision to leave the police force until after I had made it, but she was clearly relieved when I told her. I had been a policeman since I was a teenager; she had encouraged and helped me throughout, and my father and she had been very proud of me as I climbed the ladder. I thought of so many of my friends, in all walks of life, as well as my senior colleagues, whose parents had not lived to see their success; I have always realized how fortunate I have been. Whatever their pride in their four sons, it is still less than ours in them.

I returned to work to find a thoughtful and welcome letter from Councillor Stephen Murphy thanking me, on behalf of the Police Committee, and placing on record their appreciation of me as an outstanding police officer in the Greater Manchester Force. I was glad to receive it, and it meant a great deal to me.

The new year arrived, and with it an offer of a new job. Phil Redmond, the Chairman of Mersey Television, an independent television company based in Liverpool, offered me the post of General Manager of Brookside Productions Limited, which produces the popular weekly drama series *Brookside* for Channel Four, and I accepted. I was attracted to the new challenge of a world about which I knew very little, and I was impressed by Redmond's business flair. I took very little time in deciding to join him, and I looked forward to my new work.

As 1987 got into its stride I noticed an even greater edginess in Mr Anderton. He was alternately warm and effusive, almost brotherly, and icily cold, abrupt and rude. He withdrew to his office for days on end, or disappeared without telling anyone, except possibly his staff officer. The continuing press speculation about declining morale within the Force, and his evaporating public popularity, which means so much to him, was clearly affecting him. He was at times forgetful, irritable and barely in control of his anger at anyone who criticized or questioned him. Addressing a big and important meeting of senior officers at Police Headquarters on 15 January, he profusely thanked a Chief Superintendent who had made an unsolicitedly statement assuring him, despite press accounts, of the wonderful morale and spirit of the Force. Mr Anderton said, 'I know that that is the case, the people out there [gesturing in the direction of Manchester] are one hundred per cent behind me. It is only a small segment of the press who are not.' I sat next to him at the meeting and reflected on recent articles in practically every newspaper, as well as on the BBC and ITV. His outburst and the speech of the Chief Superintendent were received in virtual silence.

I carried on fully as before in acting as his Deputy, and did not relinquish any of my responsibilities for disciplinary hearings or policy meetings; but it had become an almost impossible task. Running parallel with the domestic and internal questions of police effectiveness (the 1985 crime figures for Greater Manchester had shown a big increase in the crime rate and a fall in the detection rate), outside in the wider world the Stalker affair still burned fiercely away. On 15 January Peter Archer MP, Labour spokesman on Northern Ireland, asked what was happening to my report. The House of Commons should be told, he said, 'otherwise speculation is inevitable that some people in high positions wanted to prevent him investigating it'. Tom King responded by saying that it was important 'to get as much as possible in the public domain as soon as possible'. He ended by saying, not entirely accurately, that 'the whole of Mr Stalker's team continue their work under the direction of Mr Sampson'. Of course, the 'whole team' no longer existed. John Thorburn had retired, and other members of my original group, one of them a Detective Superintendent, had not been involved in the Sampson investigation into the Hayshed tape.

The effects of Mr Anderton's 'cesspit' speech about AIDS sufferers continued to reverberate. Police Committee efforts to discipline him 'for bringing discredit on the police force' were defeated by twenty-one votes to twenty. There was an unashamed air of defiance about him. I have known him for a long time and had seen the signs before. When he is under stress, or political pressure, he plays to the public conscience. I had once heard him say to a Police Committee, 'I now know how Christ must have felt on the Cross', merely because he was being subjected to a fairly forceful line of questioning. The fact is, however, that even people who dislike him will support him if faced with the stark choice between a professionally strong and stubborn police chief and hostile militants of the Left. Policing issues in Manchester, which in the past have cried out for reasoned debate, have too often been reduced to barren arguments of ideology between two 'sides' who would not listen to the other's point of view. There had, in the years between 1981 and 1986, been much energy wastefully spent in this way, and James Anderton's superb handling of the media, through a big and efficient Police Press Department, almost always won the day. He came to believe that public opposition to hard-line Marxist politicians, who unashamedly seek to exercise much tighter controls over the police, represents personal support and affection for him.

On 18 January 1987 James Anderton gave a radio broadcast on a BBC religious affairs programme in which he spoke about his faith and his move from Methodism to Catholicism. In it he said that he believed that 'God speaks through him' and that he was a Prophet of the Lord. His revelations came as no real surprise to me, since he has always privately indicated that he felt the Divine Presence within him; but the timing of it, coming so soon after the AIDS speech controversy, took his senior officers by surprise. My immediate reaction was that he had begun the process of deliberately defying the Police Committee to discipline him. I spoke to him the day afterwards and saw the same light in his eyes I had seen five weeks earlier on the day of his AIDS speech. When he is under stress James Anderton unashamedly, proudly even, turns to religion. He stands alongside his God and looks his enemies in the eyes. This latest broadcast had been a way of reinforcing the sincerity of his remarks about moral degenerates, homosexuals and sodomites. It was an aggressive personal statement of faith. The press, of course, were delighted with it, and the Force was swamped with calls.

I was privately angry about it, because of the avoidable publicity we were once again being subjected to. I was repeatedly asked by the press and politicians for personal comment, but refused to make any. Mr Anderton obviously had at that time a compulsion to share his inner faith with the world, even though it caused awful problems for the Force as a whole. It created a brittle and unhappy atmosphere; policemen and women doing their difficult job on the streets felt that the Chief Constable had let them down. It was they who had to deflect the taunts and insults of street-corner pundits, not the man who had caused them to be made. Senior officers were asking themselves, and me, whether the Chief Constable was ill. The Police Committee called an immediate meeting and agreed to travel to the Home Office later that week with the Chief Constable to discuss what they saw as this latest blow to the morale and standing of the Force. Anderton did not speak to me all week, probably because he knew I was not likely to tell him what he wanted to hear. He again locked his door and diverted his phones, and I saw clear signs of a man at his limit. Those who undoubtedly would have argued with him about the wisdom of what he had done, such as myself and at least two of the Assistant Chief Constables, were not asked for our opinions. It had been a feature of his behaviour for many years that he rarely discussed his controversial speeches with anyone before he made them.

On Wednesday, 21 January, Anderton was scheduled to accompany Her Royal Highness the Duchess of Gloucester on a full day's public visit to Manchester. He came into my office in the morning looking drawn and physically ill. He was obviously not sleeping, and the press presence outside his house and elsewhere was understandably upsetting him. He asked me to undertake his official duties all that day by accompanying the Royal visitor, and he put out a press statement explaining that because of the intense press interest in him he did not wish to embarrass the Duchess of Gloucester and was therefore withdrawing from the visit. If anything, my standing in for him probably created even more press speculation about his health. For me it was a very pleasant occasion. It was to be the last of hundreds of occasions over a period of fifteen years when I had had the privilege of accompanying Royal visitors on their visit to Greater Manchester, and because I had not expected it I enjoyed it all the more.

James Anderton's visit to the Home Office was a huge media event, and he used it to the full to reinforce his message of personal sincerity and genuine religious belief. He refused the offer of being driven directly through the secure gates of the Home Office in Queen Anne's Gate, London, and decided instead to walk through the milling crowd of pressmen and television crews. The result was pandemonium, and it made its impact that evening on the national television news bulletins. The result of the meeting, however, was that a sort of truce was declared, and from then on James Anderton became a different man. His new Chairman, Councillor Murphy, is a moderate Labour politician, and not a 'Marxist' councillor with whom James Anderton could be seen to be in conflict. He is also the first Labour chairman who does not represent a socially deprived inner-city area; his Wigan constituency does not provide the same opportunities for headlines as does, for example, Manchester's Moss Side or Salford.

During mid-January 1987 I did not see the Chief Constable for many days. The story was always the same — his driver or secretary would tell me he was 'in London', but I did not ever hear that directly from him. His staff officer acted as Anderton's intermediary between us. It was all so childish, and he never told me why he was acting in this way. My suspicion is that he saw my return to work as some sort of a personal defeat for him, and that this practice of distancing himself from me was a way of expressing his annoyance.

On 27 January I told Anderton that I had been invited to appear on a BBC Television programme entitled *Open Air* to be produced 'live' on 29 January from Manchester. This programme deals with issues of the day, and the producer had asked me to contribute to a discussion on media coverage of sensitive cases, such as the treatment of rape victims or tragedies like the Manchester air disaster. The discussion was also intended to touch upon press intrusion into private lives. It seemed to me a perfectly suitable programme for the police to contribute to, and I had accepted, having made it clear I would not discuss my own case. Mr Anderton did not make any comment when I told him; he returned to his office and wrote me a hand-written note that said: 'In the light of my lengthy discussions in London, and the need we all recognise to give the Force a period free from media attention, and the risk, however remote, of further controversy, I have to say that if the invitation had been extended to me I would refuse. I suggest you do the same.' Of course I did so and cancelled my acceptance, although I still think the police should have been represented in a debate that was to become even more significant later in the year following the media coverage of the Zeebrugge disaster and the Hungerford shootings.

That note told me a great deal. It told me that James Anderton had been exhorted to curtail his public pronouncements and that he had agreed to keep himself out of the headlines. I know that in years past, as a matter of principle and independence, he would have been very reluctant to accept any such 'practical' advice; but in this instance I am sure he saw the wisdom of what was discussed at the Home Office. I firmly believe that the patience of influential politicians and civil servants was finally exhausted and, as his presidential year of ACPO approached, James Anderton very sensibly read the writing on the wall. He obviously wanted me to leave the Force quietly so that he could put the events of the past year behind him and make a fresh start with his new Committee. I saw the position thus: the Home Office would support Anderton, and the moderate Labour group would keep their more outspoken and militant colleagues off his back, but only if he withdrew from the public arena and kept his opinions to himself. And that is exactly what has happened. The irony of it is that his Presidential year as spokesman for the Association of Chief Police Officers has probably been the quietest ever. The Chief Constable who everyone expected to speak boldly and often, in police-related matters, said virtually nothing for eleven months, and his year of office slipped quietly and anonymously by, until in September he called for the castration of sexual offenders. I believe the police force generally has missed having a robust voice on some important occasions, but there has been undoubted benefit to the seven thousand men and women of the Greater Manchester Police Force.

Kevin Taylor, on the other hand, had not been quiet during this time. Weary and angry at the manner in which his business has been ruined by police investigators who had not yet asked him a single direct question, he obtained evidence of alleged serious police malpractice in obtaining information about me and him in May 1986, information that had led firstly to the raid on his home, and subsequently to the Sampson enquiry. Taylor's wife placed the facts before Bury Magistrates, who issued personal summonses against James Anderton, Chief Superintendent Peter Topping, and Detective Inspector Stephenson for perjury and other serious criminal offences. The Chief Constable appealed to the High Court against the issue of the summonses, and for the moment they are not being proceeded with. For legal reasons I am unable to discuss them further, other than to say that the resultant publicity focused public attention once again on the events involving me that had taken place the previous year.

The calendar moved into March 1987, and I was keenly aware that in two weeks' time I would be leaving the police force. I had had almost three months to reflect on my decision to go, and had not regretted it. I was still a knowledgeable and professional senior policeman, and I still had enthusiasm and love for the job I was doing. I knew that, given different circumstances, I could have continued for many more years as the Deputy Chief Constable of the Force. But not as Deputy to James Anderton. During my service I have worked for bosses who have often been inadequate or ineffective, but there has always been someone above them who possessed the qualities they did not. I could always find a rationalizing argument that compensated for the temporary imposition above me of an over-promoted or inexperienced supervisor; there had always been someone else to admire and respect. Now, as second-in-command of the Force, it was absolutely imperative that I work harmoniously again with James Anderton, and I knew by this time that I could not continue to work with a man who clearly did not want me there. I was working with a hard and inflexible man, whom I could never again rely on or be comfortable with.

There will be many who disagree with this assessment, including several of my friends and senior colleagues, and of course they are entitled to do so. They will say he is a warm and friendly man, compassionate and open in his beliefs, often misunderstood but nevertheless sincere in his Christian values. They may be right. James Anderton is a complex and contradictory personality whose mercurial changes of mood are often difficult to understand. My judgment is mine and mine alone, but it is based on over thirty years of professional and personal contact with him on a very regular, almost daily, basis.

Even the last few days had their surprises. Assistant Chief

Constable Donald Shaw was still seeking to ask me about events at the Hayshed, despite assurances given in Parliament that the matter had been finalized many months before. He asked me whether I knew of, or had traced, a second copy of the Hayshed tape. I told him that I had put all my energies into getting my hands on the first copy but that, yes, I did believe there was at least a second complete copy of the entire events at the Hayshed, including the actual shooting dead of Tighe and the policemen's conversations before and after. I gave him the name of a British Army major based in Germany who I believed had heard it and would know where it might be found. I had no idea whether it was an authorized version or not, and I told Mr Shaw so. That was one of the unanswered questions on my list to be tackled after I had returned to Belfast on 2 June 1986. I was frankly surprised at the length of time the enquiry into the tape still seemed to be taking. Mr Shaw was asking fairly fundamental questions nine months after my removal from the enquiry, and exactly twelve months to the day after the Director of Public Prosecutions for Northern Ireland had given his full authority to me for the RUC, Army and MI5 to tell me all they knew and to hand over the tapes. I had expected no more than a few weeks' work after my return to Belfast in June 1986 before matters could be regarded as being finalized. I now found it hard to imagine why there had been such a long delay in asking me questions about the Army's involvement, an involvement that had been known to some members of my team for over two years. The political pronouncements about delivery of Mr Sampson's report and the urgency and importance of the continued investigations into the deaths at the Hayshed and Lurgan and Mullacreavie Park did not seem to square with the stage the investigation had apparently reached. Mr Sampson had not spoken to me, John Thorburn had left, and yet nothing seemed to have moved on.

At 5.30 p.m. on Monday 2 March, James Anderton came

into my office. He had not spoken to me for almost two weeks. He was holding a letter that he said was from Sir Thomas Hetherington, the then Director of Public Prosecutions for England and Wales. He would not allow me to read it but told me I was being asked urgently to provide a 'statement to support criminal proceedings against your friend Kevin Taylor'. Anderton said that the DPP was seeking evidence to show that Kevin Taylor had used a company credit card for private reasons on a holiday some years before. I asked what the statement needed to contain: was he referring to the American trip we had made together five years earlier? Mr Anderton replied that he was, but said that he personally did not know what essential points were needed in the statement and that he would instruct a senior detective to come to see me 'within the next day or so' to formally record the statement for me. He left the office and I telephoned the detective he had named, to let him know when I was free. He declined to come to my office and said he had been instructed only to deal with me through the Chief Constable. I told him that the Chief Constable wished him to come to see me, and he replied that he would prepare a draft statement that he would submit to the Chief Constable for me to sign. The whole thing was quite ridiculous. We were in the same building, he knew what was needed, I knew what I was competent and willing to say, the Director of Public Prosecutions wished urgently to receive the information, and the Chief Constable had approved it.

I did not make an issue of it and decided to wait for the draft statement to arrive, via Mr Anderton. It came seven days later, on 9 March, four days before I left the police force. It was peppered with significant inaccuracies, the most puzzling and important being, yet again, reference to a 'flight from New York'. I had told Mr Sampson eight months earlier that Mr Taylor and I had not been within fifteen hundred miles of New York and that we had not flown back to the United

Kingdom from there. I had presumed that West Yorkshire police officers had corrected this serious mistake, and yet here it was surfacing again, uncorrected, eight months later. I returned the draft statement to Mr Anderton on 11 March with a note pointing out the errors and asking for them to be put right before I signed it. The matter was not pursued. Mr Anderton did not mention it and an amended statement has never been sent to me for signature. It was a strange affair, and I cannot explain it. Either it was another mistake by Mr Sampson, which, despite my corrections, was passed to the DPP, or else there was confusion involving a different Mr Taylor.

I arrived at the last few days, and all that was left for me to do was to clear my desk and office and quietly leave, which I did on Friday 13 March. I went with Stella to a farewell lunch at Salford Police Station, a place that held some particularly happy memories for me, and returned to my office at Police Headquarters in the middle of the afternoon. The only piece of paper waiting on my desk was a freshly typed 'Job Description' for my successor. I had never received one on my appointment, and I read it with great interest. Among other things, it stated simply and unequivocally that 'An official car and driver may be provided for use on duty within or outside the County of Greater Manchester. Such use would include travelling to and from social events, sporting events or functions as well as ceremonial, civic or other appropriate official duties.' The timing of its arrival on my desk was, I am sure, accidental, but the sad irony was inescapable. At last it was being acknowledged that my use of police cars had been perfectly proper. It was saying I had done nothing wrong. That single sentence, had it been written a few months before, would have saved me many thousands of pounds and would have consigned most of Mr Sampson's huge report to the dustbin. It had come too late for me, of course, but in a perverse way it threw into sharp focus the monumental triviality of it all, and I drew some grim satisfaction from that.

I sat at my empty desk in a bare office that was no longer mine, and I thought about the lifetime I had spent as a Manchester policeman. I felt no different in either enthusiasm or health from the teenager who had launched himself out on his first beat in April 1958. I remembered the colleagues I had worked with and the marvellous people I had met. I was grateful for the privilege of being born a Manchester man and of spending my working life absorbed in and committed to the life of the great City and the region. I knew, deep in my heart, that under the circumstances it was time to go; but that did not make it easier. I recalled, in every detail, my first day as a policeman, and now I was on my last. It is a day that comes to all professionals who have spent a lifetime doing one job; I was no one special, except that in my case it had happened eight years sooner than I had planned. I sat looking out over Manchester for two hours. Mr Anderton was in but his door was closed. It was Friday afternoon, my final day in Police Headquarters, and he knew I would never return. Eventually I said my farewells to my senior colleagues and to my secretary and left my warrant card on my desk. It was 4.30 and I went home. Mr Anderton did not come out of his office. I was no longer a policeman.

# Conclusions

Conclusions. The word carries a weight of certainty. Absolute certainty must elude me in this affair. Nevertheless, I believe that the account I have given in this book gets as close to the 'truth' — whatever that word may mean — as is possible at this moment.

The notion of writing a book about the Stalker affair came later to me than to others, and I have had time to look back over the past three and a half years and to reflect on what happened to me and, more importantly, to my investigation. There are some incontrovertible facts, and perhaps we should look at those first.

It cannot be disputed that in a five-week period in the mid-winter of 1982 six men were shot dead by a specialist squad of police officers in Northern Ireland. The circumstances of those shootings pointed to a police inclination, if not a policy, to shoot suspects dead without warning rather than to arrest them. Coming, as these incidents did, so close together, the suspicion of deliberate assassination was not unreasonable. The later disclosures to the courts of police malpractice and deviousness made an investigation independent of the RUC both desirable and inevitable. In the spring of 1984 I was appointed to head that investigation, and during the next two years, with a small team of Manchester police officers, I undertook the job in a manner that I know could not have been more professional or thorough.

In September 1985 I submitted to the Chief Constable of the RUC a first report that recommended the prosecutions of eleven of his police officers, ranging in rank from constable to Chief Superintendent, for a variety of criminal offences, including conspiracy to pervert the course of justice and perjury. In that report I also asked for access to a secret MI5 tape recording that I believe would have supported further charges against other police officers of perjury and possibly murder and attempted murder. The Chief Constable kept this report for five months before passing it, in February 1986, to the Director of Public Prosecutions, who within a few days gave me the authority I sought to listen to the tape and to carry on with my investigation. I had made no secret of the fact that those enquiries would involve the formal interview of a number of very senior police officers (including the Chief Constable) about the parts they had played in events during and after the shootings. It was well known to Home Office and other government officials, including MI5 officers, that my renewed enquiries would, by law, have involved discussions with the Northern Ireland Police Authority if at any stage I suspected disciplinary offences on the part of those senior officers.

Three days before I was to return to Northern Ireland to recommence my work, on 28 May 1986, I was forever removed from the investigation, and as I write this, well over two years after the date upon which I first delivered my report to Sir John Hermon recommending prosecutions, there has still been no announcement either supporting or rejecting those recommendations. There has been only silence.

In May 1984 when I was appointed to the investigation I was the relatively young Deputy Chief Constable of a major British police force with possibly twenty years remaining before retirement, and with the likelihood of further promotion to the position of Chief Constable, or perhaps further. Less than three years later, at the age of forty-seven, I had left the police force.

Those are facts. But what lies behind them? Firstly, it is important always to remember that my investigation was neither welcomed nor seen as necessary in Northern Ireland police circles. It was regarded by many as a further imposition on an already overburdened and beleaguered police force, and a harmful raking of old embers. The six dead men, including the boy Michael Justin Tighe, were said by the police to be terrorists engaged in war against the Crown, and my endeavours to find out what happened before and at the times of their deaths were resented and resisted in some quarters. In the cruel arena of Northern Ireland what had happened was seen as yesterday's news, and there was no great rush of enthusiasm to help me discover the truth of events that were then close to two years old. Such a period is a lifetime in Northern Ireland, and much had happened; many others, including policemen, had died at the hands of terrorist groups on both sides, and in a certain sense these six deaths were just names on the files. Politically, however, my investigation was important and its progress was carefully watched. The Dublin government saw the activities of the RUC as a crucial subject of debate in the Anglo-Irish talks, and it was seeking reassurances from the British government that there was neither a shoot-to-kill policy nor a cover-up. The confidence in the RUC of the minority Catholic population in the Province lies at the very heart of a successful campaign against the IRA and INLA on both sides of the border, and if real progress is ever to be made the RUC has to be seen as being honest and neutral in its relationships with *all* the people of Northern Ireland. The RUC has tried hard to shed its sectarian image, but the publicity surrounding this investigation was a setback. The shadow of the deaths of these five men, all Catholics and unarmed, and of the boy Michael

Tighe, lay and still lies darkly across many of the community efforts being made by the RUC. I believe that in high political and legal circles my investigation was welcomed, and that even in that bruised and cynical land there were real hopes that it might, in a significant way, prove to be an agent of change in the attitudes of the police and the public towards each other.

The Northern Ireland Office and, no doubt, central government kept themselves informed through Sir Philip Myers of the course of events, and I doubt if there was any great consternation when I first ruffled a few feathers in the RUC. I suppose that my findings of either inefficiency or deliberate ineptitude in the RUC's investigation of the deaths of the five men in the two incidents in Lurgan and Armagh City may have raised an eyebrow or two, but nothing of what I was at that time finding was politically embarrassing.

I do not doubt, however, that my discovery of the existence of the MI5 tape of the killing of Tighe in the Hayshed, and my pursuit of it, created very real anxiety. I was breaking new ground in my demands for access, and anti-terrorist operators within MI5 and the Special Branch were bitterly unhappy about even speaking to me. It is probable that Sir Philip Myers, or indeed the then Northern Ireland Secretary of State, Mr Douglas Hurd, did not even know of the existence of the tape until I began asking for it, because permission for its installation had been given under the general authority of the previous Northern Ireland Secretary, Mr James Prior. I can imagine the earnest discussions that must have taken place about the comparative importance of protecting police and MI5 operational practices and tactics, and my investigation into the death and possible murder of young Tighe.

Government, as we know, often has to take a broad view. I, on the other hand, as an investigator, could take a narrower view. I knew what my objectives were, and with my officers I set out to achieve them openly, deliberately and, I have to say, obstinately.

By the time my interim report was delivered to Sir John Hermon in September 1985 not he, Sir Philip Myers, or my own chief, James Anderton, was in any doubt that I had passed my own personal point of no return. The wording of my report, and my analysis and argument in respect of those eleven police officers, left no room for uncertainty. I unequivocally recommended prosecutions, and backed up those recommendations with hard facts and new evidence. My report also made it absolutely clear that I suspected that other, very senior, officers had certain accusations to answer. In the report I said I would, in due course, be calling for answers from those officers. The interim report went on to outline what I thought was badly wrong with some areas of RUC activity and supervision. I was also not particuarly complimentary about aspects of its management and accountability. Until the delivery of my report in September 1985, my views had only been guessed at. Thereafter they were available to anyone who was allowed to read them.

Let me turn now to events in Manchester, and in particular to my connection with Kevin Taylor. It is claimed in the Sampson report that my friendship with Kevin Taylor became of concern to James Anderton and Sir Philip Myers in June 1984, within a few weeks of my commencing the investigations in Northern Ireland. Sampson says that in June 1984 a remark about Taylor and myself made in Manchester by a businessman to a senior policeman during a game of golf led to the submission of a report by Chief Superintendent Topping to James Anderton, who in turn told Sir Philip Myers. I do not question the existence of Topping's report, but I do not believe that it was seen at that time as having any value. That, I believe, came much later when reasons for removing me from the Northern Ireland investigation were being discussed. Apart from the fact that the policeman (now retired) and the businessman (whom I know quite well) have since emphatically denied to newspaper reporters and to me that they said anything that could remotely be construed as accusatory or sinister, I can see no reason why, if there existed the concern that is now claimed, I was not either asked then about the extent of my friendship with Taylor, or taken from the enquiry before I had had a chance to start it. In June 1984 I had made only one journey to Northern Ireland, merely to meet the Chief Constable and to look at our office and hotel accommodation, and to delay matters then would have caused no inconvenience and would have cleared the air before the enquiry was begun. It is my firm opinion that Topping's report was regarded at that time as dross and that there was no concern whatsoever about my friendship with Kevin Taylor. This became an issue only *after* I had delivered my critical report to Sir John Hermon on 18 September 1985. Indeed, I would go further and say I do not believe that there was any serious interest in Kevin Taylor until around that date. I make these claims for very good reasons: firstly, because on 26 August 1986 James Anderton told me so in my uncompromising conversation with him after I had returned to work; and secondly, for reasons that I have never before publicly disclosed.

During the middle months of 1985 vacancies for two Chief Constables' posts were advertised nationally. In both cases I was personally contacted by Sir Philip Myers and encouraged by him to apply for them. One was at Strathclyde, a large and important region centred on Glasgow and having a police force that is the biggest in the United Kingdom outside of London. With almost eight thousand police officers and three thousand support staff, it is larger than either of the two biggest English provincial forces, Greater Manchester and West Midlands. At Sir Philip Myers' suggestion I sent to Glasgow for the application forms, and filled them out. This vacancy in Strathclyde Police occurred at the very height of my efforts to obtain the tape of the Hayshed shooting, my clashes with Sir John Hermon and my visits to MI5. I had been a Deputy Chief Constable for not much more than a year, and this apparent Home Office support for my application came as a surprise, since normally a two-year stint as Deputy Chief Constable is insisted upon before appointment to Chief Constable. The thought crossed my mind that the sudden possibility of my becoming a Chief Constable so soon might not be entirely unconnected with the stage my investigations had reached in Belfast. I have since reflected what the outcome might have been had I called a truce with the RUC Special Branch and ceased my efforts to obtain the tape. I think there might have been an oblique message implicit in the suggestion that I try for this job. Whether that is so or not, in the event, I did not post the application. I was flattered, since Strathclyde is a fine police force, but I felt vaguely uneasy about taking such a job during a demanding investigation that would prevent me from doing it properly, and after family discussions I decided not to look for a move to Scotland at that particular time.

Within a few weeks, in the summer of 1985, I had conceded temporary defeat in my efforts to obtain the tape, and I had seen that the Chief Constable's post at Bedfordshire was about to become vacant. I discussed my intended application with Sir Philip Myers and James Anderton. They were both supportive, and I went ahead with my application with their full knowledge and approval; indeed, James Anderton agreed to be nominated as one of the two professional and character referees necessary in high-level applications such as this. In the event, the job went to a local man — Alan Dyer, who was then Deputy Chief Constable of Bedfordshire — a man I know and respect. Nevertheless, the encouragement and support I received from both Sir Philip Myers and James Anderton to apply for these two important Chief Constable posts is quite irreconcilable with the claim made by Sampson that I had been under a cloud for over twelve months and that both of them were worried and anxious about my friendship with Kevin Taylor. I do not believe that either would ever allow himself to be part of a process that could place a tainted or suspected man in the office of Chief Constable, whether of Strathclyde, Bedfordshire or anywhere else. The idea is quite unthinkable. Neither would I ascribe any other motive to them connected with my Northern Ireland enquiry. While I had verbally discussed my concerns over the RUC with both of them, I had not at that stage begun to draft my report, and neither of them knew the results of my findings or the strength of my eventual recommendations.

These overt acts and friendly approaches by two of the men involved only a few months later in my removal from duty convince me more than anything else that they had at that time (mid-1985) absolutely no reason to believe that I was not a suitable person to become a Chief Constable. In my view, serious efforts to find reasons to take me out of Northern Ireland did not begin until some time after September 1985, when it became known what my report contained and what my intentions were in respect of the Chief Constable of the RUC. Furthermore, whatever information the RUC informant, David Burton (Bertelstein), had provided to the police in February and March 1985, no misgivings about my becoming a Chief Constable were communicated to me by either Sir Philip Myers or James Anderton. My friendship with Kevin Taylor was very well known to both of them. This suggests to me that he was not at that time seen as any impediment to my advancement or as a man with whom a prospective Chief Constable should not associate.

Within a few weeks, however — by September 1985 — all that had changed. Kevin Taylor found himself the subject of a concerted police investigation, an investigation that has since then been carried on secretly and unremittingly, involving,

Taylor claims, camera surveillance and telephone intercepts at his home and office. It has resulted in his near-ruin. At fifty-five years of age, without a criminal conviction of any kind, he has been broken in business if not in spirit, his money gone and his life left in tatters. I must, of course, stand aside. It has been a cruel and unreal spectacle, and I feel immense sorrow for him and his family. I believe that the investigation into Kevin Taylor was — is — a means to an end and that efforts to discredit him have been dragged out for as long as possible. The enquiry into him runs parallel with the Northern Ireland investigation. I cannot accept, based on my own lifetime's experience, that such an investigation should take so long. In the two and a half years that police investigators say they have been looking into his business, his bank accounts and his life, international terrorists and mass murderers have been investigated, tried, convicted and imprisoned. Kevin Taylor's case drags on.

Taylor's experience is typical of so much associated with this bizarre story. It has been characterized by delay and hindrance. There was a two-year delay in calling for an initial independent investigation into the killing by police of five unarmed men and a boy; there was delay by Special Branch in telling RUC investigators and the courts the truth; this was followed by prevarication and obstruction for a further two years in refusing me access to the MI5 tape, and then delay in sending my report to the man who had urgently called for it, the Northern Ireland Director of Public Prosecutions. There was delay in telling me of his decision; and delay in allowing me to resume my investigation. Later, in May and June 1986, it was many weeks before I was told of the accusations against me; now, as I write, eighteen months after Colin Sampson took over my investigation, there is still absolute silence about its outcome. Indeed, I do not know for sure whether the report has been delivered to the RUC. Over five years have passed since six men were shot dead by police, and inquests have still not taken place — a legal process that should take place within a few weeks of a death in order to discover its cause. The only thing that can preclude an inquest is a criminal charge, and none has so far been brought.

I find all this in some sense quite incredible and in another sense quite understandable. In Northern Ireland, time has a different rhythm. It can govern political as well as physical survival, and is traded and exploited in ways that are incomprehensible to those of us who live on the mainland. My investigation, and the haste with which my team and I pursued it, threatened a delicate balance. We went to Belfast, Lurgan and Armagh unburdened by old loyalties, debts or interests. We wished to act as quickly and productively as we could, and I now realize how little we appreciated that what we were doing was disconcerting and disturbing to the people who live and operate there. They, of course, have seen it all before. They have witnessed the brisk arrival in the Province of bureaucrats, military personnel and other strangers from the mainland who all think they have the answers to intractable questions, and they have learned to smile patiently while the latest pioneer attempted to re-invent the Ulster wheel. They know, with the perfect wisdom of those who have lived through eighteen years of bombs and atrocities, that things, if they change at all, change only slowly, and they look with well-concealed contempt upon those who think they can set the pace. I was no doubt seen as a mainland careerist who did not comprehend their world, and an important part of the RUC set out to *make* me understand that in Northern Ireland the survival and strength of the police is paramount. If the police fail, then government fails. There was nothing in their attitude towards me or my team that was personal; I doubt if it would have mattered who we were. It was a demonstration to us that life in the Province will — indeed, must — go on in its time-honoured way.

Sir John Hermon is a powerful and confident Chief

Constable who obstructed my efforts to obtain the Hayshed
tape or transcript because he felt that to agree to my demands
without a fight would constitute surrender on his part and
would jeopardize the greater good — viz. the safeguarding of
the Province from terrorism. The struggle between him and
me was not just one between two equally determined men, it
was between conflicting philosophies: of balancing broad
responsibilities in an imperfect world, and of pursuing truth
*because* it is an imperfect world. I lost the battle. I have no
anger at losing — in truth I realize I tilted at one powerful
windmill too many — but I am entitled to feel sad about it
because in the final analysis I believe both Sir John Hermon
and I have the long-term interests of the RUC and the future of
policing in Northern Ireland at heart. It should never have
been a battle, although I respect, if not admire, the way in
which Sir John Hermon took the fight to me. He protected the
Force and himself from intrusion by me into its anti-terrorist
efforts and practices, and he succeeded. I believe he was
wrong to do so and that co-operation with me at the time I
asked for it would have served those admirable aims much
better. But having made what I still believe was a sadly short-
sighted decision, he carried it out in a skilful manner. The
truth is that I was expendable; he was not.

The decision that resulted in my removal was, I think, a
political one, based on the coming together of common
interests that were threatened by what, in June 1986, I was
about to do. In September 1985, and in the five months that
followed, my interim report was read with anger and fear at
senior levels within the RUC. I have been told that there was
outrage at my recommendations that eleven policemen be
prosecuted for matters that were then three years old. The
report was not merely critical of the RUC. It went further, and
its contents did not reflect well on the Home Office
Inspectorate. Procedures and processes within some sections
of the Force were in a sorry state. Dangerous practices,

slackness, loose supervision and fundamental inefficiency, all of which should have been discovered long before I found them, remained unnoticed. It was not a happy story.

In March 1986, Sir Philip Myers obtained from me a clandestine copy of my report, and the reading of it at his offices in Colwyn Bay must have had the effect of a cold douche. Its contents did not merely threaten the stability and reputation of the RUC, they raised disturbing questions about the effectiveness of the political controls and supervision exercised over it. In March 1986 my interim report was seen for the first time as much more than just the result of a criminal investigation; it had become a very damaging political document. Until then only policemen had seen it, but now it was on the desks of lawyers and government officials in Belfast and London. There followed a month of absolute silence, and then, in April 1986, I made the first moves in my renewed investigation by going to Belfast for an appointment with Sir John Hermon, an appointment he did not keep.

The question of the existence or content of the Hayshed tape had by this time become secondary, in my view, to the action I intended to take when I next returned regarding the very senior officers of the Force. My message to Sir Philip Myers, that I would soon seek to discuss the disciplinary implications of their behaviour, must have created enormous consternation. Such a move could have presented the Northern Ireland Office and the Northern Ireland Police Authority with a grave problem: that of deciding whether or not to support me should I request suspension and removal from duty of one or more of those officers. The risk of allowing me even to make such a request must have been too great, and I believe that in April 1986 a government decision was made to end my involvement in the enquiry. A decision of this importance I feel sure would be unlikely to have been made at anything less than the highest levels. The advantages of my report were now outweighed by the disadvantages, and I had in short become an embarrassment.

The implementation of the decision had to be rapid, and a plausible reason had to be found. For once, time was not on the side of the RUC, since I was preparing to return to Belfast. Also, the month of July was looming, and with it the testing Protestant 'marching season', when Ulster Loyalists in their tens of thousands take to the streets in powerful and challenging displays of their solidarity and strength. Tension was building up as early as April, and the RUC were already making plans to deal with massive Loyalist marches, flags flying and drums beating, through the exclusively Catholic areas of Portadown and Belfast. It is not an overstatement to say that the Anglo-Irish negotiations hung at that time by a thread — and the main strand in that thread was the willingness or otherwise of the RUC to crush Loyalist provocation and to ban or divert their marches through sensitive Catholic areas. Dublin — and America — watched carefully, and the Catholic community in the North sensed that this was a very special year; half-hearted efforts on the part of the RUC, or apparent acquiescence to Loyalist demands, would have resulted in violent counter-attacks and political upheaval. The Chief Constable stood firm, however: resolute and courageous decisions to divert historically important Protestant marches were made. A good deal of violence occurred between the police and Loyalist marchers, and many policemen were injured, threatened and even driven from their homes for helping to enforce the bans; but the overall result in that summer of 1986 was an honest success for the RUC and personal triumph for Sir John Hermon and Mr Tom King. Police action had relieved pressure on the Anglo-Irish talks and the tension was dramatically reduced. The Province breathed again after a summer of desperate anxiety.

Had I been allowed to continue in the way I had intended, the story might have been very different. I would have returned to Belfast on 2 June 1986 and, while my team under Chief Superintendent John Thorburn sought out the truth of the existence or otherwise of the Hayshed tape, I would have made early preparations to interview the Chief Constable and other very senior officers. After that, based on the hard information I already had, I would almost certainly have discussed and considered a formal statutory disciplinary process that would have involved officials of the Northern Ireland Police Authority and the Home Office. Sir Philip Myers would, without doubt, have been drawn into the matter. Once commenced, this procedure is very slow; but more importantly, it cannot be kept secret. By the end of June the engine of discipline could have been in motion. The impact on plans for policing the July marches, on police and Army anti-terrorist efforts, and on the Anglo-Irish talks would have been shattering. The winners in the short term would have been the terrorist groups on both sides, who would undoubtedly have exploited to the full the collapsed morale of the Force. Alongside that, was my investigation, or indeed my reputation, so very important?

By instinct and training I am a policeman. I have dealt in facts and evidence all my life, and I am satisfied only when I can place the final piece in the jigsaw of my case. Sometimes, as then, this is not possible, and I must look at what I *have* managed to fit together. As I have said, this story cannot be truly complete — not unless someone breaks ranks and emerges with the missing pieces. But an uncompleted jigsaw may show the outline of the missing pieces. In this story, the outlines of some of the players are present, but I do not know who they are. I have probably never met them, but the importance of what I was doing in Northern Ireland in 1985 and 1986 would mean that they paid close attention to me. I fully expected that to be the case, and looking back I am not in the least surprised at the action that was taken. I am astonished only by the amateurishness of it.

I will never know what was said in Whitehall and in Belfast during March and April 1986; but I am almost certain that Sir John Hermon did not keep his appointment with me on 30 April 1986 because he had been asked not to do so. I do not believe that he knew at that stage why he was to avoid me. I am convinced that the raid, ten days later, on Kevin Taylor's house (on 9 May 1986) was a trawling expedition to try to obtain evidence against him that would, because of his friendship with me, provide grounds for further delaying my return to Northern Ireland. John Thorburn and I had left some broken bones behind us after our visit to the Special Branch in Belfast on 30 April. I do not doubt now that there had been, for some time, a gently simmering interest in Kevin Taylor on the part of the Greater Manchester Police that was brought to the boil only after the contents of my interim report became known in late 1985 and early 1986. It was then that the Taylor investigation suddenly became even more intense, and this intensity increased during the spring of 1986 as I prepared to recommence my work in Northern Ireland. I was drawn into it when, on 9 May 1986, Taylor's house was searched under a warrant for suspected fraud. This warrant was used to remove, among other things, half a dozen photographs of my wife and me talking to people at a party given five years before. Those innocuous photographs then became the basis upon which a secret decision was made in Scarborough, Yorkshire, on 19 May by Sir Lawrence Byford, Sir Philip Myers and James Anderton to commence a disciplinary investigation into me and to take me forever away from Northern Ireland. Ostensibly these men were gathered there to attend a Police Federation Annual Conference. This meeting was referred to by Sampson in paragraphs 28 and 29 of his report, in which he confirms the presence of Byford and Anderton, though not that of Myers. I have independent corroboration, however, of the fact that Myers was also present.

By comparison with the depth and extent of my investigation, the pretexts used for my removal were flimsy. I cannot impute mischief or malevolence to anyone, but nevertheless I believe, as do many members of the public, that I was hurriedly removed because I was on the threshold of causing a major police scandal and political row that would have resulted in several resignations and general mayhem.

Mr Anderton's handing me an entirely unnecessary file of papers outside the Moss Nook Restaurant in Manchester in the knowledge that within a few hours I was to be removed from duty was both bizarre and inexplicable; but then so was much of his subsequent behaviour after my return to work. What I can say is that he always seemed to me to be more sympathetic and understanding of the problems of policing in Northern Ireland than of the difficulties experienced over many months by his own police officers who were attempting to investigate serious matters there. He would, I know, have welcomed an invitation to become the Chief Constable of the RUC at some time in his career, and at that time, two or three years ago, it was a matter he mentioned often.

Colin Sampson, although present at those closed discussions, did not in my opinion take part in any real sense in the decision to remove me. It seems to me that he was edged into the untenable position of having to take on my almost completed and supposedly urgent RUC enquiry, and at exactly the same time to commence an investigation into me that was based on little or no foundation, without benefit of either statements or evidence. Whether this was a very clever or a supremely stupid move on the part of the Home Office and the Police Complaints Authority I have never quite concluded, but publicly it was certainly seen as the latter. Mr Sampson put together a report that made recommendations in respect of me that were to be ultimately rejected. I am sure he would approach it all very differently if he could turn back the clock to May 1986.

I have tried hard in a personal sense to heal my own wounds, and any scar traces that do remain are there because of the lasting pain that was caused to Stella, my daughters and my parents, rather than to me. I do not seek martyrdom. I have to say that in a peculiar way I have drawn some consolation from my belief that I am just another casualty of the political situation in Northern Ireland. This is not the first time that honourable men have, for short-term gains, made dishonourable decisions. I was a policeman for too long to expect life to be fair, and I am honest enough to admit to myself that I pushed powerful people and institutions rather harder than a more sensible man might have done. To that extent I should have expected, if not completely accepted, the events that subsequently took place. For my part I can rest easily in the knowledge that I tried, with the sterling help of John Thorburn, to do an honest and professional job of work. That knowledge is shared also with members of my team, some of whom will join the next generation of senior officers; I hope they learned valuable lessons from their two years in Northern Ireland with me.

I believe that what I said in my interim report was, in its own way, important, and I know that although it will never be admitted, many of the recommendations I made for change in the RUC have already been implemented. On 16 July 1987 the *Guardian* announced that the government had ordered an 'immediate investigation' into the way the RUC controls its undercover squads. The report referred to a letter of the previous day from Mr Tom King, the Secretary of State for Northern Ireland, to a Conservative MP, which said, 'It has been agreed that certain matters of organisation should be more fully explored by way of a special investigation by Her Majesty's Chief Inspector of Constabulary'. (At the time of writing this is Mr Stanley Barratt, who was appointed in succession to Sir Lawrence Byford.) The Chief Constable, Sir John Hermon, told the *Guardian* that he 'welcomed the enquiry'. This brief ministerial letter, couched in discreet terms, in effect says that lessons have been learned, matters are being put right, and there is now no need for Parliamentary concern over the supervision of RUC undercover squads. It is, as I see it, a final acknowledgement that the entire matter, in organizational terms, is over. In November 1987 the RUC issued an official Code of Conduct that was designed to govern relations between the Force and the people of Northern Ireland.

The human questions remain, however. Perhaps one day Mr and Mrs Tighe will learn exactly how and why their seventeen-year-old son died in a hail of police bullets.

As I write these concluding paragraphs I realize how close I am to the end of a book that I felt needed to be written, and I am aware of the many questions that remain unanswered. The fact that there have been no prosecutions resulting from the events in Northern Ireland in the winter of 1982 makes it impossible to reach any conclusions about the attitude of the authorities towards them. One might ask what was to be gained by replacing me, a Deputy Chief Constable, with a senior Chief Constable at the head of most of my own Manchester team. I think the political danger of my investigation's having an adverse effect on the policing of Protestant marches must be taken into account here. Delay was vital at that moment. The eighteen-month period that has elapsed since Mr Sampson took over now seems to indicate that he has decided that suspensions or disciplinary action against senior officers was not justifiable. I believe that the objective of my removal has now been met: time has been bought, individual policemen and politicians have survived, and with them the essential life of the Province. Even if prosecutions were now to be brought against some or all of those eleven policemen, they would not have the dramatic impact they would have had when I first found evidence for them over three years ago. Five years after the events themselves, the reasons for bringing charges have become obscured, and witnesses are not as willing or available as they once were. To be absolutely blunt, this case is now, in November 1987, quite stale, and it could reasonably be argued that because of the passage of time and the diminishing quality of the evidence, the public interest does not now demand prosecutions. That would be a perfectly proper legal and moral stance to take. In the context of Northern Ireland it would also be an eminently sensible one. It also illustrates very well what I mean about time being a priceless commodity.

Other questions nag away, and irritate all the more because I know they will never be answered. They are questions that have recurred during the fifteen months since the Manchester Police returned me to work, and they crop up regularly in conversations with people who have followed the switchback course of the Stalker affair. Why, they say to me, was the decision made to take me out of Northern Ireland *before* any investigation was begun into my alleged breaches of police discipline? Why, if the reason for my removal was not in fact to take me from Northern Ireland, was I not allowed to return to the investigation when I went back to duty? And finally, why, despite the often expressed urgency of the matter, is there still complete silence about the investigation eighteen months after I was relieved of it? These are valid questions, and I have tried to look for answers. In doing so I have drawn my own conclusions, and I must leave readers of this book to draw theirs.

# Afterword

## A New Life

I have worked hard at putting the events of the final year of my police career behind me. After I left the force I spent four rewarding months as General Manager of the Channel Four television series *Brookside* before leaving to begin writing this book and, subsequently, to commence a short-term contract with BBC Television. My exposure to the wholly new world of television production was very stimulating. The demands of making a twice-weekly and highly regarded television drama series left no time for looking back. The Chairman of the company, Phil Redmond, pretty well left me to get on with it, and I surprised myself by the quick and easy way in which I took to the people and the process, and by the positive manner in which they seemed to take to me. I enjoyed my stay at Brookside, and given different circumstances I would have been happy to be there still; but I had not fully reckoned with the continuing public interest in the Stalker affair and in me as a man.

I thought it would soon come to an end, at least until there were developments in Northern Ireland. But interest remained and the letters continued to arrive. It has become a feature of my life that people recognize me in the street and in shops and restaurants, and I have now accepted that, at least for the moment, I am public property. This interest is not by any means confined to the Manchester area, and I am increasingly accepting invitations from around the UK and abroad to address meetings, dinners, seminars and lectures to talk not just about policing but also about other matters. While at Brookside I began writing on a free-lance basis for a number of newspapers, notably the London *Evening Standard* and the *Daily Express,* and in September 1987 I joined the National Union of Journalists. These demands, together with occasional broadcasting opportunities, were always likely to conflict with my full-time Brookside job. Eventually the decision was made when I decided to write this book. Phil Redmond, himself a writer, understood the position, and I left the company sadly, but on good terms.

Since then, for the first time in my life, I have worked outside an organized environment, writing, travelling and having time to think about the future. Slowly I have been able to shed the constraints of expressed thought and opinion that are so rightly placed on a serving police officer, and I have come to regard myself as a writer/journalist who used to be a policeman rather than an ex-policeman who dabbles in writing. Words are now my living. As the months go by I feel increasingly free to comment on the work of my former colleagues. I have resumed the life of an ordinary member of the public, but with a much more informed and objective eye. The attitudes of former senior colleagues towards me vary. Most of them, I believe, regard me as a professional and honest commentator on the police world and as a man who left the police force because it was the right thing to do. Others, but only a few in number, clearly see me as a threat — especially when I am wearing a press badge.

A question often asked of me is 'Do you miss the police force?' Yes, I do. I miss above all the comradeship of shrewd and resourceful people with whom I have spent long days and nights, and I miss the constantly demanding and fascinating work. I have lost not a fraction of my respect for the great majority of policemen and policewomen, who do their straightforward and honest best in an increasingly violent and difficult environment. If I could live my life over again I would still gladly join them. I am proud to have been invited to remain a member of the Association of Chief Police Officers after I left the force.

I have very few regrets, but one of them is that my enthusiasm and knowledge are no longer of any practical use to the police. I am conscious of the enormously expensive training and preparation that has been invested in me in recent years. I am sad that at forty-seven years of age I felt obliged to leave the force, and that the public were not given a full return on that investment.

In these final paragraphs I shall try to acknowledge the help I was given in writing this book. The impetus to do so was slow in coming, and I needed encouragement to sit down and actually begin it. This was provided by my immediate family and two or three close friends, and I am deeply grateful to them for their confidence in me.

I now count among my friends a number of people I had not even met when, in May 1986, this affair first became public; but the bonds are now strong and whatever happens in the future those people will have played an important part in my life. Several of them are members of the press and newsgathering agencies who would not thank me for naming them, but they know who they are and I would like to pay tribute to their courtesy and professionalism.

I wish to acknowledge by name only a handful of people and to thank them for the trust and faith they showed in me. Firstly, Rodger Pannone and Peter Lakin for their untiring commitment and skills; Mike Unger for his many kindnesses and for administering the legal fund, acts that he never allowed to get in the way of his first duty as a newspaper editor; Suzie Mathis for the positiveness of her friendship;

John Thorburn and my team for their loyalty; Charles Horan for his example as a detective; Mildred Marney for her superb typing of the manuscript; and Derek Johns of Harrap for his help and advice.

Finally I would like to mention the fifteen thousand or more members of the public who wrote from this country, Ireland and abroad, either to me or to the *Manchester Evening News*, during the last six months of 1986. They more than anyone have a right to learn of my conclusions about the Stalker affair. It is for them that this book was written.

# Appendix

## *Chronology*

| | |
|---|---|
| **1939**<br>*April* | John Stalker born in Manchester. |
| **1956/57** | Cadet in Manchester City Police. |
| **1958**<br>*April* | Constable in Manchester City Police. |
| **1961** | Joined CID. |
| **1962**<br>*August* | Married to Stella. |
| **1964**<br>*October* | Promoted to Detective Sergeant. |
| **1968**<br>*June* | Promoted to Detective Inspector. |
| **1972** | Meets Kevin Taylor. |
| **1973** | Positively vetted by Special Branch and Government Security Services. |
| **1974**<br>*April* | Promoted to Detective Chief Inspector in Greater Manchester Police. |
| **1976**<br>*June* | Promoted to Detective Superintendent. |
| **1978**<br>*February* | Promoted to Detective Chief Superintendent: Head of Warwickshire CID. |

**1979**
*March-September*  Positively vetted again by Government agencies. Attended Senior Command Course at Police Staff College, Bramshill, Hampshire.

**1980**
*April*  Promoted Assistant Chief Constable, Greater Manchester Police.
Vetted again by Government agencies.

**1981**
*December*  Nine-day holiday aboard sailing yacht with Kevin Taylor in Florida.

**1982**
*January*  Kevin Taylor's fiftieth birthday party at his home.
*(late)*  Positively vetted again by Government agencies. Clearance given for access to highest-security classified material.
*27 October*  Three RUC policemen killed by IRA land-mine at Kinnego Embankment, Lurgan.
*11 November*  Toman, Burns and McKerr shot dead by Special Squad of RUC officers.
*24 November*  Tighe shot dead and McCauley badly injured by members of same RUC Squad.
*12 December*  Grew and Carroll shot dead by members of same RUC Squad.

**1983**
*June*  Director of Public Prosecutions orders a reinvestigation into all three incidents. Deputy Chief Constable McAtamney of RUC given the task. DPP waives Official Secrets Act.
*All year*  Stalker attends Royal College of Defence Studies, London. Extensive world-wide travel.

**1984**
*March*  Stalker appointed Deputy Chief Constable of the Greater Manchester Police.
*May*  Asked to head further investigation into the deaths of the six men. Selects his team to do it.
*24 May*  Meets Sir John Hermon. Draft terms of reference accepted.
*June*  Commences work in Northern Ireland. Obstruction encountered from Special Branch from beginning.

277

| | |
|---|---|
| *November* | Stalker learns of existence of MI5 tape recording of the shooting of Tighe and McCauley. |

**1985**

| | |
|---|---|
| *28 January* | Stalker meets MI5 in London, who agree to release of the tape recording. |
| *February* | Stalker learns he is targeted by a terrorist group. |
| *15 February* | McCauley trial at Belfast Crown Court. Police evidence excluded because of lies. |
| *20 February* | Stalker writes to RUC Special Branch asking for tape and informant information. Telephone reply refusing request. |
| *5 March* | Stalker writes to Chief Constable, RUC, asking for tape and identity of witnesses to the shooting. |
| *13 March* | Reply from Sir John Hermon. Request refused. |
| *9 April* | Stalker writes to Hermon asking him to reconsider. |
| *9 April* | Stalker writes to Deputy Chief Constable McAtamney requesting suspension from duty of two Special Branch Superintendents. No response to either letter. Advice sought from Sir Philip Myers. |
| *22 April* | Stalker writes again to Hermon asking for access to tape and requesting suspension of police officers. |
| *22 April* | Immediate reply. Both requests refused. |
| *29 April* | Stalker writes to Hermon asking to be released from his responsibility to report to RUC and asking for access to Director of Public Prosecutions. |
| | No response from Hermon but Sir Philip Myers asks Stalker to go to Belfast to see Hermon. |
| *9 May* | Meeting in Belfast. Hermon promises to 'reconsider' his refusals. |
| *13/14 May* | DPP and Home Office told of apparent progress being made by Stalker. |
| *15 May* | Meeting with Hermon in Belfast. He agrees to release the tape – if it exists – subject to approval of MI5. |
| *16 May* | Hermon telephones Stalker. MI5 must vet tape before he releases it. |
| | No response from either RUC or MI5. Hermon 'too busy' to speak to Stalker. |

| | |
|---|---|
| *May and June* | Sir Philip Myers and James Anderton aware of, and support, Stalker's intentions to apply for Chief Constable posts in Strathclyde Police and Bedfordshire Police. |
| *4 June* | Further letter sent to Hermon asking for tape. |
| *14 June* | Meeting called by MI5 in London. Hermon refuses to release tape unless it is 'in the public interest to do so'. |
| *18 June* | Hermon telephones Stalker refusing access to informant. |
| *20 June* | Sir Philip Myers cannot assist Stalker further. |
| *26 June* | Stalker writes to Hermon informing him of fresh evidence pointing to offences of unlawful killings by RUC. No response. |
| *1 July* | Preparation of Interim Report. |
| *18 September* | Interim Report delivered to RUC Headquarters, Belfast. |
| *September (late)* | Kevin Taylor tells Stalker of CID enquiries at Taylor's bank. |
| *October (early)* | Detective Superintendent tells Stalker that Taylor is not under police investigation. |
| *October (late)* | Determined enquiries now made into Kevin Taylor's businesses. |
| *23 November* | Stalker sees Taylor for last time at Autumn Ball at Hotel Piccadilly, Manchester. Anderton raises no objections. |
| *24 November* | Ango-Irish Agreement signed by Prime Ministers of United Kingdom and Ireland. |

## 1986

| | |
|---|---|
| *15 February* | Hermon sends Stalker's Interim Report to DPP. |
| *4 March* | Sir Philip Myers asks Stalker for clandestine copy of the Interim Report. |
| *4 March* | DPP instructs Hermon to give Stalker access to tape and all information. |
| *30 April* | Hermon fails to keep appointment in Belfast with Stalker. Special Branch records obtained, but not the tape. |
| *April* | Stalker hears that a secret police surveillance squad is formed in Manchester to investigate a policeman. |
| *9 May* | Taylor's home and offices searched by Manchester CID. Business accounts and an album of photographs taken away. |

| | |
|---|---|
| *12 May* | Hermon writes to Stalker, asking to see him before enquiries are recommenced. Appointment made for 19 May. |
| *14 May* | Sir Philip Myers tells Stalker to cancel the appointment. No explanation given. Arrangements made for Stalker to return on 26 May. |
| *19 May* | Meeting to discuss Stalker in Scarborough between Sir Lawrence Byford, Myers, Anderton and others. |
| *23 May* | Sir Philip Myers again instructs Stalker to cancel his visit to Belfast. Arrangements made for return on 2 June. Stalker determined to go. |
| *27 May* | Dinner in Moss Nook Restaurant, Manchester with Stalker, Anderton, Colin Cameron and Peter Taylor from BBC TV. |
| *28 May* | Telephone calls to Stalker from Mr R. Rees and Anderton. Told he is suspected of disciplinary offences. |
| *29 May* | Stalker told by Colin Sampson, Chief Constable of West Yorkshire, that he had been 'removed forever' from Northern Ireland investigation. Instructed to stay at home. |
| *6 June* | Public announcement that Sampson would now head the RUC investigation. |
| *9 June* | First disciplinary interview with Stalker. Sampson provides no details. |
| *16 June* | Stalker's mother admitted to Intensive Care Unit. |
| *16 June* | BBC Panorama programme reveals existence of Hayshed tape. |
| *23 June* | Second interview with Sampson. Questions asked about Taylor's birthday party five years earlier. |
| *30 June* | Stalker formally suspended from duty. |
| *5 July* | Stalker's mother returns home. |
| *9 July* | Home Office refuse to separate Sampson's enquiries into RUC and Stalker. |
| *July (mid)* | Protestant marching season begins in Northern Ireland. Violent and bloody confrontations with RUC. Police actions please Dublin government. |
| *12 July* | Hermon suspends the two Superintendents; fifteen months after Stalker's request. |
| *17 July* | Third interview with Sampson. Questions asked |

|  | about 1981 holiday and Hotel Piccadilly Ball in November 1985. Also Stalker's use of police cars. |
|---|---|
| *29 July* | Fourth and final interview with Sampson. More questions about police cars. |
| *2 August* | Councillor Norman Briggs, Chairman of Police Committee, dies on holiday. Replaced by Councillor David Moffat. |
| *August (mid)* | Unlawful leaking of confidential Sampson Report to the press. |
| *22 August* | Police Committee vote overwhelmingly to reinstate Stalker to post of Deputy Chief Constable. |
| *23 August* | Stalker returns to work. |
| *26 August* | Anderton confirms that investigation into Stalker did not commence until after April 1986. Press release by Anderton welcoming Stalker back to work. |
| *1 September* | Press release by Anderton denying conspiracy against Stalker. |
| *3 September* | Press release by Anderton emphasizing his authority over Stalker as Chief Constable of Force. |
| *6 September* | Journalist hands Stalker a photocopy of Sampson's report into him. |
| *12 September* | Anderton installed as President of Association of Chief Police Officers (ACPO). |
| *18 September* | First anniversary of delivery to RUC of Stalker's Interim Report. Still no decision made. |
| *September (mid)* | Councillor Moffat replaced as Chairman of Police Committee by Councillor Stephen Murphy. |
| *26 September* | Stalker receives legal bill of £21,980 for defending himself in disciplinary matter. |
| *17 October* | Police Committee refuse to contribute towards Stalker's legal costs. Public donations begin to arrive at Police Headquarters. |
| *22 October* | Anderton effectively halts public donations. Warns of disciplinary offences if Stalker accepts. |
| *6 November* | Home Office have no objections to public donations, subject to Police Committee approval. |

| | |
|---|---|
| *17 November* | Police Committee agree subject to ACPO involvement. |
| *21 November* | ACPO refuse to donate to or endorse the fund. |
| *26 November* | John Thorburn leaves the police. |
| *5 December* | Police Committee give clearance to public legal fund. Donations begin again to arrive. |
| *11 December* | Anderton gives widely controversial speech about AIDS sufferers. |
| *15 December* | West Yorkshire Police still investigating RUC. Ask Stalker about the tapes. |
| *16 December* | Moors murders reopened. Myra Hindley taken to scenes of the murders. Stalker not told. |
| *18 December* | Stalker decides to leave the police force. |
| *20 December* | Moors murders search called off for the winter. |

**1987**

| | |
|---|---|
| *January* | Anderton gives his 'Prophet of God' speech. |
| *March* | Stalker leaves the police. |

# Index